Lowell Edmunds
Toward the Characterization of Helen in Homer

Trends in Classics –
Supplementary Volumes

Edited by
Franco Montanari and Antonios Rengakos

Associate Editors
Stavros Frangoulidis · Fausto Montana · Lara Pagani
Serena Perrone · Evina Sistakou · Christos Tsagalis

Scientific Committee
Alberto Bernabé · Margarethe Billerbeck
Claude Calame · Jonas Grethlein · Philip R. Hardie
Stephen J. Harrison · Richard Hunter · Christina Kraus
Giuseppe Mastromarco · Gregory Nagy
Theodore D. Papanghelis · Giusto Picone
Tim Whitmarsh · Bernhard Zimmermann

Volume 87

Lowell Edmunds

Toward the Characterization of Helen in Homer

Appellatives, Periphrastic Denominations, and Noun-Epithet Formulas

DE GRUYTER

ISBN 978-3-11-076337-9
e-ISBN (PDF) 978-3-11-062612-4
e-ISBN (EPUB) 978-3-11-062648-3
ISSN 1868-4785

Bibliographic information published by the Deutsche Nationalbibliothek
The Deutsche Nationalbibliothek lists this publication in the Deutsche Nationalbibliografie;
detailed bibliographic data are available on the Internet at http://dnb.dnb.de.

© 2021 Walter de Gruyter GmbH, Berlin/Boston
This volume is text- and page-identical with the hardback published in 2019.
Editorial Office: Alessia Ferreccio and Katerina Zianna
Logo: Christopher Schneider, Laufen
Printing and binding: CPI books GmbH, Leck

www.degruyter.com

Preface

The study of the Homeric epithets for Helen undertaken in this monograph is a first stage in a larger study of her characterization in the *Iliad* and the *Odyssey*. In the course of my research on these epithets it soon became clear that they could not be understood apart from her appellatives, her periphrastic denominations, such as "sister-in-law of warriors," and her terms of self-reproach. These kinds of reference to Helen come from characters in the epics. Almost the only epithet used of her by them is "Argive" (10/13x). Her other epithets come from the narrator. The name Helen without an epithet (23x) is never neutral but always reflects either a character's particular point of view (13/23x) or the narrator's (10/23x). The study of Helen's epithets is preceded by chapters on these other ways of referring to Helen, including on the epithet "Argive."

The question guiding my research on the epithets was whether or not they had contextual meaning. In conclusion it seems that Bryan Hainsworth's dictum holds: "relevance and redundancy [of formulas] are the ends of a spectrum" (Hainsworth 1993: 21) but in most instances these epithets, with the exception of καλλιπάρῃος (*Od.* 15.123), lie in the range of relevance. None can be described simply as a "generic epithet of women." This conclusion is another reply, preceded by many others, to Milman Parry's notion of the semantic emptiness of the epithet, which, he said, becomes merged with its noun "in the expression of a single idea" (Parry 1971[1928]: 154).

Parry's work led to another kind of research on the epithet, which should be mentioned here in order to make clear the present study's more limited ambition. Dissatisfaction with Parry led ultimately to new general definitions of the formula (e.g., Hainsworth 1968; Nagler 1974; Visser 1987; Bakker 1997). This monograph, concentrating on the contextual meaning of the epithets of Helen, is not concerned with such definitions.

The central conclusion that Parry drew from his work on the noun-epithet formula, which was that the *Iliad* and the *Odyssey* were composed orally, was to have profound consequences. The field of Homeric studies is now divided on the question of composition, adhering to one or the other of two principal models. Perhaps the most favored is a poet or two poets who composed these epics at the end of the eighth or beginning of the seventh century B.C.E. and either dictated them or wrote them down. If it was a single poet, he is anonymous; he was not called Homer (Graziosi 2002: 21–50; West 2011b[1999]: 413–21). (In this monograph the name Homer has sometimes been used as a metonym for the corpus consisting of the *Iliad* and the *Odyssey*.) Gregory Nagy long ago proposed an alternative, evolutionary model. He distinguished five stages of a progressively less fluid oral text, culminating in the completely fixed text of Aristarchus (Nagy 1992, rev. in Nagy 1996a; Nagy 1996b: ch. 5; defended in Nagy 2014). This model has been accepted and rethought in the Prolegomena volume of the English translation of the Basel Commentary (Bierl 2015: 21–31).

The results of this study of Helen's epithets could be explained on either of these models but are not applied to an argument for one or the other. As for a pre-history of oral composition and performance, few would now deny that there was one. This pre-history is often referred to as a "tradition," which is taken as the basis of diachronic interpretation (on "tradition" see the Introduction). This monograph seeks a synchronic, contextual interpretation of Helen's epithets and concludes that their traditional or inherited connotations, which can sometimes be shown, not only fail to add connotative depth but are false leads. (The term "connotations" is taken from the application of the concept of traditional referentiality by Kelly 2007: 9–14.)

The quotations of the *Iliad* come from the text of T.W. Allen, of the *Odyssey* from the text of Peter von der Muehll, with indication of divergences. Most Greek proper names and adjectives are given in Latin or Latinized transliteration.

This monograph started as a joint project with Kristen Baxter (Pennsylvania State University). Considerations of time compelled her to withdraw but I am grateful for her initial collaboration. I thank Aaron Beck-Schachter, Mario Cantilena, Leah Edmunds, Joshua Katz, Richard Martin, Patrizia Mureddu, Jordi Pàmias, and Jaume Pòrtulas for help along the way. At the end, Christos Tsagalis and Leon Wash each read the whole manuscript and to them I am especially indebted. As always special thanks go to Susan T. Edmunds, who discussed many points, small and large, with me.

Lowell Edmunds
Highland Park, NJ
April, 2019

Contents

Preface — V
Abbreviations — XI
List of Tables — XIII

Introduction — 1
Quantitative survey — 6
The name Helen with an epithet in the second half of the hexameter — 7
Helen with an epithet in the first half of the hexameter — 10

1   **Appellatives and Periphrastic Denominations** — 15
1.1   The vocative γύναι "lady" — 15
1.2   νύμφα φίλη "dear bride" — 16
1.3   φίλον τέκος "dear child" — 17
1.4   Helen's terms for her Trojan in-laws and for her family in Sparta — 17
1.5   γυνή in the nominative and in oblique cases; Helen as ἄκοιτις and ἄλοχος — 19
1.6   Leading (ἄγειν, ἀνάγειν) and following (ἕπεσθαι) — 21
1.7   Indirect description or "periphrastic denomination" — 23
1.8   Conclusion — 25

2   **Epithets of Opprobrium** — 26
2.1   κακομήχανος — 26
2.2   κρυοέσση (*Il.* 6.344) — 27
2.3   ῥιγεδανή (*Il.* 19.325) — 28
2.4   στυγερή (*Il.* 3.404) — 29
2.5   Semantic field of κρυοέσση, ῥιγεδανή and στυγερή — 30
2.6   σχετλίη (*Il.* 1.414) — 31
2.7   κύων (*Il.* 6.344, 356) — 33
2.8   κυνῶπις and adultery — 36
2.9   ἄμμορος (*Il.* 24.773) — 38
2.10   Conclusion — 39

3   **Ἀργείη** — 40
3.1   "Argive Helen" as the object of a legitimate claim — 42
3.2   "Argive Helen's" Iliadic identity in the *Odyssey* — 46
3.3   "Argive Helen" in domestic contexts — 46

3.4	"Argive Helen" as a figure of the past —— 49	
3.5	Conclusion —— 50	
3.6	Appendix —— 50	

4 The Name Helen Unmodified —— 52
- 4.1 Helen and the war —— 52
- 4.2 Three scenes —— 56
- 4.3 Helen as wife of Menelaus —— 62
- 4.4 Conclusion —— 63

5 δῖα γυναικῶν "noble among women": The Public Figure (1) —— 65
- 5.1 Helen as δῖα γυναικῶν in the *Iliad* —— 66
- 5.2 δῖα γυναικῶν of Helen in the *Odyssey* —— 70
- 5.3 Conclusion —— 72

6 τανύπεπλος "long-robed": The Public Figure (2) —— 73
- 6.1 τανύπεπλος in *Iliad* 3.171 —— 74
- 6.2 *Odyssey* 15.305 —— 77
- 6.3 Helen in the *Odyssey*: Character and Epithets —— 78
- 6.4 Conclusion —— 80

7 Other Epithets for Beauty (1): ἠΰκομος —— 81
- 7.1 Paris as the husband of "fair-haired Helen" —— 81
- 7.2 Line-final ἠϋκόμοιο used of others besides Helen —— 83
- 7.3 ἠΰκομος in line-final formulas for Helen and Thetis —— 87
- 7.4 Conclusion —— 88
- 7.5 Appendix: The semantics of the formula Ἑλένης ἕνεκ' ἠϋκόμοιο —— 89

8 Other Epithets for Beauty (2): λευκώλενος —— 93
- 8.1 λευκώλενος of Helen in the *Odyssey* —— 93
- 8.2 "White-armed" Helen in the *Iliad* —— 96
- 8.3 Athena again —— 101
- 8.4 Conclusion —— 101

9 Epithets for Beauty (3): καλλίκομος, καλλιπάρῃος —— 103
- 9.1 καλλίκομος —— 103
- 9.2 καλλιπάρῃος —— 105

9.3	Comparison of formular behavior of καλλίκομος and καλλιπάρῃος —— 110
9.4	Conclusion —— 112

10 Kinship Epithets —— 114
- 10.1 Ἑλένη Διὸς ἐκγεγαυῖα (*Iliad* 3.199) —— 114
- 10.2 Ἑλένη Διὸς ἐκγεγαυῖα (*Iliad* 3.418), κούρη Διὸς αἰγιόχοιο (426) —— 116
- 10.3 Διὸς ἐκγεγαυῖα (*Odyssey* 4.184) —— 118
- 10.4 Διὸς ἐκγεγαυῖα (*Odyssey* 4.219), Διὸς θυγάτηρ (227) —— 119
- 10.5 Διὸς ἐκγεγαυῖα (*Odyssey* 23.218) —— 123
- 10.6 Conclusion —— 124

11 εὐπατέρεια —— 125
- 11.1 Helen as εὐπατέρεια in *Iliad* Book 6 —— 125
- 11.2 Helen as εὐπατέρεια in *Odyssey* Book 22 —— 126
- 11.3 Tyro in *Odyssey* Book 11 —— 127
- 11.4 εὐπατέρεια as a catalogue epithet —— 128
- 11.5 Another example in Odysseus' catalogue and a parallel in the *Cypria* —— 129
- 11.6 Conclusion —— 132

12 Reflections on Kinship Epithets and Epithets of Beauty —— 134
- 12.1 The synchronic dimension —— 134
- 12.2 The diachronic dimension —— 140
- 12.3 Conclusion —— 144

13 Conclusion —— 146

Appendix 1: Helen's Epithets in Homer in Order of Occurrence —— 151
Appendix 2: The Name of Helen without Epithets —— 153
Appendix 3: The "On account of" Motif —— 155
Appendix 4: Helen's epithets in lyric —— 157
Works Cited —— 159
Index nominum et rerum —— 171
Index locorum —— 173

Abbreviations

B	Bernabé, Albertus, ed. 1987. *Poetarum epicorum Graecorum: testimonia et fragmenta*. Leipzig: Teubner.
Beekes	Beekes, Robert S.P. 2010. *Etymological Dictionary of Greek*. 2 vols. Leiden: Brill.
BK	Basler Kommentar = Latacz, Joachim and Anton Bierl, eds. 2000- . *Homers Ilias, Gesamtkommentar: Basler Kommentar (BK)*. Auf der Grundlage der Ausgabe von Ameis-Hentze-Cauer (1868–1913). Munich: Saur. Berlin: de Gruyter.
B-S-V 2003	Brügger, Claude, Magdalena Stoevesandt and Edzard Visser. 2003. In Bierl and Latacz, eds. 2000- . Vol. 2 (Book 2). Fasc. 2 (Commentary). Munich: Saur.
Chantraine	Chantraine, Pierre. 1968–1980. *Dictionnaire étymologique de la langue grecque: histoire des mots*. 2 vols. Paris: Klincksieck.
Chicago Homer	Ahuvia Kahane and Martin Mueller, eds. *The Chicago Homer*. http://homer.library.northwestern.edu/
D	Davies, Malcolm, ed. 1988. *Epicorum Graecorum fragmenta*. Göttingen: Vandenhoeck and Ruprecht.
D-F	Davies, Malcolm and P.J. Finglass. 2014. *Stesichorus: The Poems*. Cambridge: Cambridge University Press.
DGE^2	Adrados, Francisco R., ed. 2008- . *Diccionario griego-español*. 2nd ed. Madrid: Consejo Superior de Investigaciones Científicas.
Dindorf	Dindorf, Wilhelm. 1855. *Scholia graeca in Homeri Odysseam: ex codicibus aucta et emendata*. Oxford: Clarendon Press.
EM	Ranke, Kurt, ed. 1977-. *Enzyklopädie des Märchens: Handwörterbuch zur historischen und vergleichenden Erzählforschung*. 14 vols. Berlin: de Gruyter.
Erbse	Erbse, Hartmut. 1969. *Scholia Graeca in Homeri Iliadem (scholia Vetera)*. 7 vols. Berlin: de Gruyter.
Et. Magn.	*Etymologicum Magnum*.
Eust.	Eustathius = van der Valk, Marchinus. 1971. *Eustathius: Commentarii ad Homeri Iliadem pertinentes ad fidem codicis Laurentiani editi*. 4 vols. Leiden: Brill. Cited by vol. (Roman numeral), page number, and line number (inner margin).
Friedländer	Friedländer, Paul. 1948. *Epigrammata: Greek Inscriptions in Verse from the Beginnings to the Persian Wars*. Berkeley: University of California Press.
Frisk	Frisk, Hjalmar. 1960. *Griechisches etymologisches Wörterbuch*. 2 vols. Heidelberg: C. Winter.
H	Hirschberger, Martina. 2004. *Gynaikon Katalogos und Megalai Ehoiai: Ein Kommentar zu den Fragmenten zweier hesiodeischer Epen*. Beiträge zur Altertumskunde, 198. Munich: Saur.
Hansen	Hansen, Peter Allan. 1983–1989. *Carmina epigraphica graeca*. 2 vols. Berlin: de Gruyter.
HE	Homer Encyclopedia = Finkelberg, Margalit, ed. 2011. *The Homer Encyclopedia*. 3 vols. Chichester: Wiley-Blackwell.
LfgrE	Snell, Bruno *et al.* 1955–2010. *Lexikon des frühgriechischen Epos*. 4 vols. Göttingen, Vandenhoek & Ruprecht.
LIMC "A."	"Alexandros" = Hampe, Roland. 1981. In *LIMC* I.1. Pp. 494–529.

LIMC "H."	"Hélène" = Kahil, Lilly. 1988. In John Boardman *et al.*, eds., *Lexicon Iconographicum Mythologiae Classicae*. In *LIMC* IV.1 Zurich: Artemis. Pp. 498–563.
LIMC "M."	"Menelaos" = Kahil, Lilly. 1997. In *LIMC* VIII.1 (Suppl.). Pp. 834–41, pls. 562–65.
LIMC	Boardman, John *et al.* 1981–1999. *Lexicon Iconographicum Mythologiae Classicae*. 9 vols. Zurich: Artemis.
L-N-S	Latacz, Joachim, René Nünlist and Magdalena Stoevesandt. 2000. In Bierl and Latacz, eds. 2000- . Vol. 1 (Book 1). Fasc. 2 (Commentary). Munich: Saur.
M	Most, Glenn W. 2006–2007. *Hesiod: The Shield; Catalogue of Women; Other Fragments*. Loeb Classical Library. Cambridge, MA: Harvard University Press.
Meillet and Vendryes	Meillet, A. and J. Vendryes. 1963. *Traité de grammaire comparée des langues classiques*. 3rd ed. Paris: Librairie Ancienne Honoré Champion.
Mirto	Paduano, Guido and Maria Serena Mirto. 1997. *Omero: Iliade*. Turin: Einaudi-Gallimard.
Montanari	Montanari, Franco. 2013. *Vocabolario della lingua greca*. 3rd ed. Turin: Loescher.
M-W	Merkelbach, Reinhold and M.L. West. 1967. *Fragmenta Hesiodea*. Oxford: Clarendon Press.
Neri-Cinti	Neri, Camillo and Federico Cinti. 2017. *Saffo: Poesie, frammenti e testimonianze*. Santarcangelo di Romagna: Rusconi.
Nünlist-de Jong	Nünlist, René and Irene J.F. de Jong. 2000. "Homerische Poetik in Stichwörtern." In Graf *et al.* 2000: 159–71 = BK vol. 1.
OED	*OED Online = Oxford English Dictionary Online*. http://www.oed.com.
Paduano	Paduano, Guido and Maria Serena Mirto. 1997. *Omero: Iliade*. Turin: Einaudi-Gallimard.
PMG	Page, D.L. 1962. *Poetae Melici Graecae*. Oxford: Clarendon Press.
PMGF	Davies, Malcolm. 1991. *Poetarum Melicorum Graecorum Fragmenta*. Vol. 1 (Alcman, Stesichorus, Ibycus). Oxford: Clarendon Press.
Richardson	Richardson, Nicholas. 1993. *The Iliad: A Commentary*. Vol. 6 (Books 21–24). Cambridge: Cambridge University Press.
Schwyzer	Schwyzer, Eduard. 1939–1971. *Griechische Grammatik auf der Grundlage von Karl Brugmanns Griechischer Grammatik*. Vol. 1 (Allgemeiner Teil; Lautlehre; Wortbildung; Flexion) by Schwyzer (1939). Vol. 2 (Syntax and Syntaktische Stylistik) by Albert Debrunner (1950). Vol. 3 (Register) by Demetrius J. Georgacas (1953). Vol. 4 (Stellenregister) by Fritz Radt and Stefan Radt (1971). Munich: Beck.
SLG	Page, D.L. 1974. *Supplementum Lyricis Graecis*. Oxford: Clarendon Press.
Stoevesandt	Stoevesandt, Magdalena. 2008. In Bierl and Latacz, eds. 2000- . Vol. 4 (Book 6). Fasc. 2 (Commentary). Berlin: de Gruyter.
ThesCRA	Lambrinoudakis, Vassilis and Jean Ch. Balty, eds. 2004–2005. *Thesaurus cultus et rituum antiquorum*. 2004–2005. Basel: Fondation pour le lexicon iconographicum mythologiae classicae.
van der Valk	van der Valk, Marchinus. 1971–1987. *Commentarii ad Homeri Iliadem pertinentes ad fidem codicis Laurentiani editi*. 4 vols. Leiden: Brill.
W	West, M.L. 2013. *The Epic Cycle: A Commentary on the Lost Troy Epics*. Oxford: Oxford University Press.

List of Tables

Tab. 1: Argive Helen ch. 3 —— **40**
Tab. 2: Helen's speeches ch. 4 —— **59**
Tab. 3: Comparison of epithets of Helen in *Iliad* and *Odyssey* ch. 6 —— **79**
Tab. 4: Helen: epithets of beauty, with speakers ch. 8 —— **97**
Tab. 5: "White-armed" ch. 8 —— **99**
Tab. 6: Helen at the beginning of the Teichoscopia ch. 10 —— **115**
Tab. 7: Sequences of epithets and appellatives in *Iliad* 3 and *Odyssey* 4 ch. 10 —— **118**
Tab. 8: Helen's epithets of beauty ch. 12 —— **135**
Tab. 9: Helen's epithets of beauty in Homer compared with those in Hesiod, *Cypria* and lyric ch. 12 —— **137**
Tab. 10: Helen's kinship epithets: frequency, distribution and speaker(s) ch. 12 —— **139**

Introduction

This study deals mainly with the Homeric epithets of Helen and asks what kinds of contextual meaning they have and how they contribute to her characterization. Helen is also characterized in other ways, most obviously by her speeches, and scholarship on Helen's character (Fr. *personnage*, Germ. *Figur*, Ital. *personaggio*, Span. *personaje*) has typically focused on these speeches.[1] When she gives a speech, however, whether or not her name bears an epithet in the speech-introduction, Helen is already a character who is known to other characters and to the audience in other ways, as indicated by her appellatives (ch. 1) and periphrastic denominations (also ch. 1) and as can be inferred from the terms of her self-reproach (ch. 2). The ethnic Ἀργείη "Argive" in the *Iliad*, Helen's commonest epithet and the one used by more speakers than any other, refers to her as the object of the fighting, the prize on account of whom the war is fought, in particular from the Achaean point of view (ch. 3). Further, in twenty-three of its fifty-nine occurrences (*Il.* 40x, incl. 23.81a; *Od.* 19x) the name Helen is unmodified (ch. 4). In this use, it is not neutral but always reflects either a character's particular point of view or the narrator's.[2] These various ways of referring to Helen give her an identity or identities before she begins to speak and belong to the study of her characterization.

The definition of epithet adopted by Milman Parry from Ferdinand Brunot would include Helen's terms of self-reproach, which appear in the list of her epithets given below.[3] This definition was: "des mots ou d'expressions rapportées [à des noms] sans l'intermédiaire d'aucun verbe copule."[4] For Helen, as for other characters, and for Helen also in Hesiod, in the *Catalogue of Women*, in the *Cypria* and in the lyric poets, Brunot's "expressions" would also include adjectives, adjectives and participles with dependent nouns, and also nouns and a noun-phrase such as θαῦμα βροτοῖσι (*Cypr.* fr. 9.1 B; *Od.* 11.287; ch. 11§4). Two other

---

1 Finkelberg 2011.3: 819: The speeches are the "main vehicle for characterization."
2 Contrary to Parry 1971[1928]: 140: "...[T]he audience became indifferent to which fixed epithet the poet used in a given line. This indifference is the complement of the indifference he felt for the use *or the omission* of the fixed epithet" (my emphasis).
3 Cf. *OED* s.v. "epithet" 4.b. (*OED* online version September 2015). Dee 2000 includes these epithets in his list for Helen.
4 Brunot 1922: 633. (The title of this work as given by Parry is incorrect.) Parry 1971[1928a]: 153 n. 1: "...Brunot's definition is both precise and extensive enough to contain and define the various uses of those words in Greek and Latin poetry which have been called epithets."

noun phrases listed below for the Homeric Helen are Διὸς θυγάτηρ and κούρη Διός.

Three levels of Helen's epithets can be distinguished on a scale from disapprobation to high approbation. At the bottom are the epithets of opprobrium, all of them used by Helen of herself except for one used of her by Aphrodite (*Il.* 3.414) and one used by Achilles (*Il.* 19.325). At the middle level there is Helen's most common epithet, the ethnic Ἀργείη, used by nine speakers. There are also the familial appellatives (ch. 1). At the top are the laudatory epithets referring to her beauty and the ones referring to her as the daughter of Zeus. At this level there is also the simile in which Helen is compared to Artemis of the golden distaff, which is not discussed in this monograph.

Levels are consistently related to speaker. Opprobrium comes from the sources just indicated. Anyone, so to speak, can call Helen Ἀργείη, and of course the members of her Trojan family use the appropriate appellatives for her (and Helen appropriately names her Trojan relatives). All of the laudatory epithets come from the narrator, with two exceptions, Achilles (*Il.* 9.339) and Athena (*Od.* 22.227, where praise of Helen is not, however, the point; ch. 8). Likewise, all the kinship epithets come from the narrator, with a sole exception, which is used by Penelope (*Od.* 23.218).

Because Helen's name-epithets formulas appear for the most part in "the subtle rhetoric of the invisible but powerful narrator," comparison between the narrator's and others' perspectives is an obvious approach.[5] This distinction is now standard.[6] Its history begins with the ancient scholia (ch. 8§2) and it is the main approach taken in this study.[7]

The narrator's epithets for Helen ought to have a special authority. So one assumes, considering that he is divinely inspired and thus omniscient.[8] There is

---

[5] de Jong 2004: xiv.

[6] de Jong 1987; de Jong 1997; de Jong 2012: 28; further bibliography in Edmunds 2014: 27 n. 37. The λύσις ἐκ τοῦ προσώπου, explaining the contradictions between the words of one character and another, was already in the scholia. See in Nünlist and de Jong 2000 lemmata for "Argument-Funktion" (with many cross-references), "Erzähler," "Erzählung," "Figuren-Sprache," etc. de Jong 1987: 192–93 gave it as a rule that "the presentation by characters in character-text is conditioned by the identity of the speaker and addressee and by the situation..." See also de Jong 1997. For a survey of views of the distinction between Homer and the speakers in the epics see Edmunds 2014: 5–6.

[7] de Jong 2012: 28 discusses this approach, citing relevant scholarship, in a survey of various approaches to contextual meaning.

[8] Nagy 1976: 247–48; Nagy 1999[1979]: 17: the singer's knowledge comes from the Muses. Also Griffin 1980: 18, 128–30 and his Index s.v. "Divine perspective." See now González 2013: 7.2.3 ("The singer, instrument of the Muse").

a disparity in knowledge between the narrator (and his audience) and the heroes that was captured in Jörgensen's Law, as Jörgensen himself called it.⁹ He studied the use of the names of gods and of θεός and δαίμων and found that the narrator makes a distinction between himself and the characters whom he represents as speaking. They are usually ignorant of the identity of a god whom they have perceived as intervening in their affairs (for whom they use θεός or δαίμων), whereas the narrator, and thus his audience, always knows exactly who the god is. He knows, and imparts to his audience, what the gods know. The same is true of the epithets: the narrator's tell us the truth about Helen. Others' may or may not do so.

♦

The proposal of a study of the meaning of Helen's epithets evokes an old controversy. As is well known, Milman Parry denied that the fixed or ornamental epithet (as distinguished from the particularized epithet referring to a single character or object) had any meaning.¹⁰ (For further discussion and for a classification of Helen's epithets using Parry's scheme see pp. 5–11 below.) He held that the epithet becomes merged with its noun "in the expression of a single idea."¹¹ He made this point as insistently as he did because it seemed to him crucial to his thesis on the poet's traditional, inherited (i.e., not original) style as evidence of oral composition. Parry's view met with immediate objection.¹² Metrically equivalent

---

9 Jörgensen 1904: 381 'Gesetz'. The Law: "Der Dichter macht...zwischen sich selbst und den Personen, die er als redend einführt, den Unterschied, dass diese die Persönlichkeit der eingreifenden Gottheit gewohnlich nicht erkennen, während er selber stets aufs genaueste weiss,..." (364).
10 Parry 1971[1928a]: 149, 165; Parry 1971[1930]: 317; also 270, 305.
11 Parry 1971[1928a]: 154 (in the sentence quoted from here the second occurrence of "epithet" should apparently be corrected to "name").
12 Already in 1933, Calhoun, referring to Parry's demonstration of the formularity of the first twenty-five lines of the *Iliad*, asked "What shall we say of such art as this?" He proceeded to argue that Homer uses formulas as "freely and unconsciously" as the modern poet uses words (Calhoun 1933: 8, 9. Response by Parry 1971[1937]. For the controversy between Calhoun and Parry over ἔπεα πτερόεντα see Elmer 2011: 606.). This earliest reaction to the definition of the formula was, then, literary-critical, affirming Homer the artist against Parry. A quarter of a century later, Combellack described the stand-off between the literary critics and the Parryists: "Conscious...that in post-Homeric literature adjectives used by great poets usually mean something..., critics have naturally tried to deal with Homeric poetry in the same way. And, although in the post-Parry age criticism of this sort is no longer so simple, [it]...still...manifests itself in a number of ways" (Combellack 1959: 196; cited by A. Parry 1971: lv.) The stand-off continued. In 1967 Albert Lord in "Homer as Oral Poet" criticized an interpretive article on Homer by Anne Amory Parry (A.A. Parry 1966) for its "subjective criticism" . She replied to Lord under the title "Homer as Artist" (A.A. Parry 1971; on this controversy: Hoekstra 1991: 471–72). In 1971, in the

epithets for the same character or object, which might reflect compositional decisions, were an obvious case. Parry discussed this phenomenon but of course skeptically: "the particularized meaning of the equivalent epithet is by no means a necessary conclusion."[13] He found that there were only three such formulas that could not be explained "by the operation of analogy or by the association of words," along with some cases in which the epithet does not occur frequently enough for any conclusion to be drawn from its distribution.[14] (Such happens to be the case in the nonce use of καλλιπάρηος of Helen at *Od.* 15.123, where δῖα γυναικῶν would fit. See ch. 9.) For Parry the contextual irrelevance of the equivalent epithets was, at this point in his over-all argument, a given. If each of the two equivalent epithets was already only ornamental, each would remain ornamental wherever used, and all that had to be explained was the mental process ("the bard's mind") by which the phenomenon came about.[15] Scholars have argued against Parry's view of the equivalent epithets.[16] Today few would deny that the Homeric epithets can have contextual meaning.

The name-epithet formulas for Helen in the first and second hemistichs are, as formulas, analogous to those for other heroes and gods. Putting these formulas for Helen together with Ἀργείη/ν Ἑλένη/ν in the first hemistich, one finds a fairly complete repertory, a "system," in which, however, the components are minimally

---

introduction to his father's collected works, A. Parry entered the controversy on the side of literary criticism. He regretted the fact that after Calhoun criticism that "tried to grasp both the existence and the poetic effect of the formula, and then to show how it became part of an artistic construct, has been rare (A. Parry 1971: lxii). Parry cited: Armstrong 1958; N. Austin 1966; the tenth chapter of Whitman 1958; two articles of his own (A. Parry 1956; A. Parry 1966). Earlier in this introduction (lv n. 2) Parry cited A.A. Parry 1973 as forthcoming. The historical sketch just given covers roughly the first forty years of reaction to M. Parry.

13 Parry 1971a[1928]: 155.
14 Parry 1971a[1928]: 187.
15 Parry 1971a[1928]: 176.
16 The first twenty years of scholarship on metrically equivalent noun-epithet formulas: Boedeker 1974: 31–39; Shannon 1975; Janko 1981 (opposing Boedeker 1974 and Shannon 1975: see 251 n. 6); Cosset 1983; Cosset 1984; Schmiel 1984 (reply to Janko 1981); Beck 1986; Sacks 1987: 161–75; Olson 1994 (reply to Janko 1981); Sbardella 1994 (esp. 26–27 on the use of metrically equivalent formulas in some Homeric Hymns). Hainsworth 1978: 45 n. 5 challenged Boedeker but without argumentation. The position of Jahn 1987 is somewhat different. At the end of a study of the body-part words ἦτορ, κῆρ, κραδίη, πραπίδες, φρένες, θυμός and also the non-physical μένος, νόος and ψυχή he considers the possibility of semantic choice and reaches the compromise of what he calls a "double functionality" of meter and semantics. More recently: Brillet-Dubois 2015.

declinable, as will be seen in the following discussion.¹⁷ It is also economical, except for the well-known exception of Helen's three reply-verses in *Iliad* Book 3 (ch. 6§1) and one other exception (καλλιπάρῃος, already cited above). The fact remains that the name-epithet formulas for Helen present what could be called a normal picture. Further, all of Helen's epithets except one (ῥιγεδανή 19.325; ch. 2§3) are borne by at least one other character.

The following Parryist analysis of Helen's epithets has two purposes: to provide a survey of the epithets to be discussed in this monograph; to show how they constitute a system in Parry's sense. It is preceded by a brief quantitative survey. In this survey, data for the *Iliad* and the *Odyssey* are combined, because Helen has, with very few exceptions, the same epithets in both epics (ch. 6§3 with fig. 3; ch. 10§3 with fig. 7). Parry's scheme is followed simply for descriptive purposes. General definitions of the Homeric formula, which have been a concern of scholarship off and on since Parry's time, would be not be useful for these purposes.¹⁸ One can distinguish two sides of Parry's work: the formula, with which he began, and oral composition, the inference which he drew from his study of the formula. At present, study of the formula has receded and study of the oral aspect of Homer, in particular of performance, is to the fore.¹⁹

---

17 For the term "system," see Parry 1971a[1928]: 17: "systems of formulae of differing metrical value and containing different parts of speech." Parry's use of "system" was inconsistent. See M. Sale 2001: 59–60.
18 New definitions: notably Hainsworth 1968, i.e., already in the lifetime of A. Parry, who cites this work in passing (1971: xlix n. 3). He also cites: an earlier article (1964) by Hainsworth (xxxiii n. 1, again xlix n. 3); Hoekstra 1965 (xxi n. 2, xxxiii n. 1, xlix n. 3); Russo 1963; Russo 1966. Friedrich 2011: 54–57 traces a progressive widening of Parry's theory of the formula culminating in Nagler 1974. For overviews of this area of Homeric research, see Russo 1997; Edwards 1997, especially pp. 272–77; Russo 2011; Finkelberg 2012; Bozzone 2015: 16–24. See also the bibliography in Bakker 1997: 159 n. 9.
19 Friedrich 2011: 57 put it thus: "Das Debakel, das aus der hemmungslosen Formeljagd resultierte, gab Anlass zu alternativen Neuansätzen in der Formeltheorie. Deren Tenor war: weg von der fixierten Formel!" Friedrich 2007 is an example. Finkelberg 2004 is a *histoire raisonnée* focusing on the formula as the basis of the theory of oral composition and showing how formular studies starting with Nagler 1974 (she discusses also Visser 1987, Visser 1989 and Bakker 1997) tended willy-nilly to undermine the oral theory by expanding the definition of the formula. She continues with Hoekstra 1965 and Hainsworth 1968 (citing also Cantilena 1982, W. Sale 1989, and Finkelberg 1989). (This brief survey does not include aesthetic interpretation of the formula such as by Austin 1975 and Vivante 1982. See the survey in de Jong 1998: 123–26, and Cairns 2001: 52 on "contemporary criticism's successful overcoming of oralist objections to the literary interpretation of epic.")

Quantitative survey

The name Helen has an epithet fifty-three times in Homer. This count includes epithets used by the narrator or by a character in referring to Helen by name. It also includes epithets, mostly of opprobrium, used of Helen by herself, three times attached to an oblique form of ἐγώ (*Il.* 6.344, 24.773; *Od.* 4.145). Once a formular epithet occurs without her name (*Od.* 4.227). The list of her epithets is, then, the following:[20]

- ἄμμορος 1x *Il.*
- Ἀργείη 9x *Il.*, 4x *Od.*
- δῖα γυναικῶν 3x *Il.*, 2x *Od.*
- Διὸς ἐκγεγαυῖα 2x *Il.*, 3x *Od.*
- Διὸς θυγάτηρ 1x *Od.*
- εὐπατέρεια 1x *Il.*, 1x *Od.*
- ἠΰκομος 7x *Il.*
- κακομήχανος 1x *Il.*
- καλλίκομος 1x *Il.*, 1x *Od.*
- καλλιπάρῃος 1x *Od.*
- κούρη Διός 1x *Il.*
- κρυόεις 1x *Il.*
- κυνῶπις 1x *Il.*, 1x *Od.*
- κύων 2x *Il.*
- λευκώλενος 1x *Il.*, 1x *Od.*
- ῥιγεδανή 1x *Il.*
- στυγερή 1x *Il.*
- σχετλίη 1x *Il.*
- τανύπεπλος 1x *Il.*, 2x *Od.*

This list includes, on Brunot's definition, quoted above, Διὸς θυγάτηρ and κούρη Διός. It does not include τριτάτη (*Il.* 24.761; discussed in ch. 11) or the epithets used in oblique reference to Helen by Hector: γυνὴ εὐειδής (*Il.* 3.48 [to Paris]) and θαλερὴ παράκοιτις (*Il.* 3.53 [to Paris]).[21] (For other words for "wife" see ch. 1§5.) πολυήρατος (*Od.* 15.126) is a separate problem (see ch. 9§2). The list to be discussed in this study amounts, then, to nineteen different epithets in the *Iliad* and

---

[20] This list differs in two ways from the one given by Clader 1976: 41–44: it includes (1) epithets of opprobrium and (2) Ἀργείη, Διὸς ἐκγεγαυῖα, and σχετλίη.
[21] Of the epithets used of Helen by other characters or by the narrator the list in Clader 1976: 41–44 omits Ἀργείη, Διὸς ἐκγεγαυῖα, and σχετλίη.

the *Odyssey*. Helen has an epithet from this list thirty-five times in the *Iliad*, seventeen times in the *Odyssey*. Some of her epithets appear only in the *Iliad*: ἠυκόμος, κακομήχανος, κούρη Διός, κρυόεις, κύων, ῥιγεδανή, στυγερή, and σχετλίη. Note that six of the eight just listed are pejorative and, of these, five come from Helen herself. Two epithets appear only in the *Odyssey*: Διὸς θυγάτηρ and καλλιπάρῃος.

These epithets fall into three main categories (distinct from the three levels discussed above): kinship epithets, referring to Helen as the daughter of Zeus; the epithets referring to Helen's beauty; pejorative epithets. There are also the ethnic "Argive" and δῖα γυναῖκων. Helen's name appears in the *Iliad* and the *Odyssey* without an epithet twenty-three times (App. 2). There are five instances in Homer in which Helen has two epithets in the same line. At *Il.* 3.228 and *Od.* 4.305 she is δῖα γυναῖκων and τανύπεπλος. At *Od.* 4.184 and 23.218 she is Ἀργείη and Διὸς ἐκγεγυῖα. At *Od.* 22.227, she is λευκώλενος and εὐπατέρεια. In one instance, Helen has three epithets (κυνὸς κακομηχάνου ὀκρυοέσσης, *Il.* 6.343). (In the Hesiodic *Catalogue* Helen is three times called Ἀργείη and ἠυκόμος in the same line.[22] In a line in an anonymous lyric fragment Helen is δῖα and πολυνεικής (fr. adesp. 96 PMG).)

The name Helen with an epithet in the second half of the hexameter

Parry's paradigm case of the name-epithet formula was the one that extends from the trochaic or feminine caesura to line-end.[23] "All the chief characters of the *Iliad* and the *Odyssey*, if their names can be fitted into the last half of the verse along with an epithet, have a noun-epithet formula in the nominative, beginning with a simple consonant, which fills the verse between the trochaic caesura of the third foot and the verse-end…"[24] He found three such systems, defined by three types, e.g., δῖος Ὀδυσσεύς (– ⏑ ⏑ – –) (60x), πολύμητις Ὀδυσσεύς (⏑ ⏑ – ⏑ ⏑ – –) (81x), and πολύτλας Ὀδυσσεύς (⏑ – ⏑ ⏑ – –) (38x). At the end of a long footnote he included Ἑλένη in a list of eleven names of characters of some prominence in Homer who fall outside these systems "because the metrical value of the name is an absolute barrier to the creation of such formulas."[25] As it happens, Ἑλένη is

---

22 Fr. 200.2 M-W = 156e.2 M (not in H); fr. 204.43, 55 M-W = 110.43, 55 H = 155.43, 55 M.
23 Parry 1971a[1928]: 9–13.
24 Parry 1971[1930]: 277.
25 Parry 1971[1930]: 278 *sub fin.* (i.e., n. 2 beginning on the preceding page).

the only name in the list that has the metrical shape ⌣ ⌣ – and can thus be used after the masculine or penthemimeral caesura as the beginning of a noun-epithet formula filling the second hemistich. Helen's name is therefore not an absolute barrier to the hemistich formula.

Of name-epithet combinations used of Helen, the commonest in this position is Ἑλένης πόσις ἠυκόμοιο, preceded by Ἀλέξανδρος, thus the line:

– ⌣ Ἀλέξανδρος, Ἑλένης πόσις ἠυκόμοιο (6x).

A variant of this formula occurs five times in the Hesiodic *Catalogue*, as Ἀργείης Ἑλένης πόσις ἔμμενα[ι ἠυκόμοιο "to be the husband of fair-haired Argive Helen"[26] or ἱμείρων Ἑλένης πόσις ἔμμεναι ἠυκόμοιο "desiring to be the husband of fair-haired Helen."[27] This Hesiodic variant does not entail the Homeric lengthening of the syllable preceding the name Ἑλένη, which once began with digamma.[28] The rule for this particular kind of metrical exploitation of digamma has been stated as follows: "The poets, though unaware of the diachronic changes per se, were quite aware of their reflexes in attested formulae of the language and interpreted diachronic variants as free variants, which then led to their use as metrical alternatives."[29] Accordingly, in the Homeric formula under discussion, the potential of Ἑλένη for making position is exploited by the poet.[30] (Hesiod would have been quite capable of the same if it had suited his purposes.[31]) It is not, then, that the poet "observes" or "neglects" digamma at his whim. When he chooses at times

---

26 Fr. 200.2 M-W = 156e.2 M (not in H); fr. 204.43, 55 M-W = 110.43, 55 H = 155.43, 55 M.
27 Fr. 199.2 M-W = 108.2 H = 154d.2 M.
28 The name Helen with initial digamma has been found in two sixth-century inscriptions from the Menelaion in Sparta: *SEG* 26: 457–58; 36: 356. (Images first published in Catling and Cavanagh 1976; reprinted in Edmunds 2016a: 175, 182). In a forthcoming book, Nicole Lanérès will argue that the next-to-last word in Δεῖνι[ς]) τάδ'ἀνέθεκε) Χαρι[ ]) Ϝελέναι) ΜενελάϜο) cannot be read as Helen. Hainsworth 1993: 267 (on *Il.* 11.369: αὐτὰρ Ἀλέξανδρος Ἑλένης πόσις ἠϋκόμοιο): "the frequent lengthening of a naturally short syllable before the caesura prevents this verse from being cited for a Homeric Ϝελένη. Both epics imply Ἑ- by regularly eliding vowels before it (29x in OCT out of 58 occurrences)."
29 Hackstein 2010: 414. For this kind of diachronic picture cf. Reece 2009: 316 on ἔπεα.
30 Hoekstra 1989: 197 on *Od.* 14.68 a propos of Helen with initial digamma in the two sixth-century inscriptions from the Menelaion: "For epic poetry this means that if the abduction of Helen was among its older subjects, the digammated form of the name must have been part of early formulae. However, only a few traces of this state of affairs remain in Homer, the most notable being Ἀλέξανδρος, Ἑλένης πόσις ἠυκόμοιο." It is argued in Edmunds 2016a that Helen's abduction is the central motif in her story and might have come from Indo-European epic.
31 See the discussion of digamma in Hesiod by G. Edwards 1971: 135–39.

to remember it, he has the authority of tradition for a phrase for which he has need.³² Parry said:

> ...[T]he digamma was lost in the diction of early Greek heroic poetry neither sooner nor later than it was lost in the daily speech, but the singers who had to compose in a rigorous and therefore highly conservative verse-form, still used the old phrases and verses because that was their way of making poetry, because to have given up the traditional phrase wherever the loss of digamma now caused hiatus or failure to make position, would have been to destroy the diction almost entirely.³³

At other times the poet finds expedients to correct for the loss.³⁴
The other name-epithet formulas in the second half of the line are:
- Ἑλένη Διὸς ἐκγεγαυῖα (2x *Il.*, 1x *Od.*)
- Ἑλένης ἕνεκ' ἠϋκόμοιο (1x *Il.*)
- Ἑλένης πάρα καλλικόμοιο (1x *Od.*)
- Ἑλένη φέρε, δῖα γυναικῶν (1x *Od.*)
- Ἑλένης πόσις/ν ἠϋκόμοιο (6x *Il.*)
- Ἑλένης ἕνεκ' ἠϋκόμοιο; (1x *Il.*)

One can compare Kirk's tabulation of epithets for Aphrodite:³⁵
- δῖ' Ἀφροδίτη (4x *Il.*, 1x *Od.*)
- χρυσέης / χρυσέηι / χρυσέην Ἀφροδίτης (etc.) (5x *Il.*, 5x *Od.*)
- φιλομμειδὴς Ἀφροδίτη (5x *Il.*, 1x *Od.*)
- Διὸς θυγάτηρ Ἀφροδίτη (8x *Il.*, 1x *Od.*)
- ἐϋστεφάνου τ' Ἀφροδίτης (1x *Od.*), cf. ἐϋστέφανος/ου Κυθέρεια/ας (2x *Od.*)

The fourth and fifth items in this list are half-verses extending from the trochaic or feminine caesura to line-end, and they come under Parry's rule, quoted above. (φιλομμειδὴς and Διὸς θυγάτηρ are metrically interchangeable.³⁶) Despite the

---

32 So "Anlaut mit 'positionsbildendem' etymologischem Digamma" (Krieter-Spiro 2009: 120 on *Il.* 3.329) is not the whole truth.
33 Parry 1971[1934]: 393. On the loss of digamma in initial prevocalic position in particular see S. West 1988: 70 on lines 3–4, with references to scholarship on this matter.
34 See Reece 2009: 178–89 for an example of nu-ephelcystikon (and, through metanalysis, its far-reaching consequences).
35 Kirk 1985: 326, with alternate forms and references somewhat amplified here. Cf. another, somewhat fuller (but less convenient for present purposes) table of Aphrodite's epithets: Boedeker 1974: 20.
36 This violation of economy is the theme of Kirk's discussion *ad loc.*

vastly smaller number of examples for Helen, it is clear that her epithets come under the same description as those of the other chief characters.

Helen with an epithet in the first half of the hexameter

Parry defined a far smaller set of noun-epithet formulas in the nominative occurring between the beginning of the line and the penthemimeral caesura, without exception used as the subject of a verb in the preceding line.[37] The metrical shape of the name Helen makes such a formula impossible but again something similar is achieved, by means of formulas between the beginning of the line and the feminine caesura (τανύπεπλος 3x). In these cases the verb appears in the second half of the same line. There is one example of Ἀργείη Ἑλένη, Helen's most frequent epithet, in the first half of the line with the verb at the beginning of the *following* line (*Il.* 6.323–24).

Ἀργείη, which always occurs in the first half of the line (9x *Il.*, 4x *Od.*), is, however, usually in the accusative (9x in all), when either in line-initial position (3x) or in the second-third feet (6x). In the latter position, the name Helen following the epithet creates an hephthemimeral caesura, e.g. (*Il.* 7.350),

δεῦτ' ἄγετ' Ἀργείην Ἑλένην καὶ κτήμαθ' ἅμ' αὐτῇ

or, in the nominative (4x in all, 2x in this position), e.g. (*Od.* 4.184):

κλαῖε μὲν Ἀργείη Ἑλένη, Διὸς ἐκγεγαυῖα

In other words, the noun-epithet combination is itself mobile between the initial and the mid-verse positions. One concludes that, for the purpose of the composition of a line in which the accusative was wanted, the Argive Helen formula did duty.

Helen's formulas thus constitute a fairly complete syntactical repertory, with a preference for the nominative case in the second half of the line and a preference for the accusative in the first. It was possible to use the name-epithet formula in the dative but this case was avoided. It occurs only once (Ἶρις δ' αὖθ' Ἑλένῃ λευκωλένῳ ἄγγελος ἦλθεν, *Il.* 3.121). The dative is formulaic, however, in a certain prepositional phrase in lines beginning – ⏑⏑ ἀμφ' Ἑλένῃ (cf. App. 3).

---

[37] Parry 1971a[1928]: 55.

To conclude this survey of the epithets, Parry's statement that "Helen is the only woman in Homer who clearly has distinctive epithets of her own" requires comment. He proceeds to list:[38]
- Ἑλένη Διὸς ἐκγεγαυῖα
- Ἀργείη Ἑλένη
- Ἑλένῃ...εὐπατερείῃ.

By distinctive Parry meant "used for only one god or hero." None of the three epithets listed by Parry is distinctive of Helen. To begin with Ἀργείη, this epithet is in fact used twice of Hera in the *Iliad* (4.8; 5.908; cf. Hes. *Theog.* 11–12). Διὸς ἐκγεγαυῖα is used also of Athena (*Il.* 6.229; cf. Hes. *Op.* 256, of Dikē; *Theog.* 76: Διὸς ἐκγεγαυῖαι, of the Muses). εὐπατέρεια is used also of Tyro (*Od.* 11.235). These three epithets seem, then, to have been generic, to use the term that Parry contrasted with distinctive, even if they are not abundantly attested.[39] In fact, Helen's only distinctive epithet is ῥιγεδανή, used by Achilles (*Il.* 19.331). Not only does Helen lack distinctive epithets but she also falls outside Parry's rule that "For most of the principal Homeric heroes, there exists a line consisting entirely of their names in the vocative case and certain of their titles."[40] All of Helen's epithets, except some of the epithets of blame that she uses of herself and Achilles' ῥιγεδάνη (*Il.* 19.325), are shared with other women but sometimes with only one other woman or mainly with one other.

◆

The reason for this use of the same epithets of different women can be assumed to be the reliance of the composer on an inherited stock of epithets. From the time of Parry, this inheritance has been referred to as "tradition."[41] Scholarly opinion is, however, divided on the usefulness of this notion. In the matter of the epithets, for some scholars, who take a diachronic approach to the interpretation of the Homeric texts, tradition is a principle. Nagy speaks of the epithet as "like a small theme song that conjures up a thought-association with the traditional essence of an epic figure, thing, or concept."[42] John Miles Foley's referred to "traditional

---

38 Parry 1971a[1928]: 97.
39 Parry 1971a[1928]: 64.
40 Parry 1971a[1928]: 140.
41 A. Parry 1971: xxvii–xxviii: "The term 'traditional' had in the M.A. thesis [of M. Parry] represented an intuitive and aesthetic perception. In the French *thèse*, it became an inescapable scientific inference."
42 Nagy 1990a: 23. Most recently: Nagy 2016d. This view of the formula rests on a larger theory. The formula is "a fixed phrase conditioned by the traditional themes of oral poetry" and "meter

referentiality." "Traditional elements," he said, "reach out of the immediate instance in which they appear to the fecund totality of the entire tradition…, and they bear meanings as wide and deep as the tradition they encode."[43]

The concept of tradition underlying these statements goes back to a theory adopted by Parry from the anthropologist A.L. Kroeber (1876–1960), with whom Parry studied during his years at the University of California in Berkeley (1921–1923). Krober's theory of culture emphasized the collective accumulation of knowledge and skills and minimized the importance of the individual. In an essay published in 1917, he called culture in his sense "superorganic."[44] The influence of this concept on Parry is clear already in his M.A. thesis (1923).[45] In 1952, long after Parry's death, Kroeber retracted the superorganic as "unwarranted reification."[46] The critical term that Kroeber used of his own theory would later be used of the Parryist concept of tradition: "Within the discipline of Parryist studies of Homer, it is only a small step from…a 'superorganic' view of tradition to one that predicates verbal action of a reified Tradition."[47] Only a year after an anthropologist made this statement, a classical scholar made the same criticism: "Instead of defining tradition, Homerists tend to reify it."[48] Not all Homerists are liable to this charge, however; a dossier of those who "undervalue" tradition can also be constructed.[49]

John F. García, the anthropologist who made the critique of Parry, was thinking of formulaic composition (so "verbal action" suggests). In the superorganic view, as the quotations from Nagy and Foley show, tradition not only produces the formulas but also gives them meaning. These two sides of tradition can be

---

is diachronically generated by formula rather than vice versa." Cf. already Nagy 1976: 244: "the diachronic viewpoint suggests that the prime regulator of the Homeric epithet in particular and formula in general is traditional *theme* rather than current *meter*" (his emphasis). The formula so conceived comes from the deep past, and in fact Nagy's concept is based on comparative metrical studies in Greek and Sanskrit. See Nagy 1974 (summary on formula and meter at 140–49).

43 Foley 1991: 6. For uptake of this concept see Edwards 1997: 275. Cf. Dué 2012: "Every formula is traditional, but every formula carries with it many layers of accumulated meaning, meaning that resonates through time and even across geographical distances." For reflections on "traditional referentiality": Kelly 2007: 9–14.
44 Kroeber 1917.
45 García 2001: 68–69, with quotations from the thesis.
46 Kroeber 1952: 23, in the introduction to the reprint of Kroeber 1917. García 2001: 67 discusses the retraction. (Parry died in 1935).
47 García 2001: 70–71.
48 Scodel 2002: 4.
49 Ready 2018: 62–64.

distinguished as the signifier and the signified, to invoke Ferdinand de Saussure's well-known opposition.⁵⁰ On the side of the signifier, few scholars would hesitate to call the diction of Homeric epic traditional. On the side of the signified, it is more difficult to speak of a majority opinion. According to a view held by many, the process of oral composition in performance, precisely because it had to accommodate its audiences, tended to homeostasis or equilibrium of past and present.⁵¹ In this view, tradition is subtly brought up to date, while the present is ostensibly kept at a distance by the traditional style, i.e., by tradition in the first of the two senses distinguished above.⁵² The phenomenon of homeostasis can also be described as the conferral of value on an object by projecting its origin into the past. This conferral takes place in the performance, which itself is felt as traditional by the audience.⁵³ In sum, the signifier, the style, is traditional; that which is signified may be non-traditional.

This distinction is borne out in the study of Helen's epithets. On the one hand, they are traditional and, on the other, they have been used to signify a new Helen. As traditional, these epithets have come from someone more powerful than the narrator, from the one or the ones who composed the *Iliad* and the *Odyssey*, who were not themselves the inventors of these epithets.⁵⁴ They and those who preceded them inherited a repertory of epithets to express the possible aspects of women. The epithets for beauty, for example, constituted a rather extensive sub-set, of which each woman has a share.⁵⁵

Helen's epithets of beauty are in some instances the same as those of other women. Thus Helen is at various times like Penelope (ch. 5), Thetis (ch. 7), and Andromache (ch. 8). The kind of composition that produced such similarities is

---

50 Saussure 1972: 99–38 = 1986: 66–67 (where the terms signification and signal are used).
51 The question remains of what historical period is reflected in the *Il*. Cantilena 2012b, whose discussion has been followed in this paragraph refers to Morris 1986 for the reflection of the eighth and seventh centuries B.C.E. in the Homeric epics. Cf. Wickert-Micknat 1982: 2–3; Morris 1997: 558. Crielaard 2002 argues for the *Il*. and the *Od*. as "poetry of the present." Cf. Bierl 2015: 180–81; 185.
52 Cantilena 2012a: 85–86; Canfora 2012b: 155.
53 Scodel 2002: 31–32: "'Tradition' is in constant flux and will be redefined as its context changes. For those inside the tradition what matters is that they are able to feel that the performance is traditional, that it repeats crucial elements of performances of the past."
54 For the distinction between author or poet and narrator: de Jong 2004: ch. 1. For the present discussion the distinction between author and implied author (Ducrot and Todorov 1979[1972]: 329–30) is unnecessary. This distinction is applied to Homer by Rabel 1997.
55 For a list: Wickert-Micknat 1982: 121–22; for a bibliography on epithets for female beauty in archaic and classical Greek verse: 121 n. 735. There is no difference between goddesses and human women or between human women of different social levels.

evident at the level of the typical scene (sacrifice, dining, arming, etc.).[56] The same diction describes different characters doing the same things, without implying that these characters are somehow alike. In the same way, in the matter of a resemblance between Helen and another woman it does not extend beyond the aspect indicated by the epithet.[57] Besides this kind of limited similarity, which may even be sub-perceptual for a listening audience, there is also the pointed, apparently self-conscious, use of someone else's epithet, as an epithet of Athena is used of Helen in the *Odyssey* (4.227; ch. 10§4). Sometimes an epithet used of Helen can be seen, unexpectedly, as belonging to a class of women to which she does not belong (ch. 9). What has been said of Helen's epithets of beauty applies also to her kinship epithets, of which she has three that she shares with goddesses (ch. 10), besides εὐπατέρεια, used only of her and Tyro (ch. 11). Taken together her kinship epithets, like her epithets of beauty, can be seen as a selection from and a new distribution of an inherited stock.

---

[56] See Nünlist-de Jong s.v. "Typische Szene."
[57] In these cases, Lohmann's "distant connections" are not operative. Cf. Lohmann 1970: 181: "der Dichter mit bestimmter poetischer Absicht für den aufmerksam Hörer oder Leser erkennbare und auf sein Mitdenken und Erinnern berechnete Verbindungslinien zwischen teilweise weit auseinanderliegenden Szenen zieht."

1 Appellatives and Periphrastic Denominations

Helen is addressed as νύμφα φίλη "dear bride," φίλον τέκος "dear child," and γύναι "lady."[1] Both Paris and Menelaus use the last of these appellatives of Helen (*Il.* 3.438; *Od.* 4.148, 266). Helen likewise uses the appropriate appellatives in addressing Priam (3.172; §3 below) and Hector (6.344, 355; §4 below). All of these terms emerge, then, within family or marital relationships. Further, Helen's terms for her Trojan in-laws to some extent overlap with the ones that she uses to refer to her family in Sparta (§4). In addition to the terms used by Helen herself and others addressing her, there is a group of words for Helen as wife: γυνή in cases other than the vocative and three other words (§5). The word γυνή refers specifically to Helen as a prize by capture, a finding corroborated by the verbs referring to her abduction (§6). Finally, while all of the words that have been mentioned might be called "periphrastic denominations" of Helen, this chapter distinguishes this phenomenon from appellatives used by persons addressing Helen directly.[2]

1.1 The vocative γύναι "lady"

Both of Helen's husbands address her as γύναι, Paris when he asks her not to rebuke him for his failure in the single combat (3.438), Menelaus twice, deferring to something that she has just said (*Od.* 4.148, 266). (Hector addresses Andromache as γύναι at *Il.* 6.441 and Priam thus addresses Hecabe at 24.300.) Antenor's γύναι "lady," when he addresses Helen at *Il.* 3.204 on the wall of Troy, comes from the xenos of the Achaeans. As he recalls, he entertained Menelaus and Odysseus when they came to Troy on an embassy before the fighting started (*Il.* 3.204–24; cf. Apollod. Epit. 3.28; Herodotus 2.118).[3] Further, his son is the husband of Laodicē, one of Priam's daughters, thus a sister of Paris and the sister-in-law of Helen

---

[1] On the form and semantics of νύμφα, the Iliadic vocative of νύμφη: Kirk 1985: 281 on line 130.
[2] A full definition of denomination would be "the way in which a character is referred to in a literary text, either (1) by means of a proper name or a series of proper names..., or (2) by means of some form of indirect description" (de Jong 1993: 290). This paper deals with the second type, which will be referred to as "periphrastic denomination."
[3] The episode was narrated in the *Cypria* (Arg. pp. 42.55–57 B = p. 32.72–74 D = p. 116 Arg. 10c W); treated by Bacchylides in a dithyramb (15(14) S-M); dramatized by Sophocles in Ἑλένης Ἀπαίτησις ("The Demand for Helen's Return") (frs. 176–180a Radt [*TrGF* 4.177–80]). It was depicted on a Corinthian crater (ca. 560 B.C.E.) (*LIMC* "M." 9*) and on an Attic red-figure cantharus (ca. 425 B.C.E.). The *Il.* refers to this episode a second time: Paris bribed Antimachus to oppose

(*Il*. 3.121–24). (For Laodicē as sister-in-law see §2.) His form of address assumes some degree of acquaintance.[4]

1.2 νύμφα φίλη "dear bride"

Assuming the guise of Laodicē, Iris addresses Helen as νύμφα (*Il*. 3.130). The narrator, expressing Helen's point of view, calls Laodicē γάλοως (*Il*. 3.122).[5] Eustathius remarks on the distinction between the two terms for sister-in-law: γάλως τε γὰρ νύμφης ἐστὶ γάλως καὶ ἡ νύμφη γαλόῳ ἐστὶ νύμφη (I.617.23). "The sister-in-law is the 'sister-in-law" of the bride and the bride is the 'bride' to the sister-in-law." Homeric Greek has, then, two different, non-synonymous words for the two women's relations to the man through whom they are related, one for his sister, used by his wife, and one for his wife, used by his sister. νύμφα occurs only twice in Homer, the other time in the Odyssey, where Eurycleia thus addresses Penelope (4.743).[6] From these two examples it can be concluded that the word is a "form of address used (by another woman) of women married into a household."[7] (Cf. νύμφα of Helen in Stesichorus fr. 209 PMG / PMGF = fr. 170 D-F.)

1.3 φίλον τέκος "dear child"

Priam twice calls Helen φίλον τέκος (*Il*. 3.162, 192). It is a common term of affection for a child, either parental or on the part of an older person speaking to a

---

the return of Helen to Menelaos (11.122–25 [narrator]). Antimachus even urged the Trojans to kill Menelaus on the spot (11.138–42 [Agamemnon]). (This n. is largely taken from Edmunds 2016: 142.)

4 Krieter-Spiro 2009: 83 on line 204: "verwandtschaftlich-familiär." In *LfgrE* s.v. γυνή this place is listed under "Anrede" at B 2 d but it is not defined or commented on.

5 In this place the form is γαλόῳ. The same form occurs as a nom. plur. at *Il*. 22.473; gen. plur. γαλόων at *Il*. 6.378, 383; 24.769.

6 S. West in Heubeck, West and Hainsworth 1988: 239 on lines 743–44: "This may seem a surprising way to address a woman who has been married for over twenty years, but it reminds us that Eurycleia has been a member of Odysseus' household for longer than Penelope."

7 Thus *LfrgE* s.v. νύμφη II.5. Bettini 1998: 332 n. 71 proposed a more general, perhaps too general, definition. Despite a thorough survey of νύμφη and related terms in Greek literature, Andò 1996: 54 is far off the mark when she says of νύμφα at *Il*. 3.130 and *Od*. 4.743 "nel primo caso si intende forse sottolineare con questo termine un tratto distintivo della vicenda di Elena e il suo sostanziale ruolo di 'amante' nel poema iliadico, mentre nel caso di Penelope il riferimento implicito è al suo stato di ventennale privazione dell'uomo."

younger person.[8] The adjective φίλον as used by Priam has another connotation, too. It applies not only to family members but also to in-laws, as when Oedipus, apropos of his expulsion from Thebes, says to his brother-in-law Creon: τὸ συγγενὲς τοῦτ' οὐδαμῶς τότ' ἦν φίλον "This family relationship was then in no way dear to you" (Soph. *OC* 771). (For that matter the word φίλος can be extended to friends, guests, and servants in one's household.[9]) Thus Helen's addressing Priam as φίλε ἑκυρέ "dear father-in-law" (*Il.* 3.172) is symmetrical with his addressing her as φίλον τέκος.[10] (The word ἑκυρός is used in Homer only by Helen speaking to or about Priam [*Il.* 24.770].)[11] Priam's form of address to Helen is not, then, merely formulaic, as might appear from an unanalyzed collection of examples of the phrase.[12]

1.4 Helen's terms for her Trojan in-laws and for her family in Sparta

Of the appellatives for Helen five, then, occur in Book 3 of the Iliad, and two in Book 4 of the *Odyssey*. Those in the Iliad, except for Antenor's use of γύναι, all have to do with her family relationships in Troy, as does Helen's appellative for Priam (§3). In Book 6 she addresses Hector as δᾶερ "brother-in-law" (344, 355), and he addresses her as "Helen" (360), the only time in the *Iliad* and the *Odyssey* that her name appears in the vocative (see ch. 4§2.2). In Book 24 she is the third woman, after Hecuba, his mother, and Andromache, his wife, to lament over the body of Hector (762–75).[13] In this lament, she addresses him as δαέρων πολὺ

---

8 5.373 (Dione to Aphrodite); 8.39 (Zeus to Athena); 9.437 (Phoenix to Achilles), 444 (id.); 14.190 (Hera to Aphrodite); 18.63 (Thetis of Achilles); 21.509 (Zeus to Artemis); 22.38 (Priam to Hector), 183 (Zeus to Athena); 24.373 (Priam to young man = Hermes); *Od.* 4.611 (Menelaus to Telemachus); 16.25 (Eumaeus to Telemachus); 19.474 (Eurycleia to Odysseus); 23.5 (Eurycleia to Penelope). There is a variant φίλε τέκνον / τέκνον φίλε (*Il.* 22.84; *Od.* 2.363, 3.184, 15.125, 15.509).
9 Landfester 1966: 21–22.
10 She says: αἰδοῖός τέ μοί ἐσσι φίλε ἑκυρὲ δεινός τε·. Cf. Hector to Helen: μή με κάθιζ' Ἑλένη φιλέουσά περ· οὐδέ με πείσεις (*Il.* 6.360). On αἰδοῖος of family members see Tsagalis 2008: 114 n. 8.
11 Fullest list of attestations of this word in *DGE*[2] s.v. It is the standard word. See the chart (organized from woman's point of view) in Miller 1953: 46.
12 As at Wendel 1929: 98–102, 125. (Wendel is not useful for the present study because he aims at generalizations that cover not only Homer but all of Greek poetry down through fifth-century drama. Even his surveys of Homeric usage are too general.)
13 At 24.762 she uses the gen. plur. (quoted in text above); at 24.769 she uses the gen. plur. to refer to her other brothers-in-law. At 3.180 she uses the nom. sing. to refer to Agamemnon. At

φίλτατε πάντων "by far the dearest of all my brothers-in-law" (762). She recalls that he was kind to her, in spite of the fact that her husband (noun πόσις, 763) is Paris, who brought her to Troy (and, implicitly, brought the war along with her).¹⁴ Not only did she never hear a harsh word from him, but, if any of her in-laws reproached her, he restrained them. She specifies brothers-in-law (noun δαήρ), sisters-in-law (noun γάλοως, cf. *Il.* 3.122, discussed above), wives of brothers-in-law (noun εἰνάτερες), and mother-in-law (noun ἑκυρή), adding that her father-in-law (noun ἑκυρός) was always kind to her (769–70).¹⁵ Although she does not refer to any particular reproach, the list of affines in itself, with the distinction between father-in-law (always kind) and mother-in-law (by inference not always kind), suggests that anyone of them might have reproached her in the long period in which she was at Troy (765–66).¹⁶ Helen's lament is a personal reminiscence.¹⁷

In Book 3, she is equally concerned about the family that she left behind in Sparta. She uses four kinship terms: αὐτοκασιγνήτω (238, of her brothers), δαήρ (180, of Agamemnon), μήτηρ (238, of Leda; cf. 6.345), παῖς (175, of Hermione), and also πόσις (429, of Menelaus).¹⁸ The second and the last in this list of four overlap

---

14.156 the narrator uses the acc. sing. to describe Hera's perception of Poseidon. The report of Homeric usage by Huld 1988: 424 discusses the etymology of this word and Homeric phonological innovation. He points out that after Homer it is "exceedingly rare...employed only half the number of times that it occurs in epic diction." It "represents an isolate in Greek kinship terminology, the synchronic mark of a relic word."

14 On her reasoning: Richardson 1993: 357 on *Il.* 24.763–67. For useful discussions of the speech, with many bibliographical indications: Tsagalis 2004: 161–65; Perkell 2008: 104–107. Helen's lament is one of ten by close friends or family members in the *Il.* For an overview and bibliography see de Jong 2012: 185–86 on 22.477–514.

15 Richardson 1993: 157 on *Il.* 22.473: γαλόως and εἰνάτερες "tend to cluster around Helen and Andromache."

16 If Di Benedetto 1994: 128 n. 30 is right that the opening line of Helen's speech (762) echoes the opening line of Hecuba's (748), is it a kind of tact on Helen's part vis-à-vis a difficult stepmother? But Macleod 1982: 155 on line 770: "Priam's tenderness toward Helen is shown in 3.161–70. The frankness about Hecuba, in her presence, is natural, and was no doubt tolerable, in a lament."

17 One can take the speech's degree of formularity as an indication. Hainsworth 1968: 111–12 analyzes the speech and concludes "The formulaic density, at least as it can be demonstrated by exact repetition, is sharply reduced in comparison with the battle scenes." He goes on to show how a great deal of "the phraseology apparently not available from stock...echoes familiar word-associations."

18 Cf. Priam's inviting Helen to look from the wall of Troy ὄφρα ἴδῃ πρότερόν τε πόσιν πηούς τε φίλους τε ("in order that you may see your former husband and *pēoí* and dear ones"). On *pēoí* see Gates 1971: 27–28. "A meaning...which gives fairly good sense in all the Homeric and Hesiodic passages is 'kinsman living at a distance', 'kinsman outside ego's household'."

with the terms for her Trojan family. Although she does not express fear of reproach from her Spartan family (it could be taken for granted in the case of Menelaus), she surmises that her brothers, who she wrongly assumes are present at Troy, have withdrawn from the fighting because they dread the many reproaches that are hers (αἴσχεα δειδιότες καὶ ὀνείδεα πόλλ' ἅ μοί ἐστιν, 3.242).[19]

1.5 γυνή in the nominative and in oblique cases; Helen as ἄκοιτις and ἄλοχος

The vocative of γυνή was discussed above (§1). This word is used of Helen also in the nominative and in oblique cases five times, all in Book 3 (and also in Hector's indirect reference to her in line 48, on which see §7 below). In all these places this word refers to Helen as a prize by capture, implicitly a bride by capture, and disposable as such according to the captor's wishes.[20] The word ἄλοχος ("the one sharing the same bed"; < ἁ-λοχ-, in which the alpha is copulativum) has the same sense.[21] Menelaus, invoking Zeus Xenios, refers to the Trojans as "you who recklessly carried off my wedded wife and many of my possessions" (οἵ μευ κουριδίην ἄλοχον καὶ κτήματα πολλὰ / μὰψ οἴχεσθ' ἀνάγοντες, 13.623–27; see §6 below on ἀνάγοντες). Of course it was not the Trojans who carried Helen off but Paris and he did in fact violate xenia.[22] He will not, however, return Helen to Menelaus for that reason, although he can be persuaded by his brother Hector to make Helen the stakes in single combat with Menelaus. The herald announces the duel to Priam: μαχήσοντ' ἀμφὶ γυναικί· / τῷ δέ κε νικήσαντι γυνὴ καὶ κτήμαθ' ἕποιτο ("They will fight over the woman, and, whoever is the winner, the woman and the possessions will follow him").[23] Iris presents the terms to Helen (3.136–37):

---

19 Cf. Krieter-Spiro 2009: 94 on this line: "αἶσχος 'Häßlichkeit' i.S.v. 'häßliche Rede, Schmähung, Vorwurf'," though probably not "wegen Ehebruchs." On account, rather, of the *consequences* of her infidelity. Van Leeuwen 1912: 118: *Non dubitabat Helena quin Thersitae illi, qui aerumnas bellicas aegre ferrent, de se quamvis immerenti iactarent verba criminosa.*
20 *LfgrE* s.v. γυνή B4d: "Frau als Beute, Kampfpreis." The other places in Book 3 referring to Helen as such: 72 = 93, 157.
21 See Coray 2009: 131 on 19.298.
22 Cf. Aesch. *Ag.* 399–402, where Paris is the example of the one who is overcome by Ἄτη and brings ruin upon his city: οἷος καὶ Πάρις ἐλθὼν / ἐς δόμον τὸν Ἀτρειδᾶν / ᾔσχυνε ξενίαν τράπε-/ζαν κλοπαῖσι γυναικός.
23 ἕποιτο is future potential (Schwyzer 2.324, citing this place).

> μακρῆς ἐγχείῃσι μαχήσονται περὶ σεῖο·
> τῷ δέ κε νικήσαντι φίλη κεκλήσῃ ἄκοιτις.
>
> They will fight over you with long spears
> and you will be called the dear wife of the one who wins.

Paris retains possession of Helen, although the victory in the single combat was clearly Menelaus', as Agamemnon says (3.456–60). She is called the ἄκοιτις "wife" of Paris later that day when she obediently follows him to bed (ἅμα δ' εἵπετ' ἄκοιτις, 3.448 [narrator]).[24] At the council of the Trojans in Book 7 Paris proclaims (7.362–64):

> γυναῖκα μὲν οὐκ ἀποδώσω·
> κτήματα δ' ὅσσ' ἀγόμην ἐξ Ἄργεος ἡμέτερον δῶ
> πάντ' ἐθέλω δόμεναι
>
> I will not give back the woman.
> But the possessions, all that I brought from Argos to my house,
> I am willing to give all of them back.

Idaeus reports to the Argives: κουριδίην δ' ἄλοχον Μενελάου κυδαλίμοιο / οὔ φησιν δώσειν ("He says that he will not give back the wedded wife of renowned Menelaus," 7.392–93). The admission that Helen is or was in fact the wedded wife of Menelaus does not, in Paris' mind, oblige him to return Helen to Menelaus. She remains his prize, by a kind of pre-legal ius in re.

Helen was always a prize, disposable as such, and will continue to be one after the death of Paris. Menelaus had Helen as his wife in the first place because he won her in a contest with other suitors, an episode in the life of Helen narrated in the Hesiodic Catalogue but not referred to in the *Iliad*, where it is replaced by a kind of feudal loyalty to Agamemnon.[25] After Helen's second husband, Paris, is killed by Philoctetes in single combat, she marries Deïphobus (*Il. Parv.* Arg. 1 p. 74. 10 B = p. 52.11 D = Arg. 2e (p. 187) W). Priam has chosen Deïphobus in preference to Helenus, who in anger either retires to Mount Ida or, in the minor tradition, deserts to the Greeks (Conon FGrH 26 F 1 (XXXIV); Apollod. Epit. 5.9). Deïphobus

---

24 Later, she will say that she wishes that she had been the wife of a better man (ἀνδρὸς ἔπειτ' ὤφελλον ἀμείνονος εἶναι ἄκοιτις, 6.351). That she had and has no choice in the matter is a given; it is nevertheless part of the pathos of this speech, on which see Stoevesandt 2008: 117 on lines 350–53, 351; Graziosi and Haubold 2010: 178 on line 351. Paris has referred to Helen as his ἄλοχος shortly before (6.337).
25 Edmunds 2016a: 114–17.

had another rival for Helen in Idomeneus (Ibycus fr. 297 PMG = 297 PMGF; Simonides fr. 561; both from schol. T Hom. *Il.* 13.516.) In other words, there was another contest for Helen, with Priam as the arbiter.[26] Ultimately, with the success of the Argives, Menelaus will kill Deïphobus and will lead Helen down to the ships.[27] Thus Menelaus will have won Helen again, this time in combat, and the circle will be complete. All of these extra-Iliadic sources are consistent with the Iliad with respect to the status of Helen.

1.6 Leading (ἄγειν, ἀνάγειν) and following (ἕπεσθαι)

Helen is well aware of her status as an object of competition.[28] Even if she was inspired by Aphrodite with passion for Paris and left Sparta of her own volition,[29] the moment she boards his ship she becomes this object. The verb that she uses of her action so indicates. She says: "Indeed my husband is god-like Alexander, who brought me to Troy" (ἦ μέν μοι πόσις ἐστὶν Ἀλέξανδρος θεοειδής, / ὅς μ' ἄγαγε Τροίηνδ', 24.763–64). (The verbs that Helen uses in 24.766, ἔβην and ἀπελήλυθα, simply express the physical movement on her part that follows from the action of Paris designated by ἄγαγε.) When Helen and Paris reach Troy they are married.[30] Later, having returned to Sparta, Helen says of herself in Troy: "I bemoaned the blindness that Aphrodite / gave me, when he led me thither from my dear fatherland" (ἄτην δὲ μετέστενον, ἣν Ἀφροδίτη / δῶχ', ὅτε μ' ἤγαγε κεῖσε φίλης ἀπὸ πατρίδος αἴης, *Od.* 4. 261–62).[31]

---

26 In *Il. parv.* Arg. 1.6–7 B = Arg. 6–8 D = Arg. 2b W (pp. 181–84) a prophecy of Helenos causes Philoctetes to be brought from Lemnos. Only with his bow could Troy be captured. Other sources include two further conditions to the prophecy: the fetching of Neoptolemus from Scyros and the theft of the Palladion (see W loc. cit.).
27 Μενέλαος δὲ ἀνευρὼν Ἑλένην ἐπὶ τὰς ναῦς κατάγει, Δηΐφοβον φονεύσας, *Ilioupersis* Arg. 14–15 B = 21–22 D = Arg. 2d (p. 234) W; cf. *Od.* 8.516–18 (Demodocus, whose version perhaps implies that it was Odysseus who slew Deïphobus); Apollod. *Epit.* 5.22. Cf. Zeus at *Il.* 4.19: αὖτις δ' Ἀργείην Ἑλένην Μενέλαος ἄγοιτο.
28 López Gregoris 1986: 22: "Helena conoce cuál es su status como esposa de cualquier varón, status que no cambia aunque cambie el marido."
29 Krieter-Spiro 2009: 73 on lines 173b–74: "freiwillig."
30 As presupposed by the *Il.* (e.g., ἄκοιτις, 3.447) and as in the *Cypria* (Arg. 19–20 B = 26–27 D = Arg, 2e W (p. 93)). The marriage is shown on a Corinthian crater and on a *lebes* found at Smyrna (Edmunds 2016a: 305: items 16–17). Köstler 1950: 193 n. 99: "Daß die zweite Ehe durch ein doppeltes Verbrechen, das der Entführung und das des Bruches der Gastfreundschaft zustande kam, tat der Gültigkeit der Ehe keinen Abbruch." Quoted by Reichel 1999: 294. Contrary to Ebbott 1999: 3, Helen had no reason to consider her marriage to Paris blameworthy in itself.
31 On ἄτη in this passage: Cairns 2012: 11–12.

The compound ἀνάγω is used in the same sense. As Hector says to Paris, "Mingling with foreigners you brought back a beautiful woman" (μιχθεὶς ἀλλοδαποῖσι γυναῖκ' εὐειδέ ἀνῆγες, 3.48). Paris' action is described in the same way by Menelaus in a denunciation of all the Trojans: "You who willfully left and carried away my wedded wife and many possessions" (οἵ μευ κουριδίην ἄλοχον καὶ κτήματα πολλὰ / μὰψ οἴχεσθ' ἀνάγοντες, 13.626–27). The narrator, apropos of the Sidonian women whom Paris brought (ἤγαγεν, 6.291), refers to "that journey on which he brought back Helen" (τὴν ὁδὸν ἣν Ἑλένην περ ἀνήγαγεν, 6.292).[32] In short, ἀνάγω is the compound of ἄγω in the sense "abduct."[33] The verb used of Menelaus' leading Helen to the ships (κατάγειν) expresses the opposite of the action describing Paris' bringing Helen from Sparta to Troy.[34]

Paris uses another verb to refer to his abduction of Helen: ἔπλεον ἁρπάξας ἐν ποντοπόροισι νέεσσι ("I sailed away in ocean-faring ships, having snatched you from lovely Lacedaemon," 3.443–44). The verb ἁρπάζειν is the vox propria for stealing a woman.[35] Hector is right, then, when he says to Paris: σέο δ' εἵνεκ' ἀϋτή τε πτόλεμός τε / ἄστυ τόδ' ἀμφιδέδηε, "because of you the battle cry and war burn around this city" (6.328–29). Here εἵνεκα + genitive has a causal sense, whereas when the name Helen appears in this prepositional phrase the sense corresponds to Latin causā or gratiā + genitive (for the distinction between these two senses see ch. 7§5).

The action on Helen's part corresponding to the verb ἄγειν and the compound ἀνάγειν is expressed by the verb ἕπομαι. She says to Priam: "How I wish that evil death had been pleasing to me when I followed your son hither" (δεῦρο / υἱέϊ σῷ ἑπόμην, 3.174).[36] Here as elsewhere in Homer the two verbs, ἄγειν, ἀνάγειν and ἕπεσθαι are related diathetically as active and passive.[37] When Idaeus paraphrases Paris' terms for the single combat with Menelaus, he says: "the woman

---

[32] But at ch. 11§1 it is suggested that the perspective is not the narrator's but, by "implicit embedded focalization" (defined in ch. 7§5), Hecuba's.
[33] LfgrE s.v. ἄγω B IV 2 "entlangführen, einherführen," citing Il. 3.48, 6.292, 13.627, places discussed in the text above.
[34] See n. 25 above.
[35] LfgrE s.v. B 2a "Raub, Entführung," citing this place; DGE s.v. ἁρπάζω I.3 "raptar, secuestar, esp. de mujeres." Among Gorgias' four possible reasons for Helen's leaving Sparta with Paris, the fundamental one is clear: she was "carried off by force" (βίᾳ ἁρπασθεῖσα), although a second one, eros, played a part (ἐρασθεῖσα) (Hel. 6; 20).
[36] For ἕπομαι: LfgrE s.v. B 1bβ (col. 656), with cross-reference to ἄγω B III med. 2: "eine Frau als Gemahl heimführen" (col. 121). For the death-wish: ch. 2§7.
[37] As shown by López Gregoris 1986: 23–30, whose results are summarized by Gómez Seijo 2017: 16–17. Blondell 2013: 65, on the contrary, speaks of Helen's implicitly asserting "her own past agency."

and the possessions would follow the winner" (τῷ δέ κε νικήσαντι γυνὴ καὶ κτήμαθ' ἕποιτο, 3.255).

1.7 Indirect description or "periphrastic denomination"

Hector's rebuke of Paris when he draws back from combat with Menelaus contains three indirect descriptions of Helen, two with an epithet. Hector asks Paris if, when he sailed to Sparta with his comrades and brought back Helen, he was the kind of man which he now appears to be, i.e., a coward (3.46–53).

> ἦ τοιόσδε ἐὼν ἐν ποντοπόροισι νέεσσι
> πόντον ἐπιπλώσας, ἑτάρους ἐρίηρας ἀγείρας,
> μιχθεὶς ἀλλοδαποῖσι γυναῖκ' εὐειδέ' ἀνῆγες
> ἐξ ἀπίης γαίης νυὸν ἀνδρῶν αἰχμητάων,
> πατρί τε σῷ μέγα πῆμα πόληΐ τε παντί τε δήμῳ,
> δυσμενέσιν μὲν χάρμα, κατηφείην δὲ σοὶ αὐτῷ;
> οὐκ ἂν δὴ μείνειας ἀρηΐφιλον Μενέλαον;
> γνοίης χ' οἵου φωτὸς ἔχεις θαλερὴν παράκοιτιν·
>
> Were you such a one when in sea-faring ships
> you sailed over the sea, having gathered your trusty comrades,
> and, mingling with foreigners, brought back a beautiful woman
> from a distant land, the sister-in-law of warriors,
> a great pain to your father and your city and to all the people,
> a joy to your enemies but to yourself a shame?
> Would you not face Menelaus, dear to Ares?
> You would find out of what sort of man you have the ripe bedmate.

The implication of the opening of Hector's question (46–48) is that Paris was a better man then and not reprehensible as he is now. Hector has in mind the typical exploit of bride-capture, of which he does not disapprove in itself.[38] The epithet εὐειδής, which occurs only here in Homer, is found in Hesiod's lists of Nereids (*Theog.* 250)[39] and of Oceanids (*Theog.* 354) and four times in Hesiodic catalogues.[40] With the verb ἀνῆγες (cf. §6 above) that governs the phrase γυναῖκ'

---

[38] So Bergold 1977: 34ff. Krieter-Spiro 2009: 32 on lines 46–51 holds, on the contrary, that Hector refers to the same irresponsibility in the past as in the present.
[39] For an indication of the *Iliad*'s differentiation of itself from catalogue hexameter: Hes. *Theog.* 250 ≈ *Il.* 18.45 (ἀγακλειτή instead of εὐειδής).
[40] Hes. *Meg.* fr. 252.4 M-W = *Meg.* fr. 13.4 H = *Cat.* fr. 190.4 M; Hes. *Cat.* frs. 10(a).24 M-W = 5.24 H = 10.24 M (restored); 10(a).34 M-W = 5.34 H = 10.34 M (restored); 10(a).59 M-W = 5.59 H = 10.59 M (restored).

εὐειδέ' one can compare in the Hesiodic Catalogue the simplex ἤγαγε / ἠγάγετο, which is the normal word for bringing home a bride.[41] Contrasting Paris then with Paris now, Hector uses the diction of another kind of epic hexameter to describe Paris' action in the past.

Hector refers to Helen as νυὸν ἀνδρῶν αἰχμητάων "the sister-in-law of warriors" (i.e., of Agamemnon and those who fight in his side) or more generally "the relative of warriors" (i.e., all male affiliates of the household immediately affected by the abduction) (3.49).[42] This reference to Helen, while it is in apposition to γυναῖκ' εὐειδέ', transfers Paris' exploit to another frame of reference. Helen was already married, unlike those beautiful women brought back by other heroes, and, further, she was the in-law of warriors who would attempt, and in fact are now attempting, to recover her. Elsewhere in its few occurrences in Homer, the word νυός refers only to daughters-in-law.[43] It is a matter here of the consequences, unforeseen by Paris, of the abduction.[44]

Hector's first question (3.48–51) is, in effect, answered by a second question. First: Were you such when…? Implicit answer: No. The reason for the implicit answer comes in the form of second question, viz.: Would you not face Menelaus? Implicit answer: You would not. Explicit answer: (If you did so) you would find out… Hector's sarcasm includes reference to Helen as the wife of Menelaus, even though Paris is now married her (§5 *sub fin.*, with notes).[45] Further, Hector uses παράκοιτις to refer to Helen as wife (53; cf. §5 for the other three words for wife), the only time it is used of her. It is used of one other mortal woman, the wife of Meleager (9.590), elsewhere of Hera.[46] This word has the epithet θαλερή "blooming" (LfgrE s.v. B 3) only here. (Hera as ἄκοιτις has this epithet at Hes. *Theog.* 921 and the formula θαλερὴν…ἄκοιτιν is used eleven times of young brides in the Hes-

---

41 Frs. M-W 10a.46 = 5.46 H = 10.46 M, M-W 26.36 = 17.36 H= 23.36 M, M-W 30.29 = 20.29 H = 27.29 M, M-W 105.3 (restored) = 122.3 H; M-W 193.11 (restored) = 90.11 H = 136.11 M, M-W 251a.5 = Meg 12.5 H = 189a.5 M. Cf. *Theog.* 266, 410, 508, 901.
42 These interpretations follow Krieter-Spiro 2009: 33 on line 49.
43 22.65 (in his speech to Hector, evoking the fall of Troy, Priam describes the consequences for his sons, his daughters, their children, his daughters-in-law and for himself); 24.166 (the wives of the sons of Priam grieve for Hector); *Od.* 3.451 (Nestor's daughters, daughters-in-law and wife raise the ritual cry as a heifer is sacrificed).
44 Herodotus supplies a motive for Paris' heedlessness: he did not expect that he would pay a penalty, because the perpetrators of earlier abductions had not done so (…Ἀλέξανδρον τὸν Πριάμου…ἐθελῆσαί οἱ ἐκ τῆς Ἑλλάδος δι' ἁρπαγῆς γενέσθαι γυναῖκα, ἐπιστάμενον πάντως ὅτι οὐ δώσει δίκας· οὐδὲ γὰρ ἐκείνους διδόναι, 1.3.1).
45 For sarcasm etc.: Krieter-Spiro 2009: 34 on lines 52–53.
46 Hera: 4.60; 14.346; 18.184, 365; 21.479. Hera once uses this word of Thetis (24.60).

iodic Catalogue. For Hera as καλλιπάρῃος, an epithet appropriate to a marriageable young woman: ch. 9§2.) Hector not only refers to Helen as Menelaus' wife, he characterizes her as the young bedmate she was at the time of the abduction, a poignant loss for Menelaus and one likely to provoke the response that it has in fact provoked.

1.8 Conclusion

As Helen well knows, she is the wife of the one who happens to have her in his possession.[47] As her appellatives and the words for "wife" that are used of her show, Helen's fundamental identity at Troy is that of wife. As the wife of Paris she is an in-law of the royal family, as the appellatives used of her and by her attest. She has only two friends among her in-laws, Hector and Priam. Her only other Trojan friend is Antenor, the xenos of the Achaeans in Troy. His daughter, her sister-in-law, is the one whose appearance Iris assumes when she brings Helen the news of the single combat. The blame that Helen suffers in Troy is discussed in the next chapter. Helen sees herself also as a member of the family that she left behind in Sparta. When she returns to Sparta she becomes again the wife (ἄλοχος) of Menelaus and he gives order to her as such, along with the servants (αὐτίκ' ἄρ' ᾗ ἀλόχῳ ἠδὲ δμῳῇσι κέλευσε, 15.93).

---

[47] López Gregoris 1986: 22: "Helena conoce cuál es su status como esposa de cualquier varón, status que no cambia aunque cambie el marido."

2 Epithets of Opprobrium

The blame of Helen in the *Iliad* comes from four sources: The most abundant is Helen, who uses four pejorative epithets of herself. These are κύων, κακομήχανος and κρυοέσση, in the same line (*Il.* 6.344, to Hector), and κυνῶπις (*Il.* 3.180, to Priam). She calls herself κυνῶπις also at *Od.* 4.145–46, addressing Menelaus and taking his presumed point of view.[1] When she uses στυγερή (*Il.* 3.404, to Aphrodite), she is not blaming herself.

The second source of blame, no doubt far more abundant, is Helen's Trojan in-laws. We never hear them speaking of her, but from Helen's lament over Hector in Book 24 it is clear that they did reproach her (ch. 1§4). So when Helen uses pejorative epithets of herself, to trusted in-laws, apologetically, these epithets are in the nature of quotations of what the others say about her. She blames herself preemptively.[2] A third and a fourth source are Achilles, who refers to her as ῥιγεδανή (*Il.* 19.325), and Aphrodite, who rebukes her as σχετλίη (*Il.* 3.414).

None of the seven epithets to be considered in this chapter, κακομήχανος, κρυοέσση, κυνῶπις, κύων, ῥιγεδανή, στυγερή, and σχετλίη, belongs to a recurring combination with the name Helen. Furthermore, the only one that could be considered a standard personal epithet of opprobrium is σχέτλιος (in the vocative also of Achilles, Hector, the Cyclops, and Odysseus, but in the feminine singular in only one other place, *Od.* 23.150).[3]

2.1 κακομήχανος

When Helen calls herself κακομήχανος "contriver of mischief" (*Il.* 6.344) he mischief that she has in mind was, as she immediately makes clear, the war: she wishes that she had died before τάδε ἔργα "these events," as she calls them, took place (348). Only two others in Homer use κακομήχανος and each time this epithet refers to deadly conflict. (It appears only once in Greek of the classical period, in Bacchyl. 8.18, of thieves.) In the *Iliad*, Phoenix quotes Peleus' advice to Achilles when he left for Troy: ληγέμεναι δ' ἔριδος κακομηχάνου (9.257, "desist from

---

[1] As Di Benedetto 2010: 284–85 on line 148 has shown, Menelaus deliberately overlooks her apology.
[2] Di Benedetto 1998: 335–39. Boedeker 2012: 72 n. 26: "As if pre-empting any reproach, she blames herself–to Priam (*Il.* 3.173–80), to Hector (*Il.* 6.344–58) and in the *Odyssey* to Menelaus and Telemachus (4.145)."
[3] *LfgrE* s.v. σχέτλιος B1a.

https://doi.org/10.1515/9783110626124-003

baneful strife")–precisely what Achilles does not do. As Helen is the cause of the war, at least in her self-presentation to Hector, Achilles' quarrel with Agamemnon and withdrawal from the fighting–in short his "destructive wrath"–are the cause of the episode in the war recounted in the *Iliad*. In the *Odyssey*, Penelope calls Antinous κακομήχανε (16.418).[4] As soon becomes clear, she has in mind the suitors' plan to kill Telemachus (421–22). As said above, Helen's κακομήχανος can be heard as a quotation of what the Trojans call her and a rhetorical appropriation of their term for her. They, with the exception of Hector and Priam, are the ones who regard her as the cause of the war.

Helen's death-wish, which has already been heard in her reply to Priam and will be heard again in her lament for Hector, has usually been interpreted psychologically, as revealing her true feelings about herself.[5] Her death-wishes are, however, apologetic and part of a rhetorical strategy (§7 below; ch. 4§2.2). As a scholiast said: "she persuasively avoided the shame for what happened" (πιθανῶς παρέδραμε τὴν αἰσχύνην τῶν εἰργασμένων, schol. bT 348c Erbse). The English translation just given might suggest the scholiast's judgment on the result of Helen's speech. The adverb πιθανῶς refers, however, to the rhetorical persuasiveness that the scholiast perceives.

2.2 κρυοέσση (*Il.* 6.344)

This adjective is derived from κρύος, meaning a coldness that makes one shiver, and is used only of the phenomena of battle (e.g., fear) and of death in battle (of Tartarus at ps-Hes. *Scut.* 255).[6] It is here transferred to Helen as the cause of the war.[7] Eustathius well explains: "Homer calls ὀκρυόεσσαν the one who caused the deaths of many by the battles on account of her and sent them to cold Hades."[8] If, as she says in the conclusion of her speech in Book 24, πάντες δέ με πεφρίκασιν

---

4 Cf. the other -μηχανος compounds in the vocative: ἀμήχανε, Zeus to Hera, *Il.* 15.14 and πολυμήχαν' Ὀδυσσεῦ, *Il.* 4x; *Od.* 14x.
5 For example, Reichel 1994: 265–67. Cf. n. 43 below.
6 The manuscripts have an ancient false division ὀκρυόεσση (also at *Il.* 9.64). West reads Payne Knight's κακομηχάνοο κρυοέσσης. The emendation is historically correct (Schwyzer 1.103) but should it be the reading? See Leumann 1993[1950]: 50; Chantraine 1968–1980 s.v. ὀκρυόεις; Stoevesand 2008: 116 on line 344; Reece 2009: 81–87; Graziosi and Haubold 2010: 176 on line 344.
7 *LfgrE* s.v. κρυόεις, ὀκρυόεις.
8 ὀκρυόεσσαν δὲ λέγει τὴν πολλοὺς νεκρώσασαν τοῖς δι' αὐτὴν πολέμοις καὶ κρυερῷ Ἅιδῃ προπέμψασαν (II.326.13).

"everyone shudders at me" (775), then κρυοέσση "chilling" is a good way to express their feelings about her.[9]

2.3 ῥιγεδανή (*Il.* 19.325)

In his lament for the death of Patroclus Achilles says that he would suffer nothing worse if he learned of the death of his father (19.323–35)

> ὅς που νῦν Φθίηφι τέρεν κατὰ δάκρυον εἴβει
> χήτεΐ τοιοῦδ' υἷος· ὃ δ' ἀλλοδαπῷ ἐνὶ δήμῳ
> εἵνεκα ῥιγεδανῆς Ἑλένης Τρωσὶν πολεμίζω·

> who now I think in Phthia sheds a soft tear
> for need of such a son, but I, in a foreign land
> am fighting the Trojans on account of Helen, at whom we shudder.[10]

The thought of his lonely father in Phthia provokes in Achilles the thought of Helen as the one who keeps him in Troy, and he characterizes her as ῥιγεδανή. One of those "many reproaches" from the Achaeans that Helen says are hers (3.242) finally comes out, and not from a Thersites but from Achilles (cf. ch.1 n. 19). The adjective that he uses is a Homeric hapax (and it does not occur again until Ap. Rhod. 4.1343) but as a hapax it does not characterize him or his lament.[11] This unexpected word, however, like the rare ἄκμηνος earlier in this speech (320), the alliteration, and the wordplay, show us again the "master speaker" and "formulaic artist."[12] The "sharp tone" of Achilles' voice heard elsewhere can be heard here.[13] In the line under discussion Achilles is also changing the grounds of his participation in the campaign, which he is about to resume. His original conception of his and the other Achaeans' role comes out in his rebuke of Agamemnon in Book 1: we came here in order to oblige you, seeking restitution (so to translate

---

9 On φρίσσειν, φρίκη, φρικώδης: Zink 1962: 19–22 ("shuddering" but rarely physical). Cf. LSJ s.v. φρίσσω II: "freq. of a feeling of *chill, shiver, shudder*."
10 For Achilles' lament as a whole and its parallelism with the preceding lament of Briseïs: Edwards 1991: 268–69 on lines 287–300; Tsagalis 2008: 257–58. For lines 324–25: Tsagalis 2008: 123. For Achilles' lament also: Coray 2009: 139 on 322–37. See Janko 1992: vii for a recasting of lines 328–29 in memory of Janko's own father.
11 Martin 1989: 179–80. Cf. Janko 1992: 271: "Save to Alexandrian poets in search of novelty, *hapaxes* matter little, given our scant evidence for the early Greek lexicon…"
12 Martin 1989: 64–65 on alliteration; Macleod 1982: 51–52 on wordplay; Coray 2009: 81 on 163 (ἄκμηνος).
13 Martin 1989: 144.

τιμή, to bring out its concrete sense [=Helen] here) for you and Menelaus from the Trojans (158–60).¹⁴ Helen is not mentioned by name. In Book 19, it is not we, the army, who follow Agamemnon but I, Achilles, who fight the Trojans (unique example in Homer of first person singular πολεμίζω).¹⁵

2.4 στυγερή (*Il.* 3.404)

After Aphrodite has snatched Paris from the battlefield to his bedroom (313–82), she goes to Helen on the wall of Troy, disguised as the old spinning woman whom Helen brought from Sparta, and summons her to him (383–94). Helen sees through the disguise and delivers a rebuke of Aphrodite, by common consent one of the most powerful speeches in the *Iliad* (395–412).¹⁶ Aphrodite, enraged, threatens Helen, who immediately complies and goes with Aphrodite to Paris.¹⁷ Helen's rebuke opens with questions: Why do you try to deceive me (doubting Aphrodite's ostensible purpose of summoning her to Alexander) (399)?¹⁸ Will you drive me to some further city in this region where you have a mortal favorite (400–402)? Because Menelaus has now defeated Alexander and wishes to take me home, hateful as I am (στυγερή)–is that the reason that, crafty as always, you are here (403–405)?¹⁹ The point of this question is Aphrodite's deceit, not Helen's plight, which does not come into Helen's mind until toward the end of the speech

---

14 For the basis of the Achaean alliance see ch. 1§5 with reference to Edmunds 2016a. Achilles was in any case too young to have been one of the suitors of Helen and thus he had not sworn the oath of the suitors: Hes. *Cat.* 204.49–54 M-W = 110.49–54 H = 155.49–54 M. On his age: Fantuzzi 2012: 13–14.
15 For this and other unique forms of common words in Achilles' speeches see Martin 1989: 179–96.
16 Kirk 1985: 323 on lines 399–412; Krieter-Spiro 2009: 140–41 on lines 399–412. Cf. Griffin 1980: "In terms of the story, without the gods the abduction of Helen would be what it already is in Herodotus and what it remains for Offenbach: an essentially frivolous tale of a lively wife, a lusty lover, and a cuckold. The agency of Aphrodite, her protection of the man who 'has the gifts of Aphrodite', her compulsion of Helen, make the story a significant and tragic one." What it is for Offenbach it is already for Roman poets (Ovid, *Tristia* II 371–72: *Ilias ipsa quid est aliud, nisi adultera, de qua / inter amatorem pugna virumque fuit?* Cf. Hor. *Sat.* 1.3.107–108; *Priapea* 68.9–10).
17 On this scene see Edmunds 2016a: 194–95.
18 With line 399 (δαιμονίη, τί με ταῦτα λιλαίεαι ἠπεροπεύειν;) cf. Diomedes to Aphrodite at *Il.* 5.348–49 (εἶκε Διὸς θύγατερ πολέμου καὶ δηϊοτῆτος· / ἦ οὐχ ἅλις ὅττι γυναῖκας ἀνάλκιδας ἠπεροπεύεις;). Schol. T on line 549: "Some refer it to Helen."
19 For this epithet in *Od.* see de Jong 2001: 145. It occurs in what she calls "character-language," i.e., "words which are typically used by characters, i.e., which occur mainly or exclusively in speeches..." (xii).

(410–12).²⁰ Her plight includes her status as an object of reproach in the eyes of both Achaeans and Trojans. Now there would be the additional reproach from the Trojan women if she went back to the bed of the coward Paris (Τρῳαὶ δέ μ' ὀπίσσω / πᾶσαι μωμήσονται, "all the Trojan women will blame me hereafter," 411–12). In the immediate context, just after the duel, Helen may also be thinking of the attitude of Menelaus in particular. When, at the fall of Troy, he finally recovers her, his first reaction is one of anger. For the reconstruction of the story from this first encounter to their embarkation, Proclus' summary of the relevant part of the Iliouperis is too brief to be of any help: "Having killed Deïphobus, Menelaus took her to the ships."²¹ This episode has to be reconstructed from vase paintings, which present two different versions. In one of them, found also in Euripides, Menelaus continues in a vengeful state of mind. Many vase paintings show him reacting with rage to the sight of Helen. Some show him smitten by desire.²²

2.5 Semantic field of κρυοέσση, ῥιγεδανή and στυγερή

Three of the epithets that have been discussed in this chapter belong to a semantic field.²³ κρυοέσση, as pointed out, is from κρύος, "icy cold" (LSJ s.v.). ῥιγεδανή is from ῥῖγος "frost, cold" (LSJ s.v.).²⁴ The root of στυγερός is perhaps related to a

---

20 See Kirk's analysis of this speech (n. 16 above). Krieter-Spiro 2009 holds that these lines show that Helen's desire to return to Sparta (cf. 3.139f.) has been rekindled; that her bitter imputations in lines 400–402 show her disappointment; that she has long rued her departure from her homeland and the self-reproach of στυγερὴν ἐμέ, "das häufige Motiv der Selbstbeschimpfung"...(wie 172–80, 6.344–58...)," is an expression of her regret.
21 *Iliupersis* Arg. pp. 88–89.14–15 B = p. 62.21–22 D; cf. Apollod. *Epit.* 5.22.
22 Edmunds 2016a: ch. 3§10.3.
23 The concept of semantic field is used here without discussion of its theoretical ramifications. A common-sense definition is assumed: "Groups of words in the lexicon can be semantically related by being members of a set known as a semantic field… On a very general and intuitive level, we can say that the words in a semantic field, though not synonyms, are all used to talk about the same general phenomenon…" (Akmajian, *et al.* 2001: 239–40). The field discussed has already been discussed apropos of Helen in the *Iliad* (without the term "field") by Cairns 2013: 82–84, 86, beginning with φρίκη: "…[T]he experiential network in which φρίκη belongs (in which φρίκη-type emotions are typified by the lowered body temperature, shivering, and piloerection that are their physical symptoms) encompasses a range of other terms which express complementary aspects of the same imagery."
24 The formation of ῥιγεδανός is normal: Schwyzer 1: 530. On ῥιγέω ("to shudder" as a metaphor for an emotional reaction) vs. ῥιγόω (for a physical reaction): Zink 1962: 15–18; Cairns 2013: 87 n. 32.

Russian verb expressing the idea of "cold" but the etymology is uncertain.[25] In any case, "the meanings of στυγερός in early Greek epic can be explained if one proceeds from a hypothetical base meaning of 'to experience the feeling of coldness'."[26] While this base meaning is never found as such, it is implied by the meanings of σ / Στύξ as appellative and as river name, which are associated with the idea of coldness.

These adjectives having "cold" as their base meaning are extended to death, in particular death in battle and gods of death. It is a matter of substituting the effect, i.e., cold, for the cause, i.e., death. These adjectives are perhaps extended to Helen because she is the cause of death-bringing war.[27] Helen herself testifies to the effect: πάντες δέ με πεφρίκασιν "everyone shudders at me" (Il. 24.775 again). But in general a bad wife is chilling. Concluding his precepts on choosing a wife, Hesiod says (Op. 702–703):

> οὐ μὲν γάρ τι γυναικὸς ἀνὴρ ληίζετ' ἄμεινον
> τῆς ἀγαθῆς, τῆς δ' αὖτε κακῆς οὐ ῥίγιον ἄλλο.
>
> For a man acquires nothing better than a wife,
> a good one, while there is nothing more chilling than a bad one.

The same thought in almost the same words is found also in Semonides (6W²). Helen of course violates each of Hesiod's precepts: she was probably not in her teens when she arrived in Troy; she was not a virgin; she came from somewhere else, not from her husband's locale (cf. 608–701). Even without the war that she brought upon the Trojans, she would be found chilling by Hesiod's standards.

2.6 σχετλίη (*Il.* 3.414)

Helen's rebuke of Aphrodite (cf. §4 above) provokes an angry reply (3.412–17):

> Τὴν δὲ χολωσαμένη προσεφώνεε δῖ' Ἀφροδίτη·
> "μή μ' ἔρεθε, σχετλίη, μὴ χωσαμένη σε μεθείω,
> τὼς δέ σ' ἀπεχθήρω ὡς νῦν ἔκπαγλ' ἐφίλησα,

---

[25] Chantraine 1968–1980 s.v. στυγέω; Frisk 1960.2 s.v. στυγέω for a somewhat fuller discussion of this comparison with the Russian verb and with references to other hypotheses. Beekes 2010 s.v. στυγέω rejects the comparison. For -ερό-: Meillet and Vendryes 1963: 381 (§572); Palmer 1980: 258.
[26] *LfgrE* s.v. στυγέω B.
[27] *LfgrE* s.v. κρυόεις, ὀκρυόεις B.

> μέσσῳ δ' ἀμφοτέρων μητίσομαι ἔχθεα λυγρά
> Τρώων καὶ Δαναῶν, σὺ δέ κεν κακὸν οἶτον ὄληαι."
>
> Enraged, divine Aphrodite addressed her:
> Do not provoke me, obstinate one, lest in anger I abandon you,
> and so hate you as I now terribly love you
> and contrive between the two sides a baleful hatred (against you),
> of both Trojans and Danaans, and you meet an evil doom.

Of the epithets discussed in this chapter the only one used of Helen directly to her face by someone else is σχετλίη.[28] It has its basic sense.[29] Thus the translation "obstinate." Its force here comes from Aphrodite's anger and not from some particularly strong sense of the word.[30] Helen's fear and immediate compliance–she follows Aphrodite back to the house of Paris (418–20)–are provoked by the threat of a "baleful hatred" against her that will be shared by the Trojans and the Danaans (for the idea cf. 4.444 of Eris: ἥ σφιν καὶ τότε νεῖκος ὁμοίϊον ἔμβαλε μέσσῳ "who then also cast strife into them equally," i.e., into both sides). The threat is realistic because Helen knows that there is already blame of her on both sides (3.242, 24.775, cf. 3. 411–12 for the anticipation of blame). If this present resentment of her became anger and if it were shared by Achaeans and Trojans equally, then she would cease to be the object that the former are fighting to recover and the latter to keep. The Trojans might kill her (by stoning, Kirk suggests in his note on 416–17) and the Achaeans would depart. Or the Achaeans would decide to depart, and then the Trojans would kill her.

The scene as a whole, from Aphrodite's appearance on the wall of Troy and summoning of Helen to Helen's entering the bed of Paris (380–447), has a concentration of epithets (Ἑλένη Διὸς ἐκγεγαυῖα, 418; δῖα γυναικῶν, 423; κούρη Διὸς αἰγιόχοιο, 426), which are discussed in subsequent chapters.[31] They are juxtaposed to Aphrodite's epithets and denominative in the same scene (413 δῖ' Ἀφροδίτη, 420 δαίμων, 424 φιλομμειδὴς Ἀφροδίτη, 425 θεά) and also to Helen's own

---

[28] The epithet belongs to "character-language" (on which see n. 19 above).
[29] Vanséveren 1998: 254: "L'adjectif souligne d'abord l'entêtement, l'obstination de certains personnages à persévérer dans des actes ou des idées, le plus souvent de façon négative." In an Appendix (268–73) Vanséveren gives a sequential list of occurrences in Il. and Od. (text and translation for each).
[30] There is a tendency to look outside the context for a strong sense: e.g., Kirk 1990: 325 on line 414: "a strong term"; *LfgrE* s.v. σχέτλιος "schrechlich"; Krieter-Spiro 2009: 145 on line 414: "etwa, 'Verwegene'."
[31] This paragraph has in substance been taken from Edmunds 2016a: ch. 4 §7.2.

denominatives. Paris addresses her as γύναι (438; ch. §1, §5) and when she follows him to bed, Homer refers to her as "wife" (ἄκοιτις, 447). A contrast between Helen and Aphrodite with respect to divine status is at work. After Aphrodite threatens her, Helen "sprung of Zeus" is afraid (418). Helen "the daughter of Zeus" (426) obediently sits down on the chair that Aphrodite has placed in front of Paris. The epithets seem to have concessive force: although Helen is the daughter of Zeus, she is intimidated by another, more powerful daughter of Zeus. In the list just given, Helen and Aphrodite share one adjective, δῖα. In Helen's case, it is part of the epithet δῖα γυναικῶν (423) "noble among women" (ch. 5).

2.7 κύων (*Il.* 6.344, 356)

Helen calls herself a bitch. In doing so, she uses in an oblique case a word that others use, of other men and women, in the vocative.[32] She uses of herself a word by which she might, she implicitly concedes, be addressed by someone else. As it happens, when Helen calls herself a bitch, she does so in addressing Hector as δᾶερ, as she does twice in the same speech (*Il.* 6.344–58). Their meeting takes place in the house of Paris, where Hector has stopped on his way to Andromache. Hector finds Helen and Paris in the *thalamos*, where they were last seen (3.423, 6.316). The domestic scene continues the one that began at the end of Book 3.[33] The first line of Helen's speech (6.344):

> δᾶερ ἐμεῖο κυνὸς, κακομηχάνου ὀκρυοέσσης,
>
> Brother-in-law of me, a bitch, evil-devising, chilling...

At the end of the speech Helen says (6.355–57):

---

[32] Iris to Athena (*Il.* 8.423), Diomedes to Hector (*Il.* 11.362 = 20.449), Achilles to Hector (20.449), Hera to Artemis (*Il.* 21.481), Achilles to Hector (*Il.* 22.34), Odysseus to Melantho (*Od.* 18.338), Penelope to Melantho (*Od.* 19.91). For the range of meanings in which Helen's use of this word falls: *LfgrE* s.v. B 2c. Faust 1970 gives an apparently complete list of the uses of "dog" (noun and adjs.) in Homer, dividing the examples into four categories: A. similes; B. other; C. "formal expressions," corresponding for the most part to what we would call formulas; D. metaphors. From his overview of the similes (22), one concludes that dogs have no single, focal significance. Surveying the many metaphorical uses of dog in Homer Faust only concludes: "κύων war also ein Schimpfwort" (25).
[33] Reichel 1994: 247–48.

ἀλλ' ἄγε νῦν εἴσελθε καὶ ἕζεο τῷδ' ἐπὶ δίφρῳ,
δᾶερ, ἐπεί σε μάλιστα πόνος φρένας ἀμφιβέβηκεν
εἵνεκ' ἐμεῖο κυνὸς καὶ Ἀλεξάνδρου ἕνεκ' ἄτης,[34]

But come in now and sit upon this stool,
brother-in-law, since it is especially you whose thoughts toil obsesses,
toil on account of me, a bitch, and on account of the blindness of Alexander.[35]

The introduction to this speech makes clear Helen's intention:

τὸν δ' Ἑλένη μύθοισι προσηύδα μειλιχίοισι·   343[36]

Him Helen addressed with sweet words.

Helen intends, in an awkward moment, as Hector is about to leave her house, to restore Hector's goodwill toward her and Paris. In the first line of this speech, Helen expresses the wish that she had been carried off by a gust of wind on the day she was born, before these works of war came about (348; see below in this § on this kind of wish). But since the gods appointed these ills that we see, she wishes that she had been the wife of a better man than Alexander (349–50; cf. 3.428–36).[37] In the conclusion of her speech, her thought is made more explicit. It has fallen to Hector to bear the brunt of the war that we unworthy persons, Alexander and I, have brought upon Troy. Helen's calling herself a bitch, then, is apologetic, looking to the consequences of her leaving Sparta with Alexander.[38]

The two adjectives that she uses of herself when she first calls herself "bitch" (344) support her apologetic purpose. First, she is κακομήχανος, a "contriver of mischief" (§1 above) The mischief, not otherwise specified here, is the Trojan War, and, as already in her use of "dog-faced" of herself (on which see below), she has

---

[34] West 2001b: 197–98 points out that in the three places (3.100, 6.356, 24.28) in which Paris' abduction of Helen is referred to, ἄτης and ἀρχῆς are variants. Both West and van Thiel read ἀρχῆς at 3.100 and ἄτης at 6.356 and 24.28. Cf. West 2011a: 412 on lines 28–30; Cairns 2012: 13 n. 22. Edwards 1991 on Il. 19.88: ἀάτη could be restored.

[35] Schwyzer 2: 201 on the substantivized personal pronoun in the gen. to indicate possession (citing this place): rare and emphatic.

[36] Cf. for the formula Krieter-Spiro 2009: 71 on line 171; for μειλιχίοισι in particular see Stoevesand 2008: 81 on line 214.

[37] This paraphrase of lines 348–50 attempts to bring out the force of the deictics in the Greek. Cf. Stoevesand 2008: 116–17 on lines 348–49.

[38] See Graziosi and Haubold 2010: 175: on lines 344–48: Helen's opening is an example of the rhetorical move later called *insinuatio*. It is the premise of Graver 1995 that "bitch" is real self-reproach on Helen's part: "Helen does what no other Homeric character does: she insults herself" (41).

in mind above all the consequences of her following Alexander to Troy. Second, she is κρυόεσσα, someone who has a chilling effect on others (§2)–without necessarily subscribing to the justice of their reaction to her. To continue with the speech to Hector in Book 6, she refers to the ἄτη of Alexander (357).³⁹ Blindness, *atē*, is a way to excuse a mistake.⁴⁰ It is a topos in the speeches of Agamemnon in the *Iliad* (2.111, 8.236–37, 9.18, 19.86–96; cf. Dolon at 10.391).⁴¹ Phoenix' speech in *Iliad* 9 includes a theology of the Prayers, daughters of Zeus, who intervene with their father on behalf of victims of personified Atē (502–12). When Helen then says that Zeus set an evil destiny on her and Alexander (357), she sums up her apology.

Calling herself "dog-faced" (κυνῶπις, *Il*. 3.180), on the wall of Troy with Priam, she is speaking to a friendly in-law, as in the case of Hector in Book 6. She wishes that she had chosen death instead of following Priam's son to Troy (173–74), as she wishes, in her speech to Hector, that she had died on the day of her birth (6.345–48) and as she wishes in her lament for Hector that she had died before Paris brought her to Troy (24.764). Death-wishes of various kinds are not uncommon in the *Iliad* and the *Odyssey* and may or may not be sincere.⁴² Helen's belong to the rhetoric of lament (cf. ch. 4§2.2).⁴³ They are, in Nancy Worman's phrase, "verbal guises."⁴⁴ The self-blame in "dog-faced" is the same as in "bitch." Likewise, after Helen has returned to Sparta, addressing Menelaus, she refers to the time "when on account of me, dog-faced, the Achaeans came beneath Troy, stirring up bold war" (*Od*. 4.145–46). Helen's use of this adjective of herself, is consistent, then, with her use of "bitch" of herself. She uses these words to

---

39 For the reading ἄτης see n. 36 above.
40 In Homer *atē* is either a subjective state, as here in Helen's use, or, less frequently, the objective result of that state (disaster). See Cairns 2012: 1–9 (with statistics).
41 Gill 1990: 16–17, citing Taplin 1990, on Agamemnon at *Il*. 19.86–87: "an attempt at unjustified self-exculpation." Cf. Versnel 2011: 173–74 on *Il*. 19.86–96 (Agamemnon blames Zeus and Moira and the Erinyes).
42 Helen's take the form: "I wish that I had died when..." or "before..."; also Odysseus (*Od*. 5.308–10). There are three other forms: (a) "I wish that I might die now" (Penelope: *Od*. 20.61–65). (b) "I wish that I had not been begotten" (Achilles: 18.86–87; Andromache: 22.481; Hephaestus: *Od*. 8.312). (c) "I wish that x (someone else) had died / might die / had never been born" (Hector of Paris: 3.40, 428; 6.281–85; Achilles of Briseïs: 19.59–60). See Krieter-Spiro 2009: 72–73 on 3.173a; Stoevesand 2008: 116 on 6.345–48.
43 And should be understood as in the first place rhetorical. But Helen's speeches are usually interpreted psychologically as e.g. by Reichel 1994: 265–67.
44 This phrase comes from the title of Worman 2001. Also Karanika 2014: 26: "By voicing self-blame, Helen manipulates the blame away from herself." Blondell 2013: 63 takes Helen literally as expressing "outright self-blame."

trusted persons, apologetically, conceding the terrible results of her abduction. The underlying sense of dog in these metaphorical words of self-blame, the aspect of the dog to which Helen is likening herself, is the dog's capacity for betrayal.[45] The serving women in the house of Odysseus are dogs in this sense and are so called several times.[46]

2.8 κυνῶπις and adultery

Commentators, lexicographers and others typically combine Helen's use of "dog-faced" (κυνῶπις) of herself (*Il.* 3.180, *Od.* 4.145) with Hephaestus' of his unfaithful wife, Aphrodite (*Od.* 8.319) and Agamemnon's of Clytemnestra (*Od.* 11.424, cf. κύντερον 427), and conclude that the adjective means "unfaithful to a husband."[47] But Hephaestus also uses this adjective of Hera (*Il.* 18.396), and Achilles uses it (in the masculine form) of Agamemnon (*Il.* 1.159, cf. κυνὸς ὄμματ' ἔχων 1.225). Its possible range of application, one could infer, is as wide as that of the vocative κύον.[48] Certainly women can be bitches in more than one sense. When Eurycleia calls the serving women κύνες "bitches" (*Od.* 19.372, to Odysseus), she does not mean that they are adulteresses. They slept with the suitors, as Telemachus says (22.464); whether or not they had husbands whom they were betraying is irrelevant.

If one says that betrayal is the basis of the pejorative use of the dog metaphor of three unfaithful women (without going into the contexts in the case of Hephaestus' and Agamemnon's uses), then the infidelity of these women is the form that their betrayal happens to take. Helen betrays her husband by committing adultery. As betrayed, her husband must in the first place seek amends from the seducer, and, in this case, recover his wife physically. The wife's guilt, in this logic, is secondary. Thus in Euripides' *Trojan Women* Menelaus says: "I came to Troy not on account of a woman, as they think, but against a man who, deceiver

---

[45] Franco 2003: 192–206 (under the heading "Maschera sesta: il traditore"). Graver 1995: 53–59 holds that the dog-metaphors used of Helen in the *Il.* and *Od.* are anomalous and asks "Could such a depraved and culpable Helen have figured in narratives known to early performers of epic...?" and argues in the affirmative.

[46] Franco 2003: 192–95. Dogs are fawning: *Od.* 10.216

[47] E.g., *LfrgE* s.v. κυνῶπις B.1. Lilja 1976: 22: "Helen may...chiefly allude to her erotic escapade." Cf. Franco 2003: 198, 201 for an interpretation of the epithet as referring to Helen's "seducibility." Franco means by seduction the reorientation of loyalty put into effect by the new owner of a dog or the new partner of a woman (239–40 n. 107). She cites Lys. 1.33.

[48] Cf. n. 34 above.

of his host, stole my wife from my home" (864–66). Menelaus is, however, resolved to take Helen back to Sparta and put her to death. He thus clearly separates the issue of justice from his feelings toward his wife, which are vengeful (feelings that he of course overcame).

Greek law concerning adultery preserved this logic, recognizing the guilt of the adulterer, whom the deceived husband has the right to kill (Lys. 1.26–31; Xen. *Hier*. 3.3; cf. for qualifications Dem. 23.53; Plut. *Sol*. 23.1), while it left the punishment of the adulteress to her husband.[49] In Athens he was in any case required to turn her out of his house and she was also forbidden to enter public shrines (and so to participate in cult observances) (Dem. 59.87). But the adulterer is conceived of as the perpetrator while the woman is the passive object, the one seduced.[50] The Greek language has a word for the former (μοιχός) but no corresponding word for the latter (except the verb μοιχεύω in the passive).[51] That infidelity remains a conflict between the husband and the adulterer is clear from Lysias' speech for Euphiletus, who is on trial for the premeditated murder of his wife's seducer (Lys. 1). Although Euphiletus offers a narrative that ostensibly refutes the charge against him, the fact remains that, having discovered his wife's infidelity, he does not confront her but immediately begins to plan his revenge on the adulterer.[52]

In the modern logic, the one assumed by the commentators and others referred to above, Helen is the active betrayer of her husband and he is the victim of the betrayal. The adulterer, Paris, is guilty, too, but no guiltier than Helen, whose guilt weighs upon her conscience.[53] So she calls herself "bitch" and "dog-faced." This logic has a certain conception of marriage as its premise. To take the United States as an example, marriage is the foundation of the nuclear family, consisting of husband and wife and their dependent children, which is the basic social unit. Because the traditional moral values are believed to be inculcated by the family, they are called "family values." It is not surprising, then, that adultery

---

49 Cohen 1991: 98–132, in an extensive discussion of Dem. 25.53, 59.87 and *Ath. Pol*. 57.3, argues that the law referred to in these places did not in fact sanction the murder of an adulterer, which was not the usual punishment.
50 Franco 2003: 199.
51 For "men as the natural initiators of sexual intimacy" and the relevant verbs: Cole 1984: 97 n. 4.
52 See Edwards and Usher 1985: 220–21.
53 The useful survey by Hoffmann 1990 of laws concerning adultery in the Greek city states starts with a brief discussion of Hector's rebuke of Paris (*Il*. 3.39–40). Hoffmann mistakenly assumes that Paris and Helen are adulterous lovers and argues that Paris is a paradigm for Alcibiades.

can be considered a crime, as it still is in some states.⁵⁴ Further, a marriage arises from love, is based on love and companionship, and provides personal fulfillment. For this reason, divorce proceedings in more than half the states in the United States take adultery into account. An unfaithful spouse may be liable to loss of alimony.⁵⁵ Either wife or husband, whichever is unfaithful, may have his or her share of common assets reduced.⁵⁶

When Helen uses κύων of herself, she is not referring to herself as an adulteress. A fortiori, she is not expressing guilt for adultery. (She does feel regret for the consequences of her having followed Paris to Troy and she regrets having abandoned her family in Sparta. Compare the reflections of Penelope on Helen at *Od*. 23.218–21).⁵⁷ As argued in the preceding chapter, no matter what her desire for Paris, once abducted she has a passive status. As his prize she is married to him in Troy. Earlier she was Menelaus' prize in the contest of her suitors. She becomes his prize again after the capture of Troy, at which time she is the wife of Deïphobus, to whom she has been given by Priam (see ch. 1§5).

2.9 ἄμμορος (*Il.* 24.773)

Andromache has called herself ἄμμορος when she pleads with Hector to stay in Troy and guard the walls (6.408). Priam uses δυσάμμορος of Hecuba as the mother of Hector (22.428); Andromache of Hector and herself as parents of Astyanax (22.485 ≈ 24.727); Achilles of Patroclus (19.315). Those who use ἄμμορος or its compound stand in the closest degree of affection to the one whose loss is feared or lamented.⁵⁸ When Helen calls herself ἄμμορος in her lament for Hector (*Il.* 24.773) she puts herself in the same relation to him as his wife's and his family's and in this way heightens the expression of her sorrow for herself. As pointed out earlier, much of Helen's lament is a personal reminiscence of Hector (ch. 1§4).

---

54 See e.g., Ariz. Rev. Stat. § 13–1408; Fla. Stat. § 798.01; Kan. Stat. Ann. § 21–5511; 720 Ill. Comp. Stat. § 5/11–35; Mass. Gen. Laws ch. 272, § 14.
55 See e.g., N.Y. Dom. Rel. L. § 170(4); N.H. Rev. Stat. Ann. §§ 458:7(II), 458:19(IV)(b).
56 In general, European divorce law has been liberalized since the 1960s. Fault (such as adultery) as the grounds of divorce has been replaced by separation and mutual consent. For an overview of European countries: Smith 2002: 218–20.
57 See Krieter-Spiro 2009: 71–72 on lines 172–80.
58 The only exception is Arctos, on the shield of Achilles, who is ἄμμορος of the baths of Ocean, i.e., Arctos is a star that does not set (18.489).

2.10 Conclusion

It has been necessary to digress briefly on the modern assumptions that underlie some prevailing interpretations of Helen's self-reproach. The counter-interpretation of these terms that has been proposed here begins from Helen's situation in Troy (ch. 1). She is, amongst her Trojan in-laws, except for Hector and Priam, and presumably amongst all the Trojans, the object of blame. With her self-reproach, she adopts and, in so doing, preempts this blame. (Once, in the *Odyssey*, her self-blame expresses Menelaus' presumed attitude toward her.) At the same time, in Troy she regrets the loss of those whom she left behind in Sparta, she regrets her marriage to Paris and its consequences for Troy. Regret is not guilt, which Helen has no reason to take upon herself (cf. ch. 1 on her status in Troy).[59] The only one in Homer who directly addresses a term of reproach to Helen is Aphrodite, with σχετλίη (*Il.* 3.414), which refers not to some trait of Helen's personality but to the attitude toward Aphrodite that Helen has just expressed. Achilles' ῥιγεδανή (*Il.* 19.325), on the other hand, expresses the same attitude toward Helen as the Trojans' and is part of an egocentric description of his role, in which the moral basis of the Achaean campaign, i.e., the duty of restoring Helen to her Achaean husband, is implicitly rejected.

---

[59] It is unnecessary to invoke the old Doddsian distinction between guilt culture and shame culture (Dodds 1951). For a critique of this distinction as it is applied to ancient Greece: Cairns 1993: 27–47.

3 Ἀργείη

"Argive" (Ἀργείη) is the most frequently used of Helen's epithets (9x *Il.*, 4x *Od.*) and also the most fungible in the sense that more speakers use it than any other of her epithets. She is also Ἀργεία in Alcaeus (fr. 283.4 V) and has the name Ἀργειώνη in the Hesiodic *Catalogue* (3x). In the *Iliad*, this epithet not only identifies her as non-Trojan but also refers to her as the object of contention between Achaeans and Trojans (§1).[1] It is not surprising that Helen is called "Argive" in places in which the war is said to be fought "on account of" her (*Il.* 2.161 = 2.177; *Od.* 17.118). (For formulas for Helen entailing εἵνεκα see ch. 7§5.) The possessions of Menelaus that were stolen along with her are twice connected with her Argive identity (*Il.* 3.458, 7.350; cf. *Il.* 4.19, 173–74). In the *Odyssey*, now that the matter has been settled, the epithet looks back to her Iliadic identity (§2).

Tab. 1: "Argive Helen"

Il. 2.161	Ἀργείην Ἑλένην, ἧς εἵνεκα πολλοὶ Ἀχαιῶν	Hera
Il. 2.177	Ἀργείην Ἑλένην, ἧς εἵνεκα πολλοὶ Ἀχαιῶν	Athena
Il. 3.458	ὑμεῖς δ' Ἀργείην Ἑλένην καὶ κτήμαθ' ἅμ' αὐτῇ	Agamemnon
Il. 4.19	αὖτις δ' Ἀργείην Ἑλένην Μενέλαος ἄγοιτο	Zeus
Il. 4.174	Ἀργείην Ἑλένην, σέο δ' ὀστέα πύσει ἄρουρα	Agamemnon
Il. 6.323	Ἀργείη δ' Ἑλένη μετ' ἄρα δμῳῇσι γυναιξὶν	narrator
Il. 7.350	δεῦτ' ἄγετ' Ἀργείην Ἑλένην καὶ κτήμαθ' ἅμ' αὐτῇ	Antenor
Il. 9.140	αἵ κε μετ' Ἀργείην Ἑλένην κάλλισται ἔωσιν	Agamemnon
Il. 9.282	αἵ κε μετ' Ἀργείην Ἑλένην κάλλισται ἔωσιν	Odysseus
Od. 4.184	κλαῖε μὲν Ἀργείη Ἑλένη, Διὸς ἐκγεγαυῖα	narrator
Od. 4.296	ὣς ἔφατ', Ἀργείη δ' Ἑλένη δμῳῇσι κέλευσεν	narrator
Od. 17.118	ἔνθ' ἴδον Ἀργείην Ἑλένην, ἧς εἵνεκα πολλὰ	Telemachus
Od. 23.218	οὐδέ κεν Ἀργείη Ἑλένη, Διὸς ἐκγεγαυῖα	Penelope

Whatever else the epithet means as applied to Helen, it seems to have geographical reference to Argos. But Helen was from Sparta, and thus she was Laconian, not Argive. Why, then, is she called "Argive? The answer can be sought in the first

---

[1] Whallon 1961: "Argive" of Helen "reminds that she is an Achaean, that she was stolen from the Achaeans, and that she was the cause of the war."

place not in geography but in the nomenclature for those besieging Troy.² The warriors do not have a single collective name but are called variously Achaeans, Danaans, and Argives. Strabo says: Ἀργείους γοῦν καλεῖ πάντας καθάπερ καὶ Δαναοὺς καὶ Ἀχαιούς (Homer "calls (them) all Argives, just as he calls them Danaans and Achaeans," 8.6.5).³ These names, which in Homer are synonymous, are useful metrical variants. As for Argives, they are a group addressed by their leaders, or they applaud speeches, or fight, or are victorious or defeated and killed in battle. In such contexts the army as whole or some sub-set (those killed in battle) is meant.⁴ To call Helen "Argive" is to refer to her as having the same ethnic identity as that of the besieging army.⁵ When, however, Idomeneus describes Diomedes as lord of the Argives, he must mean the people of that city (*Il.* 23.471). The *Iliad* notoriously assigns the city of Argos both to Diomedes and to Agamemnon, probably as the result of overlapping traditions in this mythically crowded corner of the Peloponnesus.⁶

It could also be argued that "Argive Helen" does in fact have geographical reference, because Argos commonly refers in Homer not to the city or the territory in the northeast Peloponnesus but by extension to all of Greece, as we would say.⁷ Helen is of course "Argive" in this broad sense. Argos can be spoken of as the common homeland, as by Odysseus who speaks of the Achaeans who set out for Troy *from Argos* (*Il.* 2.287, cf. 284). The Cretan Idomeneus fears the Achaeans will die *far from Argos* (*Il.* 13.227). Nestor can say: Let the one or two Achaeans who are thinking of leaving perish before they can return *to Argos* (2.346–49). If Argos is used in this way of all the Achaeans at Troy, it must mean all of Greece, given

---

2 The following explanation follows Latacz, Nünlist and Stoevesand 2000: 15–16 on *Il.* 1.2.
3 Oikonomaki 2018 suggests some differences in the meaning of the three terms within the *Il.* and as between the *Il.* and the *Od.* She provides useful statistical charts at the end of her article.
4 For the Argives addressed by their leaders: *Il.* 2.109, 3.82, 4.234, 4.242, 5.824, 8.228, 9.16, 15.202, 15.560, 19.175, 19.255, 23.271, 23.535, 23.658, 23.706, 23.753, 23.801. For their applauding speeches: *Il.* 2.332, 2.394. For their fighting: 5.498, 12.2, 12.415, 16.73. For their being defeated and killed in battle: 5.712, 6.107, 11.216, 12.14, 12.37, 12.178, 12.293.
5 Cf. Krieter-Spiro 2009: 157 on line *Il.* 3.458: Argive means Greek.
6 See the reflections of Cingano 2004: 64–68 and Cingano 2005: 150–51 on this problem.
7 *LfgrE* s.v. τὸ Ἄργος B VI ("'Griechenland' durch Erweiterung"), with reference to II (territory in the Peloponnesus) and V (the whole Peloponnesus). For the whole Peloponnesus cf. schol. Pind. *Isth.* 2.17: καὶ τάχα ἂν τὸν Σπαρτιάτην εἴρηκε Πίνδαρος Ἀργεῖον, παρόσον ἡ πᾶσα Πελοπόννησος Ἄργος ἐκαλεῖτο ὁμωνύμως τῇ πόλει· Ὅμηρος οὖν τὴν Ἑλένην Ἀργείαν φησὶν ἀντὶ τοῦ εἰπεῖν Λακεδαιμονίαν· Ἀργείαν δὲ εἶπεν ἀντὶ τοῦ Πελοποννησιακήν. For the geographical indeterminacy of Argos in the *Il.* see Tsagalis 2012: 191–92 and for Argos as a "thematized space," especially for Agamemnon but also for other heroes, 192–201.

that there are contingents from western and from northern Greece, from the Peloponnese, and from the islands.

In the *Odyssey*, however, the significance of "Argive" has changed. Because the Achaeans are no longer assembled in a single place and working together toward a common end, there is no longer a need for a single word to describe the many peoples of Greece and distinguish them from a foreign enemy. "Argive" is used only to recall the Achaeans at Troy.[8]

3.1 "Argive Helen" as the object of a legitimate claim

As the Achaeans are preparing to flee Troy, Agamemnon's test of morale having backfired, Hera asks Athena to restrain them (2.160–62):

κὰδ δέ κεν εὐχωλὴν Πριάμῳ καὶ Τρωσὶ λίποιεν
Ἀργείην Ἑλένην, ἧς εἵνεκα πολλοὶ Ἀχαιῶν
ἐν Τροίῃ ἀπόλοντο, φίλης ἀπὸ πατρίδος αἴης·

They would leave Argive Helen to Priam and the Trojans, fulfilling their boast,
her on account of whom many Achaeans perished
in Troy, far from their own native land.

Athena will repeat what Hera has told her, much of it word for word, to Odysseus (2.173–78), including the line with the epithet in question. In the lines quoted here, the epithet is part of a chiastic pattern: (A) Priam and the Trojans — (B) Argive Helen — (B) Achaeans — (A) Troy. Hera and Athena are speaking in terms of nationalities, making the divide between Achaean and Trojan clear. The epithet characterizes Helen in terms of her nationality and at the same time implies the Achaean claim to her (cf. schol. AbT on *Il.* 3.458 on "Argive": "the one who belongs to the Achaeans").

Stressing the claim underlying the entire campaign is a natural and effective means of persuasion for the Achaean troops. Lines 2.160–61b (quoted above) are repeated for that purpose by Agamemnon in Book 4. Menelaus has been wounded in battle and Agamemnon fears that his brother will die, causing the Achaeans to abandon both Troy and the quest for "Argive Helen" (4.174).[9] "Argive" here emphasizes that, though Helen belongs to Menelaus particularly, she also belongs

---

8 See Appendix to this chapter for a possible exception.
9 See Rousseau 1990: 337 for Agamemnon's argument: with the death of Menelaus, the Achaean army would no longer have a reason for this campaign and would withdraw, leaving Helen to

to all of Greece, and must be taken from Troy regardless of whether or not her husband is alive to reclaim her.

In contrast, when Paris proposed the duel between himself and Menelaus, he of course referred to Helen without "Argive," which would have conceded Menelaus' right to her, and without any other epithet, because it is not Helen in some particular aspect over whom he and Menelaus will fight (3.67–70).

> νῦν αὖτ' εἴ μ' ἐθέλεις πολεμίζειν ἠδὲ μάχεσθαι,
> ἄλλους μὲν κάθισον Τρῶας καὶ πάντας Ἀχαιούς,
> αὐτὰρ ἔμ' ἐν μέσσῳ καὶ ἀρηΐφιλον Μενέλαον
> συμβάλετ' ἀμφ' Ἑλένῃ καὶ κτήμασι πᾶσι μάχεσθαι.

> Now though, if you wish me to fight it out and do battle,
> make the rest of the Trojans and all the Achaeans sit down,
> and set me and Menelaus dear to Ares in the middle
> to fight together over Helen and all the possessions.

The lines are repeated by Hector at 3.88–91, and the name Helen is again unmodified. For the Trojans, of course, Helen is not "Argive"; she was taken by Paris, married to him, and has lived in Troy for many years. To call her "Argive" would be to admit the besieging army's claim to her and to contradict Troy's purpose in defending itself. Later, when Agamemnon announces the terms of the duel, he also refers to Helen by name only (3.281–85):

> εἰ μὲν κεν Μενέλαον Ἀλέξανδρος καταπέφνῃ,
> αὐτὸς ἔπειθ' Ἑλένην ἐχέτω καὶ κτήματα πάντα,
> ἡμεῖς δ' ἐν νήεσσι νεώμεθα ποντοπόροισιν·
> εἰ δέ κ' Ἀλέξανδρον κτείνῃ ξανθὸς Μενέλαος,
> Τρῶας ἔπειθ' Ἑλένην καὶ κτήματα πάντ' ἀποδοῦναι,

> If Alexander kills Menelaus,
> then let him have Helen and all the possessions,
> and let us return in our ocean-going ships.
> But if fair-haired Menelaus kills Alexander,
> then let the Trojans return Helen and all the possessions.

Agamemnon does not now stress the Achaean claim to her, as that claim is the very thing this contest is intended to determine.

Paris and the Trojans. But the passages discussed here can also be taken to mean that the Achaeans have a national claim to Helen. For the accusative form of the formula here and at 2.161 = 177 as a "pendant runover" see Tsagalis 2009: 45–46.

Helen is again "Argive" at the end of Book 3, however, where Agamemnon is again the speaker. At the end of the duel between Menelaus and Paris he addresses the two armies (3.457–60):

νίκη μὲν δὴ φαίνετ' ἀρηϊφίλου Μενελάου,
ὑμεῖς δ' Ἀργείην Ἑλένην καὶ κτήμαθ' ἅμ' αὐτῇ
ἔκδοτε, καὶ τιμὴν ἀποτινέμεν ἥν τιν' ἔοικεν,
ἥ τε καὶ ἐσσομένοισι μετ' ἀνθρώποισι πέληται.

Victory belongs plainly to Menelaus dear to Ares.
You return Argive Helen and the possessions with her,
and pay back whatever compensation is fitting,
(the memory of) which will remain even among men in the future.

Here again, in the voice of the commander-in-chief, it is a matter of the Achaeans' legitimate claim, which includes the possessions of Menelaus stolen by Paris at the time of the abduction of Helen. The legitimacy is underlined by Menelaus' victory over Paris in the single combat that was to decide who would be the rightful possessor of Helen.

The only other Trojan, besides Paris and Hector in the lines noted above, to refer to Helen by name is Antenor.[10] He advises the Trojans to return Helen and Menelaus' possessions (7.350).

δεῦτ' ἄγετ', Ἀργείην Ἑλένην καὶ κτήμαθ' ἅμ' αὐτῇ
δώομεν Ἀτρεΐδῃσιν ἄγειν·

Come then, let us give Argive Helen and with her the possessions to the sons of Atreus to take away.

By calling Helen "Argive," he reinforces his argument: because Helen is Argive and belongs to the other side, the Trojans should return her and cease fighting for her.

Helen's identity is again asserted in Agamemnon's offer of prizes to Achilles in Book 9. As Agamemnon describes the many rewards he will offer to Achilles if the warrior returns to battle, he includes twenty beautiful slave women (9.139–40):

---

10 Though Antenor is Trojan, he is a ξένος of the Argives. Most notably, he served as the host of Menelaus and Odysseus during their embassy to Troy to negotiate for Helen's return. Ancient accounts of the embassy appeared in the *Cypria* (Arg. pp. 42.55–57 B = p. 32.72–74 D), Bacchylides 15(14) S-M, Sophocles in his lost Ἑλένης Ἀπαίτησις, "The Demand for Helen's Return" (frs. 176–180a Radt [TrGF 4.177–80]). See de Sanctis 2012 for a survey of literary sources.

> Τρωϊάδας δὲ γυναῖκας ἐείκοσιν αὐτὸς ἑλέσθω,
> αἵ κε μετ' Ἀργείην Ἑλένην κάλλισται ἔωσιν.
>
> Then let him choose twenty Trojan women,
> who are most beautiful after Argive Helen.

(The offer is repeated by Odysseus to Achilles at 9.281–82.) Because the speakers are themselves Achaeans addressing their remarks to other Achaeans, the purpose of "Argive" here cannot be to assert the Achaean claim on Helen. Referring to her as "Argive" is instead a way for Agamemnon to affirm the superiority of the Achaeans to the Trojans. The valuable slave women given to Achilles may be very beautiful, but they are still inferior to the most beautiful Achaean woman.

At the beginning of Book 4, after the duel between Menelaus and Paris, Zeus rattles Athena and Hera by suggesting peace as an alternative to continuation of the war (4.18–19):

> ἤτοι μὲν οἰκέοιτο πόλις Πριάμοιο ἄνακτος,
> αὖτις δ' Ἀργείην Ἑλένην Μενέλαος ἄγοιτο.
>
> The city of lord Priam might still be dwelt in,
> and Menelaus might lead away Argive Helen.

Again Helen is the object of the war and "Argive" takes Menelaus' point of view. The use of the epithet may, however, have a secondary function in this passage. Zeus began his speech by referring to Hera as "Argive" (4.9, an epithet used of the goddess only here and at 5.908, the conclusion of the action beginning here). In the next lines Zeus mocks Hera and Athena for failing to help Menelaus, while Aphrodite saved Paris from death. The explicit critique, of course, is that the goddesses did not help Menelaus win the duel decisively, but an implicit critique may be that Hera, patron goddess of marriage, could not protect Menelaus from losing his wife. In that struggle Aphrodite was also the winner in arranging for Paris to make off with Helen. "Argive" Helen belongs in Greece with her husband, but "Argive" Hera failed to protect both the dignity of her favorite land and the dignity of the domestic sphere. This interpretation is perhaps bolstered by the narrator's use of ἄγοιτο to describe Menelaus retrieving Helen (4.19, quoted above): ἄγειν γυναῖκα is the usual expression for a man taking a wife. So Zeus is proposing that Menelaus might take his wife for the second time and return her to her proper place.[11] (Cf. ch. 1§6 on ἄγειν and ἀνάγειν.)

---

[11] Helen without an epithet is also the object of discussions about the war in other parts of the *Iliad* as well, though in these cases she is not the object of a Greek claim upon her. See ch. 4.

All of the examples of "Argive" Helen discussed up to this point (9/13 instances of this formula) appear in the accusative. The use of the accusative corresponds to the conception of "Argive Helen" that has been described above, as an object to be fought over. This Helen is discussed by others or caused to act by others but does not act herself.

3.2 "Argive Helen's" Iliadic identity in the *Odyssey*

In the *Odyssey*, as pointed out above, the word "Argive" refers to all the Achaeans but is used only when recalling the events of the Trojan War. When Helen is called "Argive" in the *Odyssey*, it is, for a similar reason, to recall her as the object or prize for which that war was fought. The epithet "Argive" invokes what can be called her Iliadic identity.

The Iliadic identity conferred by the epithet "Argive" is again clear when Telemachus reports his trip to his mother (17.118–19):

> ἔνθ' ἴδον Ἀργείην Ἑλένην, ἧς εἵνεκα πολλὰ
> Ἀργεῖοι Τρῶές τε θεῶν ἰότητι μόγησαν.
>
> There I saw Argive Helen, on account of whom
> Argives and Trojans suffered much by the will of the gods.

Elsewhere in his report, Telemachus refers to Menelaus as Ἀτρείδην, δουρικλειτόν, "son of Atreus, spear-famed" (116), and again as βοὴν ἀγαθὸς "good at the war cry" (120), and to Nestor as ποιμένα λαῶν, "shepherd of the people," epithets all invoking Iliadic identities.

3.3 "Argive Helen" in domestic contexts

The epithet appears, at first glance somewhat incongruously, in domestic scenes, one in the *Iliad*, one in the *Odyssey*. In the former, Hector has gone to the house of Paris to rebuke him for not joining in the battle (6.321–24).

> τὸν δ' εὗρ' ἐν θαλάμῳ περικαλλέα τεύχε' ἕποντα,
> ἀσπίδα καὶ θώρηκα, καὶ ἀγκύλα τόξ' ἀφόωντα·
> Ἀργείη δ' Ἑλένη μετ' ἄρα δμῳῇσι γυναιξὶν
> ἧστο, καὶ ἀμφιπόλοισι περικλυτὰ ἔργα κέλευε.
>
> (Hector) found (Paris) in the chamber handling his very beautiful arms,
> his shield and breastplate and his curved bow;

Argive Helen sat amongst her serving women
and assigned excellent work to her maids.

The war, as Hector will remind Paris, is being fought because of him: σέο δ' εἵνεκ' αὐτή τε πτόλεμός τε ἄστυ τόδ' ἀμφιδέδηε, "because of you the war-cry and battle blaze around this city" (6.328–29). The Achaeans are fighting for the woman he abducted, and, before Hector speaks, the epithet "Argive" already implies his point of view. The abduction of the "Argive" woman by Paris is the cause of the war. "Argive" Helen in the nominative at the beginning of the line is made prominent by the postponement of the verb to the beginning of the next line–the only example of this word-order amongst all the name-epithet formulas for Helen.

In the other domestic scene, in the *Odyssey*, the epithet is used when Helen orders her servants to arrange beds for Telemachus and Pisistratus (4.296–97):[12]

Ἀργείη δ' Ἑλένη δμῳῇσι κέλευσε
δέμνι' ὑπ' αἰθούσῃ θέμεναι καὶ ῥήγεα καλὰ

Argive Helen bade her servants
put beds and fair blankets in the courtyard.

It seems that the kind of explanation offered in the preceding section (§2) does not apply. The epithet would, by that explanation, impose Helen's Iliadic identity on her identity as mistress of the household in Sparta. But after describing Helen's orders in more detail and the maid's fulfillment of them, the narrator continues (4.302–305):

οἱ μὲν ἄρ' ἐν προδόμῳ δόμου αὐτόθι κοιμήσαντο,
Τηλέμαχός θ' ἥρως καὶ Νέστορος ἀγλαὸς υἱός·
Ἀτρεΐδης δὲ καθεῦδε μυχῷ δόμου ὑψηλοῖο,
πὰρ δ' Ἑλένη τανύπεπλος ἐλέξατο, δῖα γυναικῶν.

So they slept right there in the porch of the palace,
the hero Telemachus and the glorious son of Nestor.
The son of Atreus slept in the innermost part of his lofty house,
and by him long-robed Helen lay down, noble among women.

Here as earlier (183–86, cf. §2 *init.*), the narrator gives an Iliadic portrait of the four characters. Pisistratus is again the son of Nestor but this time "the glorious son," while Telemachus, who had no epithet in the earlier passage, is now

---

12 See the Chicago Homer on *Od.* 4.296 for detailed analysis of the Homeric "going to bed" scene, with critique of the interpretation of S. West 1988 *ad loc.*

"hero." Menelaus is again "the son of Atreus." Helen, who was earlier "Argive" in this scene (296), is now described in a line almost identical to one in the *Iliad* (3.171).

The scene as a whole is typical, beginning with Helen's orders. Someone arranges overnight accommodations for a guest.[13] Patroclus has the servants prepare a bed for Phoenix (*Il.* 9.658–62). Achilles has his servants prepare a bed for Priam (*Il.* 24.643–48). Aretē arranges for a bed for Odysseus (*Od.* 7.335–42). Penelope orders her maids to prepare a bed for the disguised Odysseus (*Od.* 19.317–19), and, as a test of Odysseus, she orders Eurycleia, in his presence, to move the marriage bed (*Od.* 23.177–80). This list might include Nestor's arrangements for Telemachus (*Od.* 3.397–401), though in this instance Nestor bids Telemachus to sleep in the bed prepared for him, instead of ordering his servants to prepare the bed. A variation on the scene occurs when Eumaeus, lacking domestic servants, himself prepares a bed for Odysseus (*Od.* 14.518–22).

The typicality of the scene extends to the host's retiring to his own bed to sleep with a partner: Patroclus and Achilles lay down with Diomedē and Iphis (*Il.* 9.663–68), Achilles goes to bed with Briseïs (*Il.* 24.675–76), Nestor lays down with his wife (*Od.* 3.402–03), and Alcinoüs with Aretē (*Od.* 7.346–47). The partners have appropriate epithets: Patroclus' consort Diomede is καλλιπάρηος, "fair-cheeked" (ch. 9§2), Achilles' consort Iphis is εὔζωνος, "fair-girdled," Briseïs is καλλιπάρηος (ch. 9§2), Nestor's wife is his ἄλοχος δέσποινα, "lady wife," and Aretē is Alcinous' γυνὴ δέσποινα, "lady wife." The epithets that Helen has when she retires to bed, describing her as a public figure, are inappropriate. The next morning, however, still in bed, she is καλλίκομος (ch.9§1). In particular, Helen's epithets implicitly identify her as the wife who has been recovered after the long war. Helen's epithet "Argive" at the beginning of the scene, it now turns out, belonged to the same characterization of her as the long-lost and now recovered wife.

---

13 See Arend 1933: 101–103 for a more extensive and detailed analysis of this type of scene; also Taplin 1992: 78–82.

3.4 "Argive Helen" as a figure of the past

In the two domestic scenes discussed in the preceding section the formula "Argive Helen" appeared in the nominative (2/4x), appropriately, because she is, after all, an agent in her own household. In the two remaining instances the nominative formula refers to the *Odyssey*'s "historical" Helen.[14]

In Book 4, when Telemachus is visiting Sparta, all begin to weep over the apparent loss of Odysseus. The narrator names, in this order: "Argive Helen", Telemachus (with no epithet), Atreïdes Menelaus, and Pisistratus (in the periphrasis "son of Nestor") (183–86). Menelaus has the epithet Atreïdes in the *Iliad* usually as the commander of the Achaeans (4.156, 291, 316; 15.64, 87) or as warrior (14.470; 15.52, 121; 17.147). Menelaus has himself already evoked memories of the war and the service of Odysseus (98–107; cf. 151–53). In this larger context of Trojan War recollection, Helen appropriately has the epithet "Argive" (4.184). In the scene of grieving, then, the two representatives of the Trojan War generation have appropriate epithets, while of the two sons representing the next generation one has no epithet and the other an epithet formed on his father's name.

In Book 23 Penelope tells Odysseus (23.218–21):

οὐδέ κεν Ἀργείη Ἑλένη, Διὸς ἐκγεγαυῖα,
ἀνδρὶ παρ' ἀλλοδαπῷ ἐμίγη φιλότητι καὶ εὐνῇ,
εἰ ᾔδη, ὅ μιν αὖτις ἀρήϊοι υἷες Ἀχαιῶν
ἀξέμεναι οἶκόνδε φίλην ἐς πατρίδ' ἔμελλον.

Neither would Argive Helen, born of Zeus,
have joined in love and bed with a foreign man
if she had known that the war-like sons of the Achaeans
were going to bring her home again to her native land.

In this concise summary of the beginning and the course of the Trojan War, Helen has the expected epithet. Penelope knows the same epithets that the narrator uses and in effect mimics one of his verses (cf. 4.184) because she is looking back at Helen not as her cousin, as someone living at this moment in Sparta, but as the

---

14 Tsagalis 2009: 40: Helen's name in the nominative shows that "she is a typical mortal woman" whose personal name in the nominative "is not localized at verse-end as she is not an epic protagonist," although Helen is distinguished from other mortal women by the epithets referring to her as the daughter of Zeus. Tsagalis gives the ratio between Helen's name in the nominative and in the accusative as 8:17, "whereas with respect to other epic characters the situation is completely reversed" (46).

one who left Sparta with Paris. It is "external analepsis."[15] Helen is tantamount to the figure of the past whom one knows from heroic song.

Penelope, the only non-divine woman to mention Helen by name does not see Helen simply as an object to be claimed by one nation or another, but as an agent capable of making a choice. The Helen that Penelope describes did not foresee (though by implication she could have foreseen) that the Achaeans and Trojans would go to war over her and reduce her to the "Argive Helen" who was a prize to be claimed. Penelope is of course ignorant that Helen does not see herself as having had a choice but as the victim of Aphrodite (as in her tirade against the goddess, 3.399–412), who inflicted blindness upon her (*Od.* 4.261–62).

3.5 Conclusion

The identity of Helen in her appellatives and in other denominations is wife of Paris and in-law of the Trojan royal family. She is the object of the fighting, the prize, "on account of" whom the war is fought. The ethnic "Argive" in the *Iliad* expresses the Achaean view of this prize: their claim is the legitimate one and implicitly her recovery is a matter of national pride. Because she is the object of the fighting it is not surprising that "Argive Helen" usually appears in the accusative case. It appears in the nominative once in the *Iliad*, in a scene in which "Argive Helen," the foreign woman, and the now passive Paris, who brought her to Troy, are found together by Hector; and three times in the *Odyssey*, in which this epithet is "historical."

3.6 Appendix

There is perhaps an exception to the rule proposed in this chapter concerning "Argive" in the *Odyssey*, viz., that it is used only to recall the Achaeans at Troy. In *Odyssey* Book 3, Nestor explains how Orestes avenged the death of his father by murdering his mother Clytemnestra and her lover Aegisthus, and then ἦ τοι ὁ τὸν κτείνας δαίνυ τάφον Ἀργείοισιν / μητρός τε στυγερῆς καὶ ἀνάλκιδος Αἰγίσθοιο, "having slain him he held a funeral feast among the Argives for his hateful mother and feeble Aegisthus" (3.309–10). These events do not occur as part of the Trojan War, and therefore do not observe the usage of "Argive" observed in the rest of the *Odyssey*. It may be that here "Argive" means residents of the city of

---

15 Cf. Nünlist and de Jong 2000: 159 s.v. "Analepse."

Argos. The murders of Clytemnestra and Aegisthus took place, of course, in Mycenae, but Argos was an accepted alternative for Mycenae. Strabo says (8.6.19):

διὰ δὲ τὴν ἐγγύτητα τὰς δύο πόλεις ὡς μίαν οἱ τραγικοὶ συνωνύμως προσαγορεύουσιν, Εὐριπίδης δὲ καὶ ἐν τῷ αὐτῷ δράματι τοτὲ μὲν Μυκήνας καλῶν τοτὲ δ' Ἄργος τὴν αὐτὴν πόλιν, καθάπερ ἐν Ἰφιγενείᾳ καὶ Ὀρέστῃ.

Because of their proximity, the tragedians speak of the two cities synonymously as though they were one city; Euripides even in the same drama calls the same city now Mycenae and now Argos, as in *Iphigeneia* and *Orestes*.

The relation of Sparta and Mycenae in the *Odyssey* is another problem.[16] At *Od.* 4.512–22, Agamemnon first reaches Cape Malea, apparently bound for Amyclē, not Argos, which ought to have been his destination (cf. *Il.* 2.115). Amyclē makes sense if, as Carlo Brillante proposes, the narrator has in mind the tradition according to which Agamemnon and Menelaus hold a joint kingship over Sparta and Mycenae. (The two cities are apparently imagined as closer together than they are in reality.) Several passages in Books 3 and 4 of the *Odyssey* attest this tradition (3.247–52 [Telemachus], 256–57 [Nestor], 4.544–47 [Proteus]). It is also attested in Aeschylus' *Agamemnon* and in archaic lyric. At the same time, Brillante points out, the Telemachy acknowledges the tradition affirmed by the *Iliad*, according to which Agamemnon is king of Mycenae, Menelaus of Sparta. In fact, the two traditions can be juxtaposed in a manner that seems odd to us. In the same speech, Nestor says that Aegisthus ruled for seven years in Mycenae after he killed Agamemnon (3.305), i.e., Agamemnon had been the king of Mycenae, and also that Menelaus returned, apparently to Mycenae, on the very day on which Orestes was observing, with a feast, the funerals of Aegisthus and of his mother (3.311). Here Menelaus is imagined as returning to Mycenae, whereas later, in the passage in Book 4 on which Brillante focuses, Agamemnon is imagined as returning to Sparta. Rejecting with good reason the neoanalytic explanation of *Od.* 4.512–22, Brillante argues for the copresence of synchronic variants of the *nostos* of Agamemnon, both of which the narrator wanted to acknowledge. One variant is major or Panhellenic, the other is minor or local.

---

16 The rest of this paragraph is a quotation of Edmunds 2005: 55–56 but without footnotes. The work of Brillante referred to is Brillante 2005. Burkert 2001 does not have much to say on the Sparta-Mycene question but suggests (174) that Homer tends to valorize Sparta in relation to Argos.

4 The Name Helen Unmodified

Of the twenty-three occurrences of the name Helen without an epithet (App. 2) about half (11/23x) refer to Helen as the object for which the war is fought (9/23x) or as the one who has caused the sufferings of the Achaeans (2/23x). Only twice does the narrator refer to Helen in this way and each time it is a matter of focalization, i.e., of the perspective of one of the characters.[1] In other words, it is always a matter of how one character or another sees Helen. In particular, the unmodified name Helen is itself part of a formula in which it is coupled with the possessions (κτήματα) stolen from Menelaus by Paris at the time when he abducted Helen. Her passive status as wife (cf. ch. 1) is even clearer in this formula (§1.1). She has also been a source of suffering for the Achaeans, as she has been, in their eyes, for the Trojans also (§1.2; cf. ch. 2§§5, 7).

The other twelve occurrences of the name Helen without an epithet are in three scenes in the *Iliad* and the *Odyssey* (§2). These scenes are Helen on the wall of Troy (§2.1), Hector and Helen at the entrance to her home (§2.2), and the departure of Telemachus (§2.3). The narrator is almost always the speaker (9/12x) and his reasons for the use of the unmodified name vary (§2 *init.*). When it is a character in these scenes and not the narrator who uses the name Helen unmodified, he (Hector) is speaking to her or she is referring to herself. In a third instance, in quoting Proteus, Menelaus uses the name unmodified (§3). Hector, Helen herself, and Menelaus, then, each uses the name in this way once (= 3/12x); each time the use is dialogic.

4.1 Helen and the war

"Argive" Helen and the possessions of Menelaus that were stolen along with her are coupled in a formular line in which the epithet is implicitly part of the speaker's argument that she should be returned to her own people (*Il.* 3.458 ≈ 7.350; ch.3 intro.). More often, in other formulas concerning Helen and the possessions, she is simply Helen or she is "the woman."

---

[1] See Nünlist and de Jong 2000: 163 s.v. "Fokalisator." The "focalizer" (the usual term in English) is the one from whose perspective the events are presented. It may be the narrator or a character. In the latter case, the term "secondary focalization" is used. de Jong earlier spoke of "embedded focalization," which "means that the narrative 'embeds' in the narrator-text a character's focalization, that is, his perceptions, thoughts, feelings, or words (indirect speech)" (1997: 296).

4.1.1 Helen and the possessions of Menelaus

After he has been chided by Hector (ch. 1§7 *sub fin*.), Paris offers to face Menelaus in single combat: συμβάλετ' ἀμφ' Ἑλένῃ καὶ κτήμασι πᾶσι μάχεσθαι ("set me together (with Menelaus) to fight together for the sake of Helen and all the possessions," *Il*. 3.70). Whoever wins, Paris goes on to say, κτήμαθ' ἑλὼν εὖ πάντα γυναῖκά τε οἴκαδ' ἀγέσθω ("Let him fittingly take all the possessions and the woman and take them away," 3.72). Paris' words are repeated by Hector when he stands between the two armies and proposes the duel. Hector's repetition thus preserves the two versions of the terms ("Helen and the possessions": 70 ≈ 91; "the possessions and the woman": 72 = 93). When Idaeus brings the news of the duel to Priam, he says that Paris and Menelaus will fight ἀμφὶ γυναικί· / τῷ δέ κε νικήσαντι γυνὴ καὶ κτήμαθ' ἕποιτο ("over the woman; the woman and the possessions would follow the winner," 254–55). (For the diathetic relation of ἕπομαι and ἄγω / ἄγομαι see ch. 1§6.) Helen's identity has now, in the terms of the duel, been reduced to the zero-grade. She is no longer wife or in-law and her own point of view is irrelevant. Iris has told her that Paris and Menelaus will fight "over you" (περὶ σεῖο, 137) but as the rest of Iris' announcement makes clear, the disposition of Helen has nothing to do with her own wishes (ch. 1§5). Helen has become simply "the woman," having the same status as the possessions stolen by Paris.

This Trojan attitude is seen even in the old men on the wall. They refer to Helen's beauty but do not refer to her by name, saying that there is no blame in fighting over "such a woman" (τοιῇδ' ἀμφὶ γυναικὶ, 3.157), i.e., such a beautiful woman. In their minds, however, even her beauty is not sufficient reason to keep her at Troy (159–60). Within the time-frame of the *Iliad* the only Trojan who speaks of "Helen" (and not "the woman") and the possessions is Hector, first when he announces the duel of Paris and Menelaus (3.91, quoted above), and second when, about to face Achilles, he considers, and immediately rejects, the possibility of restoring everything to the Achaeans in return for his life (*Il*. 22.111–25). (On Hector as the only one to address Helen as Helen: 2§2 below.) The narrator, apropos of the sons of Antimachus, when they are slain by Agamemnon, recalls an incident from before the beginning of the war when the Achaeans sent an embassy into Troy to ask for the return of Helen. Antimachus, bribed by Paris, "would not allow (the Trojans) to give Helen to yellow-haired Menelaus" (οὐκ εἴασχ' Ἑλένην δόμεναι ξανθῷ Μενελάῳ, *Il*. 11.125). Although it might seem to be an example of "secondary focalization," tantamount to indirect speech, the fact remains that the narrator could hardly have said "the woman" in this context.[2]

---

[2] For "secondary focalization" see n. 1.

The Trojans' characteristic way of referring to Helen continues in the council scene in Book 7 (345–78), Antenor proposes that the Trojans return Helen and the possessions. Paris says that he will return them but not "the woman" (γυναῖκα, 362). The next day the herald Idaeus conveys Paris' offer to the Achaeans. He conveys Paris' refusal to return Helen in distinctly Achaean terms (7.392–93):

κουριδίην δ' ἄλοχον Μενελάου κυδαλίμοιο
οὔ φησιν δώσειν·

The wedded wife of glorious Menelaus
he says that he will not return.

Idaeus is conceding the Achaean point of view of Helen's status, perhaps diplomatically, in the hope that the Achaeans will accept the possessions. He cannot be expressing Paris' point of view, because Paris and Helen are married (ch. 1§5). Paris is the "husband of fair-haired Helen" (Il. 6x; ch. 7).

The Achaeans never refer to Helen as "the woman." Agamemnon, in referring to the terms of the duel says "Helen and all the possessions" (3.282, 285). Diomedes advises refusal of the offer brought by Idaeus (7.400–401).

μήτ' ἄρ τις νῦν κτήματ' Ἀλεξάνδροιο δεχέσθω
μήθ' Ἑλένην·

Now let no one take the possessions of Alexander
nor Helen.

Diomedes urges the Achaeans to forget about Helen (who was not in fact offered) because, he believes, Troy is doomed and victory is assured.

Odysseus, replying to Agamemnon, whom he has encountered in the underworld and the story of whose murder he has just heard, exclaims that Zeus has terribly shown his hatred of the Atreids "through the plots of women" (Ζεὺς / ἐκπάγλως ἤχθηρε γυναικείας διὰ βουλάς, Od. 11.436–37). Odysseus' odd consolation immediately (asyndetically) takes the form of two examples of these women: many of us died on account of Helen (at Troy) and Clytemnestra devised a stratagem for you (Ἑλένης μὲν ἀπωλόμεθ' εἵνεκα πολλοί / σοὶ δὲ Κλυταιμνήστρη..., 438–39). In the end, one could say, Odysseus has used his generalization about women to put the death of Agamemnon on a par with the deaths of all those who died at Troy. But it is also the case that his rhetoric has entailed greater blame of Helen than is heard from other Homeric characters.[3] Further, in implying with

---

3 de Jong 2001a: 289 on 11.438.

"on account of Helen" (Ἑλένης...εἵνεκα) that Helen intended and caused the Trojan war, he goes against the rest of the Homeric version of her role (ch. 7§5).

Eumaeus' blame of Helen takes approximately the same form as Odysseus'. He is speaking to the stranger in his house who is in fact Odysseus. First, she is the representative of a set of women, this time not all women but her own tribe, and second she caused the death of many men (14.67–69).

> ἀλλ' ὄλεθ, ὡς ὤφελλ' Ἑλένης ἀπὸ φῦλον ὀλέσθαι
> πρόχνυ, ἐπεὶ πολλῶν ἀνδρῶν ὑπὸ γούνατ' ἔλυσε·

> But he (my master) died, as I would the race of Helen had perished
> entirely, since she loosened the knees of many men.

Referring to "the tribe of Helen" he might mean all women but he might have in mind the daughters of Tyndareus, Helen, Clytemnestra, and their equally immoral sister Timandra. All are "twice-married and thrice-married, forsakers of their husbands" (Stesichorus fr. 46 PMG = fr. 223 PMGF = 85 D-F; cf. Aesch. *Ag.* 1469–71). Helen's good sister was Phylonoē.[4]

4.1.2 The sufferings of the Achaeans

The name Helen without an epithet is part of the whole-line formula: τίσασθαι δ' Ἑλένης ὁρμήματά τε στοναχάς τε ("to avenge the strivings and groans of Helen," 2.356, 590). Both semantics (of ὁρμήματα) and syntax (of the genitive) have long been in discussion. From Michael Reichel's survey of the scholarship it is clear that answers have been reached only by expanding the context of interpretation.[5] The genitive could be interpreted as subjective if "groans" (leaving aside the question of ὁρμήματα) on Helen's part correspond to her experience when she was abducted and/or now that she has been in Troy for many years.[6] As for the abduction, however, Helen went willingly, as her rebuke of Aphrodite shows (ἦ πῆ με προτέρω πολίων εὖ ναιομενάων / ἄξεις, "Will you lead me further through populous cities?" 3.400–401; cf. *Od.* 4.261–62). As for Helen in Troy, her laments

---

4 On the sisters: Edmunds 2016a: 76.
5 Reichel 2002.
6 Reichel 2002: 171–72 concludes by accepting the interpretation of the genitive as subjective. B-S-V 2003 on 2.356, invoking a "facettenreiches Bild der Helen-Gestalt," maintain that Nestor is removing all guilt from Helen, i.e., by describing her as having resisted her abduction. But the guilt of Helen is not in question in Nestor's words (or in the narrator's later).

are part of her rhetoric (see §2.2 below) and do not constitute "groans." The genitive in the formula under discussion should instead be understood as objective: "the groans over Helen." When Nestor uses the formula he refers to the groans of the Achaeans (2.354–56):

> τὼ μή τις πρὶν ἐπειγέσθω οἴκόνδε νέεσθαι,
> πρίν τινα πὰρ Τρώων ἀλόχῳ κατακοιμηθῆναι,
> τίσασθαι δ' Ἑλένης ὁρμήματά τε στοναχάς τε.
>
> So let no one hasten to return home
> before he has lain with the wife of a Trojan
> and has avenged himself for the struggles and groans over Helen.

The third of these lines is repeated apropos of the motive of Menelaus–in the voice of the narrator– in the part of the Catalogue of Ships on the Lacedaemonian contingent (2.590). Menelaus "was most of all eager in his heart to avenge himself for the struggles and groans over Helen." Menelaus would do so if he recovered Helen and the possessions that were stolen along with her (§1.1).

4.2 Three scenes

The three occurrences of the name Helen unmodified in the scene on the wall of Troy can be explained as idiomatic with the governing verbs (2§1). An epithet is missing, so to speak, in the verse introducing Helen's speech to Hector. The narrator shifts the emphasis to the unusual kind of *muthos* that Helen is about to give (2§2). Helen has the predicate adjective τριτάτη in the line introducing her lament for Hector (24.761). Again the narrator has avoided using one of Helen's epithets in a speech introduction in order to shift the emphasis, this time to Helen's preemption of third place in the sequence of women to lead the lament (2§2; on τριτάτη see ch. 11). Helen does not have an epithet when she is in the storeroom with Menelaus choosing a gift for the departing Telemachus. It is the most difficult to explain of all the uses of the name Helen unmodified (2§3). Neither Helen nor Menelaus nor Megapenthes has an epithet when they are in the storeroom in which gifts for Telemachus are chosen; they all have epithets when they leave the storeroom.

4.2.1 Helen on the wall of Troy

In the scene in which Helen appears on the wall of Troy and is questioned by Priam about the identity of three of the Achaean warriors whom he sees, the narrator thrice refers to her by her name alone. As she approaches, the Trojan elders see her (3.154–55):

οἳ δ' ὡς οὖν εἴδονθ' Ἑλένην ἐπὶ πύργον ἰοῦσαν,
ἦκα πρὸς ἀλλήλους ἔπεα πτερόεντ' ἀγόρευον·

And they, as they saw Helen coming toward the tower (where they were),
softly spoke winged words to each other.

In this "secondary focalization" the old men grasp the identity of the person who is approaching.[7] They remark on her beauty as worth fighting over (156–58) and it seems that their perception of Helen's identity might have included an epithet of beauty. But they are observing the rule that no Trojan uses a laudatory epithet of Helen. (When Antenor calls Helen "Argive" at *Il.* 7.350, the epithet is not derogatory but it is not laudatory.) They then quickly qualify their view–"let her leave" (159–60)–but without conceding the justice of the Achaean cause by referring to her as "Argive," that is, with the only epithet that they might have used.

Priam then summons Helen: Πρίαμος δ' Ἑλένην ἐκαλέσσατο φωνῇ ("but Priam called aloud out to Helen," 3.161). Here the absence of an epithet is a matter of the usage of the verb. Καλέω in both the middle and the active, when it means "summon," tends to have an unmodified object. This idiom explains Aphrodite's summoning of Helen from the wall: αὐτὴ δ' αὖθ' Ἑλένην καλέουσ' ἴε· τὴν δ' ἐκίχανεν ("she then went away to summon Helen," 383).

4.2.2 Hector and Helen; Helen's lament for Hector

In Book 6 Hector seeks out his brother Paris at his home, enters but remains near the door (318–20; see below), and finds him handling his armor (321–22). This scene continues the one contrived by Aphrodite at the end of Book 3, after she spirited Paris away from the battlefield.[8] Paris is in disgrace. Hector rebukes him

---

[7] "Secondary focalization": Krieter-Spiro 2009: 67 *ad loc*. For "secondary focalization" see n. 1.
[8] Reichel 1994: 247.

(325–31). Paris promises to return to battle (332–41).⁹ Helen then tries to persuade Hector to come in and sit down: τὸν δ' Ἑλένη μύθοισι προσηύδα μειλιχίοισιν ("But Helen spoke to him with soft words," 6.343). Here, in a speech-introduction, a name-epithet formula might have been, and was in fact, expected, as the ancient variant προσηύδα δῖα γυναικῶν shows (attested as a variant by the scribe in A; schol. A). The formular expression that replaces the name-epithet formula puts all the emphasis on the kind of speech that Helen is about to give, in which the invitation itself consists of only a few words (354).

Her speech is an apology for herself (on the self-reproach in the first line see ch. 2§§1, 2, 5) which takes the form of a lament, like her speech to Priam (ὡς ὄφελεν κτλ., 3.173–74).¹⁰ As such, it takes the form of a *muthos*, in general an inappropriate mode for a woman. In the words of Richard Martin, "Given the male, heroic in-group orientation of the word muthos, and its association with powerful self-presentation, it would seem to be a social taboo for women to employ this kind of speech." Martin goes on, however, to observe that lament is a genre of *muthos* that is available to women.¹¹

With Helen's lament can be compared the speech that Thetis gives in reply to Hephaestus' gracious welcome (18.429–61). She does not even acknowledge his greeting but begins her reply with a rhetorical question: Has any other goddess had to endure as many sorrows as I have? She proceeds to describe her unhappy marriage to Peleus (432–35a) and the son she has borne, who will never return from Troy (435b–41). She tells his story (442–56), in effect summarizing the *Iliad* up to the present, and then requests new armor for him (457–61). Thetis can be assumed to understand the protocol of the visit, which obviously does not exclude the same kind of opening lament heard in Helen's speech to her visitor, Hector.¹²

But Helen is also capable of other kinds of *muthos* and she is the only woman in the *Iliad* besides Hecuba (24.200) who speaks a *muthos*. In the scene under

---

9 The scene perhaps inspired the unusual Trojan domestic scene on a mid-sixth century amphora, in which Paris is departing for combat: *LIMC* "H." 196 = *LIMC* "A." 69*.
10 For an analysis of this speech relating it to the other Helen scenes in *Il.*: Stoevesand 2008: 115; for another analysis Graziosi and Haubold 2010: 41–44; for the scene Mirto 1997: 975–76. See also Richardson 1993: 357 on lines 762–65. For a bibliography of scholarship on this speech see Stoevesand *loc. cit.*
11 Martin 1989: 87.
12 Cf. the "emotional preamble" to an embedded narrative: de Jong 2001a: 102–103 on *Od.* 4.240–43, with many parallels.

discussion she has already rebuked Paris in a flyting speech (3.428–36).[13] Elsewhere she uses two other definable kinds, namely prophecy and the recitation of a remembered event (see Fig. 2). Of her eleven speeches in the *Iliad* and the *Odyssey* five are called *muthoi* and two are implicitly *muthoi*. Four of her speeches are explicitly *epē*. Her versatility as a speaker is in itself (as apart from the implications of the individual speeches), a part of her characterization (cf. ch. 2§7 *sub fin.*).[14]

Tab. 2: Helen's speeches. *Muthos* in parentheses: a speech that is implicitly a *muthos*.

Speech	Addressee(s)	Kind of speech	Kind of *muthos*	Epithet in introduction
Il. 3.172–80	Priam and others	muthos	lament	δῖα γυναικῶν
Il. 3.200–202	Priam and others	epos		Διὸς ἐκγεγαυῖα
Il. 3.229–42	Priam and others	(muthos)	with 3.228 cf. 3.171	τανύπεπλος, δῖα γυναικῶν
Il. 3.399–412	Aphrodite	epos		ø
Il. 3.428–36	Paris	muthos	flyting	κούρη Διὸς αἰγιόχοιο
Il. 6.344–58	Hector	muthos	lament	ø
Il. 24.762–75	Trojan women	(muthos)	lament	ø
Od. 4.138–46	Menelaus	epos		ø
Od. 4.235–64	Menelaus and others	muthos	recitation of remembered event	ø
Od. 15.125–29	Telemachus	epos		καλλιπάρῃος
Od. 15.172–78	Peisistratus and others	muthos	prophecy	τανύπεπλος

To turn to the adjective in the phrase introducing Helen's speech to Hector, her lament is introduced as "soft" or "appeasing" (μύθοισι προσηύδα μειλιχίοισι, 6.343).[15] In general, a *muthos* would not be expected to have this characteristic.

---

13 Martin 1989: 44: on the flyting speech one of the principal kinds of *muthos*. The others are: prayer, supplication, commanding, and narrating from memory. Cf. the list in Nagy 2007: 54, which includes also threats, invectives, and prophecies.
14 Worman 2002: 13–14 discusses the versatility of Helen in Greek literature of the fifth century, when she becomes the embodiment of "an enchanting style of self-presentation"; cf. 195–96.
15 *LfgrE* s.v. μείλιχ(ι)ος B 2: "besänftigend." See Graziosi and Haubold 2010: 175: on lines 344–48: Helen's opening is an example of the rhetorical move later called *insinuatio*.

This noun is modified by μείλιχ(ι)ος in just two other places, in the singular. Diomedes refers to the speech of his father Tydeus to the Thebans, implicitly contrasting it with the ambush that they set for him when he left Thebes (μειλίχιον μῦθον, *Il.* 10.288–90; cf. 4.392–97 for the ambush). This phrase also introduces Odysseus' supplication to Nausicaa (*Od.* 6.148), "a very special speech."[16] The adjective in the phrase introducing Helen's speech is twice used with προσηύδα as a substantive (Diomedes to Glaucus, 6.214; Automedon to the horses of Achilles, 17.431). A muthos is "soft," then, only in exceptional circumstances.

The lament that Helen makes, beginning with the epithets of blame that she uses of herself (cf. ch. 2§§1, 5, 7), intends to appease Hector in an awkward situation. Both these epithets and her lament are apologetic and her speech also recognizes the failure of Paris for which Hector has blamed him (350–53). Even if Hector has said that the war is "on account of" Paris (328), Helen shares the blame with her husband (εἵνεκ' ἐμεῖο κυνός, κτλ., 356).

Helen's mea culpa does not succeed. Hector replies only to her invitation: μή με κάθιζ' Ἑλένη φιλέουσά περ· οὐδέ με πείσεις ("Do not invite me to sit down, Helen, even though you love me; you will not persuade me," 360). Hector's use of the name Helen corresponds to Helen's addressing him as "brother-in-law" (δᾶερ, 344; cf. ch. 1§4). The invitation that Hector refuses has come from Helen as the wife of his brother (Paris has called her ἄλοχος in this scene, 337; cf. ch. 1§5). Hector grants that Helen is φιλέουσα, which was translated "loving" for lack of a better word. The notion of *philia* that Hector presupposes is in the first place a familial and social one, as Émile Benveniste showed in a well-known article.[17] The name Helen as used by Hector makes a striking contrast with her name as used by the narrator at the beginning of her speech. A reader may rightly say of that speech, especially of its conclusion, in which Helen looks ahead to future fame in song, "Helen considers her destiny as grand and significant as that of the heroes," but Hector has not replied to Helen in a way that fits with her characterization by the narrator.[18] In Hector's eyes, even if he is more sympathetic to her than most of the other Trojans, she has the same identity that she has for them.

The narrator introduces Helen's lament for Hector in this way: "Then Helen was the third who led the women in the wailing" (τῇσι δ' ἔπειθ' Ἑλένη τριτάτη ἐξῆρχε γόοιο (24.761). It is a formular line that has been used of Andromache and

---

16 de Jong 2001a: 159 on 148–85.
17 Benveniste 1969.
18 Graziosi and Haubold 2010: 180 on line 357.

Hecuba in preceding lines.[19] The use of the name Helen is exceptional, however. Only here is it modified by a predicate adjective. This adjective is obviously not the narrator's reminder that Helen was numerically the third woman to take this role at the prosthesis of Hector. "Third" calls attention to the implicit scale of affection that Helen has established by her characteristic spontaneity in speaking, seen already in her speech to Hector in Book 6 and again in the *Odyssey*.[20] She has assumed the third place, instead of a Trojan sister-in-law. Again as in her speeches to Priam and Hector, she laments herself, here even more egocentrically.[21] Nevertheless she moves "the numberless throng" to groans (ἐπὶ δ' ἔστενε δῆμος ἀπείρων, 776). She remains a powerful speaker.

4.2.3 Departure of Telemachus

Helen and Megapenthes accompany Menelaus to the storeroom, where they will choose parting gifts for Telemachus (οὐκ οἶος, ἅμα τῷ γ' Ἑλένη κίε καὶ Μεγαπένθης, *Od.* 15.100).[22] The function of Megapenthes will be to carry the silver bowl that Menelaus chooses as his gift for Telemachus (103, 122). Although each of the three is named, none has an epithet while he or she is in the storeroom (99–105); Menelaus once has the patronymic Ἀτρεΐδης instead of his name (102). As soon, however, as Helen begins to move from the storeroom carrying the robe that she has chosen for Telemachus and to return to public view, she is appropriately δῖα γυναικῶν (cf. ch. 5). When the gifts are presented to Telemachus both Megapenthes and Helen have an epithet (122–23; for Helen's see ch. 9). In the speech that she gives when she presents the robe to Telemachus she refers to it as a "remembrance of the hands of Helen" (μνῆμ' Ἑλένης χειρῶν, 15.126).[23] There

---

19 τῇσιν δ' Ἀνδρομάχη λευκώλενος ἦρχε γόοιο, 723, of Andromache; τῇσιν δ' αὖθ' Ἑκάβη ἀδινοῦ ἐξῆρχε γόοιο, 747, of Hecuba.
20 Graziosi and Haubold 2010: 43: "Paris' speech leaves Hector at a loss for words. And it is at this point that Helen intervenes, filling one of the heaviest silences in the whole poem." Two of her speeches in the *Odyssey* anticipate and replace speeches that Menelaus is expected to give (4.138–46; 15.172–78).
21 Egocentricity: Mirto 1997: 1518. The death wish that she expresses is, however, a convention of this kind of lament: cf. 22.431 (Andromache), 481 (Hecuba). Tsagalis 2004: 161–65 shows common features of Helen's and of Briseïs' (19.287–300) laments.
22 On Helen's gift to Telemachus see Karanika 2014: 38–40.
23 Helen's name here is without digamma. Hoekstra 1988: 197 on *Od.* 14.68 observes the undigammated form of Helen's name and, referring to the discovery of a sixth-century Spartan inscription in which the name has digamma (Catling and Cavanagh 1976), comments: "For epic poetry, this means that if the abduction of Helen was among its older subjects, the digammated

will be a future in which she is "Helen." It is the future that she imagines when in her speech to Hector in Book 6 of the *Iliad* she foresees that she and Paris will be a song for men in the future (357–58). For the audience of *Iliad* Book 6 or of *Odyssey* Book 15 that expectation has been fulfilled. She is indeed "Helen."

4.3 Helen as wife of Menelaus

In the *Odyssey* Helen is thrice referred to without an epithet as the wife of Menelaus (cf. passages in which characters use her name without an epithet to refer to her as the wife of Paris: 1§1 above). At the beginning of Book 4 Menelaus is holding a wedding feast for his two children, Hermione, born to Helen before she left for Troy, and Megapenthes, a bastard son, born to a slave woman in Helen's absence. The narrator observes (4.12–14):

> Ἑλένῃ δὲ θεοὶ γόνον οὐκέτ' ἔφαινον,
> ἐπεὶ δὴ τὸ πρῶτον ἐγείνατο παῖδ' ἐρατεινήν,
> Ἑρμιόνην, ἣ εἶδος ἔχε χρυσέης Ἀφροδίτης.
>
> The gods gave no other children to Helen,
> once she first bore her lovely child,
> Hermione, who had the beauty of golden Aphrodite.

Here the name Helen is in an oblique case. The beauty of Helen, often expressed in her epithets, is surpassed by her daughter's–*matre pulchra filia pulchrior*–, because Homer never compares Helen's beauty to Aphrodite's. The old men on the wall of Troy compare her to "immortal goddesses" in looks (3.156–58) but it is only a façon de parler.[24]

---

form of the name must have been part of early formulae. However, only a few traces of this state of affairs remains in Homer, the most notable being Ἀλέξανδρος Ἑλένης πόσις ἠυκόμοιο." West 2007: 231 n. 115 (citing the ancient grammarians on the matter) makes a similar statement. Hainsworth 1993: 267 (on *Il.* 11.369, an example of Ἀλέξανδρος, κτλ.), however, points out that in the OCT Homer vowels before Ἑ- are elided in 29 of 58 occurrences, i.e., in the 29 other occurrences the name Helen begins with digamma. But Hainsworth says of the formula Ἀλέξανδρος, κτλ.: "the frequent lengthening of a naturally short syllable before the caesura prevents this verse being cited for a Homeric Fελένη." Finally, a forthcoming book by Nicole Lanérès, to be published by the École Pratique des Hautes Études, Sciences historiques et philologiques, will argue that the next-to-last word in the inscription published in 1976 (Δεῖνι[ς]) τάδ'ἀνέθεκε) Χαρι[ ]) Fελέϙαι) Μενελάϙο) cannot be read as Helen.

24 Other women who are like to goddesses are Castianeira, the mother of Gorgythion (*Il.* 8.304–305) and Nestor's serving-woman Hecamede (*Il.* 11.638). The same kind of simile can be used of

The feast is soon forgotten and is replaced by a meal in honor of Telemachus and Peisistratus, who have just arrived.²⁵ Helen enters with her maid servants. The narrator gives a list of the presents that Menelaus and Helen received from Polybus and his wife Alcandrē in Egyptian Thebes. Helen's are accoutrements of spinning, a golden spindle and a silver basket, introduced thus (4.130):

χωρὶς δ' αὖθ' Ἑλένῃ ἄλοχος πόρε κάλλιμα δῶρα·

Besides these (the gifts given Menelaus by Polybus) his wife gave to Helen beautiful gifts.

Again the name Helen is in an oblique case. The grammatical object of the verb is very beautiful. Here the beauty of the gifts is part of the aura of Helen's entry into the *megaron*.

In the third occurrence of Helen without an epithet in Book 4, Menelaus repeats to Telemachus a conversation he had with the sea-god Proteus, who told Menelaus that he would go to the Elysian fields after death because of his marriage to Helen (4.569).

οὕνεκ' ἔχεις Ἑλένην καί σφιν γαμβρὸς Διός ἐσσι.

Because you have Helen and to them (the immortals) you are the son-in-law of Zeus.²⁶

Here Menelaus "has Helen" (accusative case) as wife. It is Helen's status as demigod, known from her kinship epithets (ch. 10), that is transferred to her husband. His status as son-in-law of Zeus was seized upon by Isocrates in his *Encomium of Helen* and inflated to Helen's deification of him (62).²⁷

4.4 Conclusion

When characters use the name Helen unmodified they are usually referring to her as the object of the war. The epithet "Argive" (ch. 2) expresses the same, usually Achaean, point of view. Both the name alone and the name with "Argive" can appear in the same phrase with the possessions stolen by Paris along with Helen. When the narrator uses her name unmodified he is describing Helen in a scene

---

men. Talthybius is "like to a god in his voice" (θεῷ ἐναλίγκιος αὐδὴν, *Il.* 19.250). Paris is regularly "godlike" (θεοειδής, *Il.* 12x), as is Priam (*Il.* 10x).
25 See de Jong 2001a: 90 on lines 3–19 on the opening of *Od.* 4.
26 σφιν refers to ἀθάνατοι (564). For the difficulties see S. West 1988: 228 on line 569.
27 Edmunds 2016a: 177–80.

with other characters and is emphasizing something other than whatever an ornamental epithet would emphasize. The storeroom scene in the *Odyssey* is exceptional. The unmodified names of the three characters in this scene may be deliberately privative. They are not in view of others and none of them does or says anything that would prompt an epithet.

5 δῖα γυναικῶν "noble among women": The Public Figure (1)

The very common adjective δῖος by itself is banal–a word that one scarcely heeds, Parry said–but in the phrase δῖα γυναικῶν, which occurs fifteen times, it is distinctive.[1] The root value of δῖος, "light," gives "divine" (of gods and demi-gods) and "noble" in the sense of conspicuously excellent (of humans).[2] This last connotation persists in the phrase δῖα γυναικῶν, which is used of the two most prominent women, Helen (5x) and Penelope (8x), especially when they appear in public or are moving from one place to another.[3] Otherwise it is used once of Alcestis (*Il.* 2.714) and once of Eurycleia (*Od.* 20.147).[4] Only the narrator uses this epithet.

Of Penelope he says four times: ἡ δ' ὅτε δὴ μνηστῆρας ἀφίκετο δῖα γυναικῶν,…"And when she, noble among women, came among the suitors,…" (*Od.* 1.332 = 16.414 = 18.208 = 21.63). She has the same epithet when she moves from one part of the house to another. "She then went to her upper-room, noble amongst women (ἡ μὲν ἔπειτ ἀνέβαιν' ὑπερῷα δῖα γυναικῶν, 18.302). Or "when she had arrived at that bed chamber, noble amongst women" (ἡ δ' ὅτε δὴ θάλαμον τὸν ἀφίκετο δῖα γυναικῶν, *Od.* 21.42 ≈ *Il.* 3.423, of Helen). When she and Odysseus are lying in bed telling each stories of the years when they were separated, "she [told] all that she endured in her house, she noble amongst women" (ἡ μὲν ὅσ' ἐν μεγάροισιν ἀνέσχετο δῖα γυναικῶν, 23.302). The narrator reports what she told Odysseus; within that report the phrase "noble amongst women"

---

1 Parry 1971[1930]: 305; cf. Parry 1971a[1928]: 137, cited in *LfgrE* s.v. δῖος B (intro.).
2 Perotti 1990: 166–67. *LfgrE* s.v. δῖος lists δ. γ. under "Special problems" under B, and gives "priority" as the meaning, citing Schwyzer 2.116 (under the main heading II. Partitiv, sub-heading 5: Der adnominale Partitiv): "die himmliche unter den Weibern" (cf. the old men on the wall of Troy). Cf. Coray 2009: 16 on *Il.* 19.6b: "δῖα (θεάων)…ist in diesen Wendungen wohl nur noch als allg. Ausdruck der höchsten Vortrefflichkeit zu verstehen." Coray's intuition of the superlative sense of the adj. fits with Schwyzer's definition of the sub-category: the gen. depends on a superlative or a positive that has the same force as a superlative.
3 Krieter-Spiro 2009: 71 on *Il.* 3.171: "ein generisches Epitheton mit Bezug auf Frauen in bedeutender Stellung gebraucht." But this epithet is used predominantly of Helen and Penelope. At *Il.* 6.343 δῖα γυναικῶν is a *varia lectio* for μειλιχίοισιν added by the scribe in A. See ch. 4§2.2
4 Alcestis: Εὔμηλος, τὸν ὑπ' Ἀδμήτῳ τέκε δῖα γυναικῶν (*Il.* 2.714). Perhaps the trace of a formula with τέκε: cf. Hes. *Cat.* fr. 190.3 M-W = 89 H = 133 M (Hippodameia). Eurycleia's epithet is part of an imposing two-line introduction to the commands that she gives to the servants (*Od.* 20.147–48). These lines show her preeminence among the servants. Eurynomē has been forgotten, as di Benedetto 2010 *ad loc.* points out. The epithet is in part contrastive, implicitly looking to the narrative past.

comes from the narrator's perspective, not Penelope's, and recreates the picture, seen earlier, of Penelope vis-à-vis the suitors. In all of these examples except the last, Penelope is on her feet and in motion to or from a place where she has been in view, and in the last her presence before the suitors is implied. The remaining example at first seems anomalous: "noble amongst women she prayed first of all to Artemis" (Ἀρτέμιδι πρώτιστον ἐπεύξατο δῖα γυναικῶν, 20.60). But she may be on her feet and the verb may presuppose a visible act, her raising her hands. One can compare the formula χεῖρας ἀνασχών (Il. 5x) / χεῖρας ἀνέσχον (Il. 3x) of persons praying.[5] The formular description of Penelope here would be consistent with the places just discussed.

5.1 Helen as δῖα γυναικῶν in the *Iliad*

The narrator introduces Helen's first reply to Priam on the wall of Troy with δῖα γυναικῶν (3.171). (This line belongs to the set of three reply-verses discussed in ch. 6§1.) Although Helen is at this point seated before Priam (162), she has just made a conspicuous arrival. The old men see her as she reaches the tower (154) and remark on her beauty (156–58). δῖα γυναικῶν, which is the first nominative epithet used of Helen (preceded by 2.161, 177 [accusatives]; 3.121 [dative]), that is, the first time that she is the subject of a verb, seems not to have a framing function here (it is clear who the speaker is) but, in the first place, to mark Helen's appearance on the wall.[6] It also serves to contrast the narrator's perspective on Helen with that of Priam and, for that matter, with Helen's own negative account of herself in this speech (cf. §1.1 below). The reoccurrence of this epithet in Helen's third reply-verse (228; cf. §1.2 below) can be explained in the same way.

5.1.1 The contrasting perspectives of the narrator and Priam in the Teichoscopia

Priam addresses Helen as φίλον τέκος (3.162), as his daughter-in-law, and in effect describes the simple speech that he anticipates ("name this man": verb ἐξονομαίνω, 166). The narrator for his part calls her δῖα γυναικῶν (3.171). In this way,

---

5 Schwenn 1927 discusses not what might be called the phenomenology of prayer but its prehistory, its form in various Greek texts, and the associated beliefs.
6 Bozzone 2015: 132 n. 89: "...[W]ho the next speaker is going to be, in a discussion scene, is often clear from context. The noun-epithet formulas at the end of the line should not be regarded as necessary information." But even if a formula does not convey new information it can still have meaning in context.

Priam's appellative seems to be over-written by the laudatory epithet and the poet's perspective seems to replace that of the kindly old king. It is not so simple. Helen's speech succeeds in maintaining both her familial or social role in Troy and also, in ways now to be explained, the superiority that she has in the narrator's, and thus also in his audience's, eyes.[7]

Helen begins by honoring Priam's address to her, speaking as his daughter-in-law (she addresses him as "father-in-law": cf. ch. 1) and with the regrets with which some of her speeches will begin.[8] It is not until the sixth line of her speech (177, the sixth of nine) that she interrupts herself, turns to Priam's question, and answers it (3.177–80).

τοῦτο δέ τοι ἐρέω, ὅ μ' ἀνείρεαι ἠδὲ μεταλλᾷς·
οὗτός γ' Ἀτρεΐδης εὐρὺ κρείων Ἀγαμέμνων,
ἀμφότερον βασιλεύς τ' ἀγαθὸς κρατερός τ' αἰχμητής·
δαὴρ αὖτ' ἐμὸς ἔσκε κυνώπιδος, εἴ ποτ' ἔην γε.

This I will tell you that you ask me and inquire after.
This is the son of Atreus, broad-ruling Agamemnon.
both good king and mighty warrior.
And as well he was brother-in-law to me, dog-faced– if it ever was.

The T scholiast remarked on line 178: "she indicates him (Agamemnon) as an individual, epigrammatically" (ὡς ἑνικὸν ἐπιγραμματικῶς αὐτὸν δηλοῖ, Erbse). The description in the following line (179) is cited by the ABCT scholia on *Iliad* 1.29 (Agamemnon is threatening Chryses) as from "the epigram" (Bekker's plausible emendation of the readings of the scholiasts), with apparent reference to the lines in Book 3 under discussion.[9] One would have, then, a two-line epigram (178–79). Hermann Köchly, comparing tristichic epigrams in the same context in *Iliad* 3 (156–58 [the Trojans elders description of Helen], 200–202 [Helen's description of Odysseus]), spoke of lines 178–80 as constituting another such epigram, and in this matter scholarship on these lines has followed him.[10] In the third of these

---

7 For this and the two subsequent replies of Helen to Priam: Tsagalis 2008: 112–34.
8 Cf. Reichel 1994: 265–67.
9 In the mss. the scholium does not have the word ἐπίγραμμα, which was conjectured by Bekker and accepted by Erbse, who reads ἔστι γάρ, ὥς που τὸ περὶ αὐτοῦ ἐπίγραμμα δῆλοι, βασιλεύς τ' ἀγαθὸς κρατερός τ' αἰχμητής.
10 Köchly 1881: 79–80. He was followed by Vox 1975, who held that Helen's οὗτος was dialogic, as part of her reply to Priam, and the epigram (i.e., lines 178–80) was not autonomous, as a real epigram would be. Elmer 2005 challenged Vox at length, maintaining that the lines are not dialogic but "inscriptional." (*Il.* 3.156–58 is a τρίγωνον ἐπίγραμμα, which can begin with any of the three lines, as Köchly points out, following the scholia.)

lines, however, which supposedly constitute a tristichic epigram, Helen makes an additional point (note αὖτε), reverting to the mode of lamentation with which she began. Both the iterative imperfect (ἔσκε) and the phrase εἴ ποτ' ἔην γε ("if it ever was") recur in Penelope's recollection of Odysseus, who she thinks has perished (*Od.* 19.315).[11]

Helen's reply to Priam as a whole shows her, then, combining two genres, lament and epigram, not an unlikely combination when one of the two main uses of the early hexameter epigram was sepulchral (the other was dedicatory). The first of these is of course on full display in Book 24 of the *Iliad* when Helen is the third woman to lead the lament over Hector (761–76). In the *Odyssey* she adopts other genres. Her staging of herself as a bard (and thus assuming what we think was a male role) will be observed (*Od.* 4.238–40; see ch. 10). At the departure of Peisistratus and Telemachus, Helen, interpreting a bird omen, gives a mantic performance (15.170–71).[12] Helen's different kinds of poetic performance are presumably received differently by their different audiences or interlocutors. Her lament, for example, at least qua lament, meets the expectations of the other mourners. As for her epigram, it is not clear that it has meaning as such for Priam, as apart from the information that it contains. Simultaneously, however, with its delivery it is heard as epigrammatic by the narrator's audience.[13] In this way, the narrator conveys Helen's skill as a speaker, which is often commented on apropos of some of her other speeches, and her skill here in the adaptation of poetic genres is a confirmation of the superiority that the narrator signaled with δῖα γυναικῶν.[14]

---

11 Martin 2003: 124–25. Hooker 1979: 394 says of εἰ that "in origin it was used to introduce a main clause, not a protasis" and holds that this original use persists here and in the five other occurrences of εἴ ποτ' ἔην γε or a slight variant thereof (*Il.* 11.762, 24.426; *Od.* 15.267–68, 19.315, 24.289). Helen is saying: "as surely as ever such a one there was." But the expected meaning "if" better brings out Helen's sense of the lapse of time and the fading of the past, now sadly out of reach. See Krieter-Spiro 2009: 74–75 on line 180.
12 Nagy 2002: 143, 146.
13 *Pace* Elmer (cf. n. 10 above), οὗτος (178) is both dialogic and epigrammatic. For its dialogic force cf. Helen's replies οὗτος δ' αὖ Λαερτιάδης (200) and οὗτος δ' Αἴας (229). For the deictic force of the demonstrative as addressed to Priam in her first response, cf. Apollonius Dyscolus: ὁ μέντοι Πρίαμος ὁρῶν τὸν Ἀγαμέμνονα πεῦσιν ποιεῖται τὴν κατὰ τοῦ κυρίου ὀνόματος, πρὸς ὃν πάλιν ὑπάγεται τὸ οὗτος δ' Ἀτρείδης ἀναγκαίως συνεχθείσης τῷ ὀνόματι τῆς δεικτικῆς ἀντωνυμίας, ἵνα ἀφορίσῃ τὸ τοῦ Ἀγαμέμνονος πρόσωπον πολλῶν συνόντων (*De constructione* in G. Uhlig, *Gramm. Graec.* vol. 2.2: 101).
14 For the similarity of lines 174–75 of Helen's speech to the funerary epigram: Tsagalis 2008: 117–18.

5.1.2 δῖα γυναικῶν in Helen's third reply-verse (228) and when she returns to Paris (423)

In her third reply-verse Helen is called both δῖα γυναικῶν and also τανύπεπλος (on the second of these epithets and the line as a whole cf. ch. 6). It could not be said that at this point in her interaction with Priam the epithet δῖα γυναικῶν is required to mark her presence; a fortiori neither does the rather unusual pairing of epithets (for this phenomenon cf. Introduction p. 7) have this function. But as with δῖα γυναικῶν in her first reply verse so here the epithet, and indeed the pair of epithets, maintains the poet's point of view, as against Helen's self-reproach and against the Achaeans' negative view of her (242). Again her speech justifies her epithets.

This time, however, it is not a matter of the imitation of poetic genres. It is rather Helen's skill in adapting an assertion that the narrator makes of himself as a bard. Helen says (3.234–35)

νῦν δ' ἄλλους μὲν <u>πάντας</u> ὁρῶ ἑλίκωπας Ἀχαιούς,
οὕς κεν ἐὺ γνοίην καί τ' <u>οὔνομα</u> <u>μυθησαίμην</u>·

Now I see all the other bright-eyed Achaeans
whom I might recognize and whose names I might tell.

These lines of course recall what the narrator said at the beginning of the catalogue in Book 2, when he called upon the Muses for aid, avowing his own inability to name all the leaders of the Danaans (484–87):

πληθὺν δ' οὐκ ἂν ἐγὼ μυθήσομαι οὐδ' ὀνομήνω,

Nor will I say or name the multitude.

Il. 2.488

What the narrator says he cannot do is what Helen says that she *could* do, producing a moment of wry humor for the narrator's audience (but not for Priam, who has never heard or read Book 2 of the *Iliad*). The lines in the *Odyssey* in which she stages herself as a bard (4.238–40) have already been mentioned. In one of these lines she says, of the trials of Odysseus (*Od.* 4.240):

<u>πάντα</u> μὲν οὐκ ἂν ἐγὼ <u>μυθήσομαι</u> οὐδ' <u>ὀνομήνω,</u>

I will not say or name all.

This line also, like the one in Helen's third reply to Priam in the *Iliad*, closely resembles the narrator's disavowal in Book 2, especially because it is also negative like the disavowal.[15] In both of Helen's "Homeric" lines, however, she uses a rhetoric that is uniquely similar to the narrator's, comparable in this respect only with the rhetoric of Achilles, which, as Richard Martin has shown, is closer than anyone else's to the narrator's own.[16] In her third reply, then, Helen's way of speaking bears out the narrator's perspective in the epithets in the third reply-verse (228).

δῖα γυναικῶν occurs a third time in Book 3 after Helen's return to the house of Paris and her show-down with Aphrodite (cf. Ch. 12): ἣ δ' εἰς ὑψόροφον θάλαμον κίε δῖα γυναικῶν ("and when she, noble amongst women, had reached the high-roofed bed chamber," 423). The similarity of this line to a line describing the movement of Penelope has already been pointed out (ch. 6§2). The noblewoman arrives at the bedchamber.

5.2 δῖα γυναικῶν of Helen in the *Odyssey*

In Book 4 of the *Odyssey*, the epithet in question occurs in a line that seems to be anomalous (304–305):

Ἀτρεΐδης δὲ καθεῦδε μυχῷ δόμου ὑψηλοῖο,
πὰρ δ' Ἑλένη τανύπεπλος ἐλέξατο, δῖα γυναικῶν.

And the son of Atreus was sleeping in an inner recess of the lofty house
and beside him long-robed Helen, noble among women, lay.

Helen is not in motion but lying down, whereas in a closely similar verse in Book 3 of the *Iliad*, discussed in ch. 6, Helen is in public, on the wall of Troy. The abducted woman has been recovered and is back in her rightful husband's bed. It can be further suggested that these epithets form a pointed contrast with the one that the narrator uses of Helen when Menelaus arises the next morning ("fair-haired," *Od.* 15.58; see ch. 9§1).

In the *Odyssey*, δῖα γυναικῶν also describes Helen as she carries a *peplos* as a gift for the parting Telemachus. "Helen, noble among women, lifting up one of these (peploi) was carrying it (τῶν ἕν' ἀειραμένη Ἑλένη φέρε, δῖα γυναικῶν, 15.107). She, Menelaus and Megapenthes are in the bedroom, where (or through which there is access to the place where) their treasures are stored. They then

---

15 See Ford 1992: 72–74 on *Il.* 2.488 and *Od.* 4.240.
16 Martin 1989: ch. 4 ("The Language of Achilles").

proceed through the house (βὰν δ' ἰέναι προτέρω διὰ δώματος, 109), to meet Telemachus. Helen has the epithet that women, she and Penelope, have when they are in motion and are making an appearance. Helen does not have another epithet until her last appearance in the *Odyssey*, when she interprets the bird omen that appears just as Telemachus and Pisistratus are departing. Here she is τανύπεπλος (15.171). It is the other epithet in the pair τανύπεπλος and δῖα γυναικῶν, and it can be suggested that it, too, is a way of presenting her in a public appearance (as at *Il.* 3.228) (ch. 6§1).

It happens that the epithet δῖα γυναικῶν occurs also in the storeroom scene in Book 6 of the *Iliad*, in the second of two plus-verses in a Ptolemaic papyrus (P480a), where it describes Hecuba. (The resemblance of the scene in the *Odyssey* to the one in *Iliad* 6.288–92 has often been commented upon.[17]) Hector has instructed Hecuba to take her finest mantle and place it on the lap of Athena, and Hecuba has gone to find the mantle (288):

αὐτὴ δ' ἐς θάλαμον κατεβήσετο κηώεντα,

She went down into her fragrant storeroom.

There follow the two plus-verses (288a–b):

κέδρινον] ὑψερεφῆ ὅς γλήνη πολλ' ἐκεκεύθει
] φωριαμοῖσι παρί[στ]ατο δῖα γυνα[ικῶν

made of cedar, which concealed many ornaments...
noble among women she stood beside the chests.

Hecuba is still in the storeroom, thus not conspicuous to other characters in the poem, except her attendants, but one could say that παρί[στ]ατο completes the action indicated in the preceding line (κατεβήσετο). Hecuba will bear the mantle to the temple of Athena on the acropolis of Troy in a public supplication.[18] (For Helen and the others, all without epithets, in the storeroom scene in *Od.* 4 see ch. 4§2).

---

17 Usener 1990: 186–88 discusses the scene in the *Od.* under the heading "Nicht-signifikante Parallelen der *Odyssee* zur *Ilias*." See his notes for earlier scholarship.
18 For speculations on connections between the plus-verse and *Od.* 15.104 see Bird 2010: 96.

5.3 Conclusion

The narrator's δῖα γυναικῶν in the two reply verses in Book 3 has the effect of elevating the figure of Helen. The speeches themselves demonstrate high skill on her part and reinforce the implication of the formula. In particular, Helen is like Achilles in her ability to use resources that are otherwise the narrator's alone. The epithet δῖα γυναικῶν occurs, however, in an unexpected context in the Odyssey in a line in which Helen is lying in bed beside Menelaus. A contrast with the epithet describing her the next morning seems to be the point.

Helen and Penelope have in common the aspect indicated by δῖα γυναικῶν; they do not have the same moral character. Helen could never be referred to by Penelope's epithets, "prudent" (πινυτή) and "wise" (περίφρων). The difference between the cousins is clear when Penelope compares herself with Helen. In a speech to Odysseus she explains her hesitation in recognizing him (23.218–24).[19] She did not want to be deceived by a stranger as Helen had been. While she does not blame Helen, she does not exonerate her. The use of the same formula preponderantly of Helen and Penelope does not, then, imply a real similarity between them. It will be suggested that this non-functional similarity is the result of a Homeric redistribution of inherited epithets for women (ch. 12§2), a redistribution in which some women, and, in Helen's case, a woman and a goddess, were going to have the same epithet, contrary to the sense of the narrative.

---

19 Heubeck in Russo, Fernández-Galiano and Heubeck 1992: 336–37 on lines 218–24. Lines 23.218–21 are quoted in ch. 3§2. See the analyses of the speech by de Jong 2001a: 557–58 on lines 209–30 and di Benedetto 2010: 1189–90 on lines 215–30.

6 τανύπεπλος "long-robed": The Public Figure (2)

The distribution of this epithet in Homer and Hesiod seems to make a crazy quilt. It refers to Thetis (*Il.* 18.385 = 18.424), to Lampetiē the messenger of Helios (*Od.* 12.375), and to Ctimenē the sister of Odysseus (*Od.* 15.363), as well as three times to Helen (*Il.* 3.228; Hom. *Od.* 4.305, 15.171). It is the narrator who uses the epithet of Helen and of Lampetiē. In Hesiodic works, it refers to Heniochē the wife of Creon (*Scut.* 83) and to Eudora, who is named in a list of the Hyades (*Astronomica* 291 M-W = 227a–b M; not in H). In these two Hesiodic places and when Eumaeus uses it (*Od.* 15.363), the epithet is in line-final position. Elsewhere it comes before the feminine caesura. One has the impression of a fungible epithet, "a generic epithet for women and goddesses."[1] Its use of Helen, can, however, be shown to have a particular significance in its context.

The element ταυν-, from *τανύς "thin," was associated with τανύω "to stretch" / τάνυμαι "to be stretched" and came to mean "stretched thin," i.e., "long."[2] In Homer and later τανύπεπλος means "of long robe" and a long robe indicates a tall woman. A scholiast comments: "If the body is extended, it is necessary that the robe be extended, too."[3] Likewise Apollonius the Sophist: τεταμένον ἄχρι πολλοῦ πέπλον ἔχουσα, ἐξ οὗ τὸ μέγεθος τῆς φορούσης σημαίνειν βούλεται "having a *peplos* that is much extended, whence he intends to signify the size of the woman wearing it" (p. 149 Bekker).[4]

A tall woman is beautiful.[5] Agamemnon prefers Chryseïs to Clytemnestra because she is no worse (i.e., better) in several respects, one of which is size: in "body or stature or intelligence or accomplishments" (οὐ δέμας οὐδὲ φυήν, οὔτ' ἄρ φρένας οὔτέ τι ἔργα, *Il.* 1.115).[6] Artemis was conspicuously tall (e.g., *Od.* 6.107–8; *Hymn Hom. Ap.* 198–99), and Eustathius mistakenly thought that Helen's height was the point of the simile in which she is "like to Artemis of the golden spindle" (*Od.* 4.122) "The poet," he said, "likens Helen to Artemis with spindle of

---

1 Edwards 1991: 192 on *Il.* 18.385–86.
2 Chantraine s.v. τανυ- A.1. Frisk s.v. τανυ- holds that in τανύπεπλος and some other τανυ- compounds a clear separation of the two senses is impossible.
3 Schol. BEQ *Od.* 4.305 Dindorf: τανύπεπλος] ἡ τεταμένον καὶ ἐπιμήκη τὸν πέπλον ἔχουσα. ὡς ἂν εἰ ἔλεγεν ἡ νεωτέρα καὶ εὐμήκης τὴν ἡλικίαν. τεταμένου γὰρ τοῦ σώματος ἀνάγκη τετάσθαι καὶ τὸν πέπλον.
4 Cf. schol. D *Il.* 3.228: περιτεταμένον ἔχουσα τὸν πέπλον ἕως ἄκρων ποδῶν καθειμένον.
5 See S. West 1988: 272 on *Od.* 5.217.
6 See Kirk 1985: 65 on lines 114–15 (an amusing note).

gold on account of the stature of her body."[7] In the context it is clear that the spindle is the point of the comparison: Helen has a golden spindle (130).[8]

τανύπεπλος indicates that Helen's height was an aspect of her beauty, although the contexts in which this epithet occurs suggest that another meaning is primary. While it is true that a tall woman is beautiful, the point of the epithet in the places in which it occurs in Homer is, like the point of δῖα γυναικῶν (ch. 5), her impressive public appearance. In its unexpected occurrence in a private scene, it can be explained as part of a contrast, perhaps humorous, with another epithet, καλλίκομος, used of Helen later in the same scene (cf. §2).

6.1 τανύπεπλος in *Iliad* 3.171

The epithet τανύπεπλος occurs in *Iliad* 3.171 in a reply-formula, one of three such formulas, all different, used of Helen in the Teichoscopia (121–244):

> τὸν δ' Ἑλένη μύθοισιν ἀμείβετο, δῖα γυναικῶν· 3.171
>
> Helen, noble among women, replied to him.
>
> τὸν δ' ἠμείβετ' ἔπειθ' Ἑλένη Διὸς ἐκγεγαυῖα· 3.199
>
> And then Helen descended of Zeus replied to him.
>
> τὸν δ' Ἑλένη τανύπεπλος ἀμείβετο, δῖα γυναικῶν· 3.228
>
> Long-robed Helen, noble among women, replied to him.

These three lines are a well-known case of the violation of formular economy, sometimes explained as intentional variation.[9] This kind of explanation, which

---

[7] Ἀρτέμιδι δὲ χρυσηλακάτῳ τὴν Ἑλένην ὁ ποιητὴς εἰκάζει, διὰ τὴν κατὰ σῶμα φυήν, I.154.31 Stalbaum.

[8] The word ἠλακάτη is often translated "distaff," incorrectly. Barber 1991: 264: "When we come to the word ἠλακάτη...we find that we have to rebuild the dictionaries written by people who knew nothing about spinning...[W]herever there is any determining context whatsoever, the only reasonable interpretation is that *ēlakatē* refers to a spindle and not a distaff." Barber discusses *Od.* 4.125–35. The dictionaries to which Barber refers now include *LfgrE* s.v. χρυσηλάκατος. For the definition of distaff: Barber 1991: 107 n. 18: "A distaff is a stick or holder from which the as-yet unspun fibers are drawn for spinning"; cf. 69–70 for fuller definition and discussion.

[9] Edwards 1969; Kirk 1985: 293 on line 3.199; Friedrich 2007: 74–75; Krieter-Spiro 2009: 71 on 3.171. For a survey of scholarship on speech introduction formulas see Bozzone 2015: 115–16.

may be correct, would still leave τανύπεπλος with only a pale significance. Kirk's critique, based on the metrical constraints of standard reply-verses, leaves the same paleness. Kirk explains the sequence of the three lines as more or less awkward adaptations of such verses. For example, the most common reply-verse is τὸν /τὴν δ' ἀπαμειβόμενος/-η προσέφη ⏑ ⏑ – ⏑ ⏑ – ⏓. Helen's name, because of its initial vowel, is unusable wherever it is placed after the formula. Kirk takes the first two lines (171, 199) as "not particularly satisfying" attempts to overcome the difficulties. The third of these lines (228), he says, replaces μύθοισιν (171) with τανύπεπλος (228), "since that does least violence to established formular systems."[10] (These three reply-verses are the only reply-verses that precede speeches given by Helen.)

On Kirk's view of the matter, discussion of the contextual significance of τανύπεπλος at 3.228 and, for that matter, of the epithets in the other reply-verses (171, 199), might seem otiose. A more promising formular interpretation begins with the observation that the accusative object of ἀμείβετο / ἠμείβετ' in the three reply-verses can be explained as a transference from the accusative normal with προσειπεῖν / προσαυδᾶν in connection with the *participle* of ἀμείβομαι.[11] This small syntactical point indicates a larger context for the explanation of the violation of economy. Hainsworth discusses the introductory lines to speeches as an example of a kind of "high stabilization." "At this point," he says, "the formulae (the celebrated personal names in the nominative singular) are grouped into highly economical sets…" and he proceeds to discuss a set of three "frames" for reply-verses:

Τὸν δ' αὖτε προσέειπε ⏑ – ⏑ ⏑ – ⏑ ⏑ – ⏓
Τὸν δ' ἀπαμειβόμενος προσέφη ⏑ ⏑ – ⏑ ⏑ – ⏓
Τὸν δ' ἀπαμειβόμενος προσεφώνεε – ⏑ ⏑ – ⏓

For present purposes, one of his statistical observations suffices. The first of these frames has thirty expressions, the second eleven, of which ten are found to trespass in the first frame. Hainsworth speculates on the reason and then adds: "The economy of the system is still further diluted by the existence of a competitor for [the first] frame, viz., τὸν δ' ἠμείβετ' ἔπειτα…and by various idiosyncratic

---

10 For a strikingly different interpretation of this violation of economy see Bozzone 2015, who argues that "[t]his lack of economy is not a sign of decay of the technique but bears witness" to youth and vitality (129).
11 Krieter-Spiro 2009: 71 on 3.171 citing *LfgrE* s.v. ἀμείβομαι.

lines..."¹² Citing this formula apropos of his set of three frames he did not refer to the three reply-verses in Book 3 but what he says holds good for them, too. Hainsworth's analysis of reply-verses restores some degree of plausibility to the three lines in Book 3 under discussion and leaves open the possibility of the contextual significance of τανύπεπλος.

First, this epithet continues the contrasting perspectives of the narrator and Priam observed apropos of δῖα γυναικῶν (171; ch. 5§1.1), maintaining the narrator's point of view against this woman's own self-reproach (173–76) and the reproach that she suffers from others (242). Second, the replacement of μύθοισιν (171) with τανύπεπλος (228), if the third reply-verse should be so described, creates a verse that is unusual in that it gives Helen two epithets. She has the same two in a verse in the *Odyssey* (4.305), and there are only three other verses in which she is described by two epithets.¹³ The pairing of the two in a single line is emphatic, perhaps climactically in the sequence of the three answering expressions describing her in the Teichoscopia. Third, within the crazy quilt there are at least faint patterns. Most obviously, this epithet is used of high-status women.¹⁴ In the *Iliad* τανύπεπλος occurs elsewhere only of Thetis, a goddess, with whom more extensive comparison proves to be possible (cf. ch. 7§3–4); in the *Odyssey*, it occurs once of Lampetiē, a minor divinity. The only other Homeric use of the epithet is in the voice of Eumaeus, who uses it of Odysseus' sister, Ctimenē (not mentioned elsewhere). Eumaeus also refers to her as ἰφθίμη "stately" (15.364 ≈ 10.106, of the daughter of the Laestrygonian Antiphatus and thus by definition a woman of large size). τανύπεπλος contributes, then, to the physical impressiveness of Helen in her first public appearance in the *Iliad*. It was argued that the other epithet in the line under discussion, δῖα γυναικῶν (228; also in the first of the three reply-verses, 371), is used of women when they appear in public or are moving from one place to another (ch. 5). The pair of epithets in the third reply-verse is climactic in its emphasis on the impressiveness of Helen's presence.

---

12 Hainsworth 1968: 115–16. He concludes: "If this is what we find in an area of high schematization we have no reason to demand as good oral craftsmanship an equal degree of schematization elsewhere..."
13 The other two pairs: Ἀργείη and Διὸς ἐκγεγυῖα (*Od.* 4.184; 23.218); λευκώλενος (ch. 8§1 for the pairing) and εὐπατέρεια (*Od.* 22.227).
14 High-status: Brügger-Stoevesandt-Visser 2003: 230 on 2.714.

6.2 *Odyssey* 15.305

In Book 4 of the *Odyssey*, however, the same line containing τανύπεπλος appears in the description of a private scene. This epithet and the other epithet in this line are the last ones used of Helen in Book 4, and Helen will not be seen again until Book 15 (304–305).

> Ἀτρεΐδης δὲ καθεῦδε μυχῷ δόμου ὑψηλοῖο,
> πὰρ δ' Ἑλένη τανύπεπλος ἐλέξατο, δῖα γυναικῶν.
>
> And the son of Atreus was sleeping in an inner part of the lofty house
> and beside him long-robed Helen, noble among women, lay.

The pair of epithets in a single line, uncommon in the case of Helen, is striking. It makes sense in the Teichoscopia, less sense in the context in *Odyssey* Book 4. As pointed out in chapter 5, δῖα γυναικῶν tends to be used of Helen and Penelope when they appear in public or are moving from one place to another. Helen has, it seems, brought her Iliadic identity, seen also in other places in Books 4 and 15, into bed in Sparta. Further, this Iliadic Helen is part of a contrast with Helen as seen next morning, still lying in bed. When Menelaus arises, Helen has a different epithet (15.58):

> ἀνστὰς ἐξ εὐνῆς, Ἑλένης πάρα καλλικόμοιο.
>
> (Menelaus) having arisen from bed, from beside fair-haired Helen

"Fair-haired" has replaced the pair of epithets with which she was last described. She is now, so to speak, without her *peplos*, and the epithet that she now has suggests another aspect of Helen (see ch. 9§1).

The epithet τανύπεπλος in the scene under discussion has been interpreted quite differently by John Scheid and Jesper Svenbro. They say of *Od.* 4.304–305: "In our opinion, the couple lies together beneath the wife's *peplos*."[15] They propose as a comparable instance a place in the epithalamium in Theocritus *Idyll* 18, in which it is said that Helen and Menelaus will lie under the same *chlaina* (16–19). But, as they acknowledge, the *chlaina* is always a man's garment. This instance and the others that they discuss all require special pleading. In short, there is no good evidence to indicate that τανύπεπλος refers to the *peplos* of Helen used as a blanket. (In a household as rich as Menelaus' bed coverings would not be

---

15 1994: 55–57 = 1996: 61–56.

lacking.) On the contrary, as the preceding discussion has shown, the connotation of this epithet is height, which, like δῖα γυναικῶν (ch. 5), makes her impressive in her public appearances. This epithet never refers literally to the garment that a woman is wearing. That there is a certain oddity in the epithets in this line in its context is undeniable; an interpretation was suggested above.

6.3 Helen in the *Odyssey*: Character and Epithets

Di Benedetto argues that with the short scene in which guests and hosts retire for the night (4.296–305) "one has a restructuring of the character of Helen." "Here Helen appears as the mistress of the house who fulfills the usual, expected tasks. In this case, it is a matter of the instructions to give to the maids in order that they prepare beds for the guests." He goes on to compare this scene with *Iliad* 24.643–76, where Achilles gives instructions for the preparation of a bed for Priam and for the herald and then goes to sleep beside Briseïs. The scene in the two places is, he says, typical and he concludes that the scene in the *Odyssey* "is not capable of accepting the Helen of remorse and regret, the Helen who sought the drug that soothed pain."[16] That Helen, however, when she was weeping for Odysseus, was Ἀργείη and Διὸς ἐκγεγαυῖα, i.e., she had two epithets, and her kinship epithets continue when she thinks of the drug (Διὸς ἐκγεγαυῖα, 4.219) and when the narrator recalls her acquiring it in Egypt (Διὸς θυγάτηρ, 4.227). This Helen, whatever she is doing, is, according to her epithets, as majestic as the Helen of her grand entrance, in which she is compared to Artemis of the golden spindle.

In short, there is no change in the characterization of Helen at the level of the epithets used of her by the narrator. There is, however, an obvious contrast between these epithets, on the one hand, and the epithet that Helen uses of herself, κυνῶπις (145), on the other. It is the same contrast as in the Teichoscopia in the *Iliad*. Further, the epithets of Helen in Book 4 of the *Odyssey*, taken together, correspond very closely to the epithets of Helen in the *Iliad* from the first mention of her up until the end of the Teichoscopia.

---

16 Di Benedetto 2010: 297–99 on *Od.* 4.296–305. On the typicality of the scene cf. ch. 5§3 and references; also S. West 1988: 212 on lines 296–305; de Jong 2001a: 104 on lines 296–305.

Tab. 3: Comparison of epithets of Helen in *Iliad* 2–3 and *Odyssey*

Iliad Books 2–3: epithets through 3.228	*Odyssey* Book 4: all epithets
2.161 = 177 (Hera to Athena; Athena to Odysseus) Ἀργείην	145 (Helen of herself) κυνῶπις; cf. 259–64
3.121 λευκώλενος	184 Ἀργείη
3.171 δῖα γυναικῶν	184, 219 Διὸς ἐκγεγαυῖα
3.180 (Helen of herself) κυνῶπις	227 Διὸς θυγάτηρ
3.199 Διὸς ἐκγεγαυῖα	259–64 (Helen's regrets) no epithet
3.228 τανύπεπλος, δῖα γυναικῶν	296 Ἀργείη
	305 τανύπεπλος, δῖα γυναικῶν

Each of these two lists contains only a single epithet that is not in the other one (λευκώλενος in the list for the *Iliad*, Διὸς θυγάτηρ in the list for the *Odyssey*). In both of these sequences, the concluding pairs are the same. When Helen lies down beside Menelaus, she is the same beautiful Helen whom the elders saw on the wall of Troy (*Od.* 4.305: cf. *Il.* 3.228). It is not the first time that the consistency of Helen's Iliadic and Odyssean identities has been observed (cf. ch. 3§2) and will not be the last (cf. ch. 10§3 with Tab. 7). This consistency is the result of the fairly systematic redistribution, in Helen's case, of an inherited stock of epithets for women and goddesses (as argued in ch. 12§2). Here is another example of the self-conscious complementarity of the *Iliad* and the *Odyssey*.[17]

In Book Fifteen of the *Odyssey*, when Telemachus departs from Sparta, Helen is no longer at the center of the action.[18] She seems to stay in bed after Menelaus has arisen and is met by Telemachus, who asks to be sent on his way (15.56–66). After Menelaus' lengthy agreement and Telemachus' reply (67–91), Menelaus gives orders to his servants and his wife, who has now arisen, to prepare a feast (92–98). "Wife" soon is "Helen" again, as she, Menelaus and Megapenthes go into the bed chamber, where their treasures are stored, in order to select gifts for Telemachus (99–108; ch. 4§2.3). They then rejoin him, and Helen and Menelaus present their gifts, each with a short speech (109–30). In this scene Helen has the epithet καλλιπάρῃος (123, on which see ch. 9§2). Peisistratus puts the gifts in the chariot. The banquet follows; then the yoking of the horses, with a libation and speeches by Odysseus and Telemachus (131–59). Just as the guests are about to depart, an eagle appears, taken by Peisistratus as an omen. He asks to whom it

---

17 Argued by Nagy 1999[1979]: §§15–18, with references to his other writings on this matter.
18 On the various type-scenes that go into the account of this departure see Edwards 1975: 53–61.

refers, to him and Telemachus or to Menelaus (160–68). Menelaus stops to think (169–70), and Helen speaks first (170–71):

τὸν δ' Ἑλένη τανύπεπλος ὑποφθαμένη φάτο μῦθον·
"κλῦτέ μευ· αὐτὰρ ἐγὼ μαντεύσομαι

And long-robed Helen anticipated him and said:
"Hear me. I will be the one to give a prophecy..."

Helen is quicker that Menelaus, as in Book 4 (116–46). She has the same self-confidence as in that Book, in her actions and in her speeches (which is not, as argued in ch. 2, belied by her self-reproach).[19] De Jong points out that Peisistratus' request for an interpretation, unusual in an "omen scene," "seems to have been inserted mainly to call attention to the fact that it is...Helen who, anticipating Menelaus..., gives an exegesis of the omen..."[20] Here, as in Book 4, τανύπεπλος belongs to the narrator's concluding description of Helen, but here it directly fits her action. The tall impressive Helen answers for Menelaus and interprets the omen.

6.4 Conclusion

τανύπεπλος describes Helen as tall and is used of her, like δῖα γυναικῶν, when she appears in public. The use of this epithet of Helen when she is lying in bed with Menelaus is exceptional (*Od.* 15.305). Comparison with the epithet used of Helen in the same setting the next morning (καλλίκομος) suggests a pointed, perhaps even humorous, contrast.

---

19 On her self-confidence: S. West 1988: 200 on 4.120ff.; Hoekstra in Heubeck and Hoekstra 1989: 242 on 15.172.
20 de Jong 2001a: 370 on lines 160–81.

7 Other Epithets for Beauty (1): ἠΰκομος

In two of Helen's name-epithet formulas the epithet is ἠΰκομος. These two constitute the only example among epithets for Helen of the same epithet in lexically and syntactically (but not metrically) different formulas. In both of these formulas Helen's hair is an aspect of her identity as the beautiful woman over whom the war is being fought. It is her beauty that strikes the old men on the wall of Troy, who say (3.156–58):

> οὐ νέμεσις Τρῶας καὶ ἐϋκνήμιδας Ἀχαιοὺς
> τοιῇδ' ἀμφὶ γυναικὶ πολὺν χρόνον ἄλγεα πάσχειν·
> αἰνῶς ἀθανάτῃσι θεῇς εἰς ὦπα ἔοικεν·
>
> It is not a matter for blame that the Trojans and well-greaved Achaeans
> long suffer woes over such a woman.
> In appearance she is terribly like the immortal goddesses.

Then they say: Let her go (3.159–60). If Helen's beauty were in fact the only reason for the struggle, the old men's line of thought would make sense and she should be returned to Menelaus and the Achaeans. But the struggle is over Helen *qua* wife (ch. 1§§5–6), and neither of her husbands and neither Achaeans nor Trojans can agree to relinquish their claim to her. The struggle would go on even if she were not beautiful. The two name-epithet formulas to be discussed in this chapter reflect this logic of the war. In one of them, the formula is part of a periphrastic denomination of Paris (§1; for this kind of denomination: ch. 1§7). In the other, Achilles says that he is fighting Ἑλένης ἕνεκ' ἠϋκόμοιο (9.339), a formula not attested elsewhere in Homer, except in a plus-verse, but found in other archaic verse (Appendix to this ch.).

7.1 Paris as the husband of "fair-haired Helen"

This epithet is used of Helen six times in a formular appositional phrase describing Paris, always in the genitive and in line-final position.[1]

---

[1] 3.329; 7.355; 8.82; 9.339; 11.369, 505; 13.766. On the "genitive of relation": Schwyzer 2.119 (1); Smyth 1301.

– ⏑ Ἀλέξανδρος Ἑλένης πόσις ἠϋκόμοιο

Alexander the husband of fair-haired Helen.

This line-final epithet is clearly useful. Helen shares it with five others: Briseïs (1x), Athena (3x, in an expanded form), Thetis (3x), Hera (1x), and Calypso (*Od.* 2x).[2] (In the *Iliad* ἠΰκομος, in the nominative, is also used of Leto [1.36; 19.413] and Niobe [24.602].) Nevertheless, the particular name-epithet formula used of Helen reveals an apparent "distant connection" between her and Thetis in particular. Metrical analysis confirms this connection (§4 below). It will be argued that this connection does not signify any similarity of Helen and Thetis but is better understood as a reflex of the formular system (cf. for discussion of this point see ch. 12§2).

The narrator is always the speaker when this formula refers to Helen. She is never present when she is so described and the epithet does not refer to a feature that anyone in the narrative perceives. (For other epithets describing Helen as fair-haired see ch. 9.) It is a way of identifying Helen as the wife of Paris and thus of identifying Paris in a certain respect.

The bT scholium on *Il.* 3.329 comments on Paris as husband of Helen saying that the poet "adorns him (by reference to) to his marriage, as 'husband of Hera' (adorns Zeus)" (κοσμεῖ αὐτὸν τῷ γάμῳ ὡς πόσις Ἥρης; cf. schol. T on 4.19). (On the marriage of Paris and Helen see ch. 1§6.) Zeus has the same formula as Paris (πόσις Ἥρης ἠϋκόμοιο, *Il.* 10.5).[3] Only Paris and Zeus are identified in this way. But Helen's epithet in the formula for Paris or Alexander has a particular connotation. He is arming (*Il.* 3.329, for the duel with Menelaus) or in battle (8.82; 11.369, 505; 13.766) or, once, in a council of the Trojans, refusing to return Helen to the Achaeans (7.355).[4] In short, it is Paris as the husband of the woman over whom the war is being fought.[5] (On the battlefield he has no martial epithet, perhaps because he is an archer and the bow is an inferior weapon in the *Iliad*.[6])

---

[2] Athena (6.92, 273, 303); Hera (10.5); Thetis (4.512; 16.860; 24.466); Briseïs (2.689); Calypso (*Od.* 8.452; 12.389).
[3] Zeus is also ἐρίγδουπος πόσις Ἥρης: *Il.* 7.411; 10.329; 13.154; 16.88.
[4] Krieter-Spiro 2009: 120 on 3.329: "Die formelhafte Bezeichnung 'Gatte der schönhaarigen Helena' nimmt wohl wie 7.355 u. 13.766 Bezug auf den Kontext, hier auf den Zweikampf mit Helenas früherem Mann..., und stilisiert so den für zwei große Parteien entscheidenden Zweikampf zu einem Duell zwischen zwei Rivalen um eine Frau."
[5] Higbie 1995: 127 compares formulas in which Zeus is the husband of Hera and speaks of "a powerful reversal of this naming pattern," which "may testify not only to the strength of the women, but the weakness of the men as well."
[6] Hainsworth 1993: 268–69 on lines 11.385–95.

Paris' identification as the husband of Helen is thus the counterpart of Helen's identification as the wife of Paris (ch. 1).

Hector's rebuke of Paris as "mad for women" (voc. γυναιμανές, 3.39 = 13.769) and "deceiver" of women (*ibid.*) fits with the identity of Paris as husband of Helen and thus as responsible for the war. Hector has in mind specifically Paris' abduction of Helen (understood by him as a deception of her), which brought the war upon Troy (3.45–51, following the rebuke; cf. ch. 1 for perspectives on the cause of the war).[7] Thus Hector's somewhat incongruous rebuke of Paris in Book 13, which follows closely upon the introduction of Paris with the formula Ἀλέξανδρος Ἑλένης πόσις ἠυκόμοιο, comes from the same grievance concerning the abduction, even if it is not mentioned in the context. It had been mentioned earlier in Book 13, by Menelaus: "you (Trojans) who for no reason went away with my wedded wife and many possessions, although you were welcomed in her house" (626–27).[8]

7.2 Line-final ἠυκόμοιο used of others besides Helen

Of the four others besides Helen who have this line-final epithet one, Hera, has already been mentioned (§1 above). Another is Athena (3x). The epithet does not associate Helen with either of these goddesses, whereas "distant connections" emerge when it is used of Briseïs and of Thetis.

7.2.1 Athena

In Athena's case there occurs the whole-line formula: τίθημι + "on the knees of fair-haired Athena" (θεῖναι / τὸν θὲς / θῆκεν Ἀθηναίης ἐπὶ γούνασιν ἠυκόμοιο, 6.92, 273, 303). After a string of Achaean successes on the battlefield Helenus counsels Hector to go into the city and bid his mother place a robe on the knees of Athena in her temple, i.e., on the knees of her statue (86–92). Hector then conveys this instruction to his mother (269–73). She takes the robe to Theano, the priestess of Athena, and Theano places it on the goddess' knees (293–303). The epithet ἠύκομος is incongruous with the others used of Athena, none of which

---

[7] Cf. Diomedes' taunt, "ogler of women" (παρθενοπῖπα, 11.385), which refers to Paris' supposed lack of valor.
[8] As pointed out by Janko 1992: 141 on lines 13.765–69.

refers to her beauty.[9] Her cult epithet in Troy is ἐρυσίπτολις "protecting the city" (305), even though she is this city's passionate enemy. It may be that the Trojans do not know of her hatred.[10] The use of ἠΰκομος of Athena by Helenus and in the two subsequent instances is probably best explained as reference to the statue itself.[11]

7.2.2 Briseïs

Briseïs is once named with this epithet by the narrator apropos of Achilles' withdrawal from the fighting: "angry over the fair-haired girl Briseïs" (κούρης χωόμενος Βρισηΐδος ἠϋκόμοιο, 2.689). In another place Achilles says that the Achaeans are fighting Ἑλένης ἕνεκ' ἠϋκόμοιο and proceeds to make explicit a comparison between Helen and Briseïs (9.339–43):

> τί δὲ λαὸν ἀνήγαγεν ἐνθάδ' ἀγείρας
> Ἀτρεΐδης; ἦ οὐχ Ἑλένης ἕνεκ' ἠϋκόμοιο;
> ἦ μοῦνοι φιλέουσ' ἀλόχους μερόπων ἀνθρώπων
> Ἀτρεΐδαι; ἐπεὶ ὅς τις ἀνὴρ ἀγαθὸς καὶ ἐχέφρων
> τὴν αὐτοῦ φιλέει καὶ κήδεται, ὡς καὶ ἐγὼ τὴν
> ἐκ θυμοῦ φίλεον, δουρικτητήν περ ἐοῦσαν.

> Why did the son of Atreus gather and army and lead it here?
> Was in not on account of fair-haired Helen?
> Of mortal men do only the Atreidae love their wives?
> Whoever is a noble man and in possession of his wits
> loves his own woman and cares for her, just as I too
> loved this woman from my heart, spear-captive though she was.

Achilles equates the taking of Briseïs from himself with the taking of Helen by Paris. He thus makes his own case a mis-en-abyme of the war as a whole.[12] In this context the formula Ἑλένης ἕνεκ' ἠϋκόμοιο is unlikely to be a chance reflex of the formular system. As pointed out above, it is the only occurrence of the formula in Homer except in a plus-verse. (For extra-Homeric instances of this formula see Appendix to this ch.) Comparing the reason for his not fighting with the Achaeans' reason for fighting Achilles uses a conventional way of referring to Helen as

---

9 Survey of her epithets in Wathelet 1995: 181–83 (without comment on ἠΰκομος).
10 Stoevesandt 2008: 37 on 6.86–101; 42 on 6.96–101.
11 Graziosi and Haubold 2010: 102 on 92.
12 Richardson 1993: 17; Edmunds 2016a: 117.

the cause of the war, one which the narrator does not use. Achilles implies a disparity between the Achaeans' project and its object, a fair-haired woman. But, as said earlier, the Achaeans would have to fight for Helen even if she was not beautiful. The narrator maintains decorum as against Achilles' view of the matter. (Cf. ch. 8§2 and ch. 10§1 for the narrator's view of Helen and the war compared with the characters'.)

7.2.3 Thetis

To turn to Thetis, she has this epithet as the mother of Achilles in contexts in which her son's role in the war is to the fore. Most notably it is Achilles as the son of "fair-haired Thetis" whose withdrawal from and reentry into the fighting are the main turning-points in the story that the *Iliad* has to tell. When Apollo rallies the Trojans he reminds them that Achilles the son of "fair-haired Thetis" has withdrawn from the fighting.[13] Hector replies to the prediction of Patroclus that he will be killed by Achilles: "Who knows if Achilles the son of fair-haired Thetis may first be struck by my spear and lose his life?"[14] But the death of Patroclus, whom Hector has slain, leads to the death of Hector himself. Hermes advises Priam, who seeks to recover the corpse of Hector from Achilles, to beseech him by his father and his "fair-haired mother" and his son.[15] The examples in this list cover the whole time-frame of the plan of Zeus, of which Thetis is the instigator (1.505–10), from Achilles' withdrawal from the fighting to the death of Hector, which was not itself a part of the plan but was its consequence, following from the death of Patroclus.[16]

It would be possible to tell the story of the Trojan War with Thetis and Achilles as the two main characters: the clash of Zeus and Poseidon over Thetis, the intervention of Themis, the marriage of Thetis to the mortal Peleus, the birth of Achilles, his wounding of Telephus in Mysia on the way to Troy, and his exploits at Troy, which ultimately made possible the recovery of Helen and the return of the Atreidae.[17] Pindar told the story in this way in *Isthmian* 8 (29–61), omitting

---

13 οὐ μὰν οὐδ' Ἀχιλεὺς Θέτιδος πάϊς ἠϋκόμοιο / μάρναται, 4.512–13.
14 τίς δ' οἶδ' εἴ κ' Ἀχιλεὺς Θέτιδος πάϊς ἠϋκόμοιο / φθήῃ ἐμῷ ὑπὸ δουρὶ τυπεὶς ἀπὸ θυμὸν ὀλέσσαι; (16.860–61).
15 καί μιν ὑπὲρ πατρὸς καὶ μητέρος ἠϋκόμοιο / λίσσεο καὶ τέκεος, ἵνα οἱ σὺν θυμὸν ὀρίνῃς (24.466–67).
16 The plan: 1.508–10 (most briefly); 11.73–83; 13.347–50; 15.592–603 (most fully).
17 Cf. Edwards in Jensen *et al.* 1999: 54: "I can envision an uncomplicated plot including a quarrel of Achilles and Agamemnon, Achilles' withdrawal, a Greek defeat, a supplication by the

Eris, the uninvited guest at the wedding of Thetis and Peleus, the Apple of Discord, the Judgment of Paris, and the abduction of Helen. These omitted events would put Helen at the center of the story as the cause of the war, as in archaic sources apart from Homer and as, implicitly, in the formula that names her as the wife of Paris, in which she is the object over whom the war is fought.[18] The epithet ἠΰκομος as used of Thetis in the *Iliad* affords a glimpse of her importance in a possible alternate telling of the story in which she and her son Achilles are the protagonists. The epithet shared by Helen and Thetis points, then, not to some fundamental similarity between them but to different versions of the Trojan War, in which their relative importance differs greatly.

In the *Iliad*, as between Helen and Thetis, the abduction of Helen is the cause of the war (ch. 1§§5–6) while Thetis is responsible, as the instigator of the plan of Zeus, only for the course of the war within the time-frame of the poem. The plan was the result of her "outrageous prayer" to Zeus (ἐξαίσιον ἀρήν, 15.598; cf. 1.508–10). Nevertheless, a compositional affinity between them is indicated not only by the epithet ἠΰκομος but also in other ways. Thetis and Helen share the otherwise rare epithet τανύπεπλος (Thetis: *Il.* 18.385 = 424; Helen: *Il.* 3.228; *Od.* 4.305, 15.171; cf. ch. 6).[19] On a larger, narrative scale, Di Benedetto has pointed out that in similar scenes of summoning, Helen, on the wall of Troy, says to Aphrodite, ἔχω δ' ἄχε' ἄκριτα θυμῷ "I have countless griefs in my heart" (3.412) and Thetis uses exactly the same sentence to Iris (24.91), who conveys the summons of Zeus, and these are the only two places in archaic epic in which it occurs. Further, in both scenes "she went" (βῆ δ' ἰέναι, 3.419, 24.95), and then, at an interval of nine lines, there occurs in line-initial position "you came" as the first word of a speech (ἤλυθες, 3.428 [Helen to Paris, beginning her rebuke of him for leaving the battlefield], 24.104 [Zeus to Thetis]). Di Benedetto, who pointed out this coincidence,

---

Greeks to Achilles in which he yielded to the third prayer (probably that of his companion Phoenix/Patroclus…), his return to battle, and a Greek victory." Edwards' plot can be found, up to Achilles' return to battle, in Thetis' speech to Hephaestus (18.429–61).

18 Edmunds 2016b: §4.2, comparing the *Cypria* (the Trojan War as Zeus' way of lightening the earth of mortals, to be achieved by the deaths of the heroes in particular), Hesiod (the Trojan War one of two wars that bring the age of heroes to an end: *Op.* 161–65) and the *Catalogue* (the war has the same purpose), proposes an archaic vulgate. It is well described *in nucleo* by Cingano 2005: 126; earlier by Kullmann 1992[1955]: 17 n. 16, except that Kullmann wrongly includes the *Iliad* prooemium. Tosetti 2006 surveys the end of the heroic age in Hes., including the *Catalogue of Women*, in the logographers, and in Apollodorus. Traces of it turn up also in Ibycus S151.1–9 PMGF and Semonides fr. 7.115–18 W^2 and it persists in Euripides. The plan of Zeus in the *Iliad* has to do with a relatively short episode in the Trojan War.

19 The others: Lampetiē the messenger of Helios (*Od.* 12.375) and Ctimenē the sister of Odysseus (*Od.* 15.363).

had to admit that it had no significance, but he believed nonetheless that "when he composed the speech in Book 24 he had in mind the one in Book 3."[20] But, lacking significance, the coincidence could be just as well explained as a reflex of the inherited system's template for composing requests conveyed by Thetis.[21] The compositional affinity between Helen and Thetis can be discerned, at a probably sub-perceptual level, in analysis of the line-final formulas in which Helen and Thetis are called ἠΰκομος (§3).

7.3 ἠΰκομος in line-final formulas for Helen and Thetis

For a metrical analysis of ἠΰκομος as an epithet of Helen, Patrizia Mureddu's comparative study of noun-epithet formulas in Hesiod and Homer provides a basis. In her classification, the epithet ἠΰκομος comes under hemistichs consisting of name and epithet and extending from either of the two principal caesuras or the hepthemimeral caesura to line-end. These hemistichs are an extensive series, in which formulas built on adonean-shaped epithets (– ⌣⌣ – ⌣̱) constitute a large sub-series having a system that uses, with few exceptions, καλλιπάρηος/-ωι/-ον for the nominative, dative, and accusative and ἠϋκόμοιο for the genitive.[22]

One can make further divisions within this sub-series. The first is between, on the one hand, (a) the name of a goddess or woman followed immediately by ἠϋκόμοιο, that is, a metrical unit consisting of two elements, name and epithet, and, on the other, (b) a longer metrical unit in which the name of a goddess or woman is followed by another word or words and then at line-end ἠϋκόμοιο. Of the former (a) there are nine examples.[23] To this list could be added, as a slight variant of this shape of the formula, the periphrastic denomination of Thetis: μητέρος ἠϋκόμοιο (*Il.* 24.466). This phrase is unique not only in the *Iliad* but in all of Greek literature. Within the latter (b) there is another division to be made: between the metrical value of the intervening words. In the formulas for Helen a single word consisting of two short syllables intervenes:

---

20 Di Benedetto 1994: 237–38; cf. 407.
21 Richardson 1993: 286 on lines 90–92 points out the similarity of Thetis' words to those of Helen in her speech at 3.399–412. Arend 1933: 57 regards *Il.* 3.121ff. as simply a shortened form of the sub-type of messenger scene in which the messenger is a divinity.
22 Mureddu 1983: 96.
23 Astreïs (Hes. *Cat.* 185.8 = 85 H = 123 M); Briseïs (*Il.* 2.689); Calypso (*Od.* 8.452, 12.389); Demeter (Hes. fr. 280.20 M-W); Doris (Hes. *Theog.* 241); Hera (*Il.* 10.5); Leto (*Hymn. Hom.* 27.21); Selenē (Epimenides fr. 2.1 D-K); Tethys (Hes. fr. dub. 343.4 M-W).

- Ἑλένης πόσις/ν ἠϋκόμοιο (*Il.* 6x)
- Ἑλένης ἕνεκ' ἠϋκόμοιο (*Il.* 1x)

In the whole-line formula for Athena discussed above (§2.1), one the other hand, one has Ἀθηναίης ἐπὶ γούνασιν ἠϋκόμοιο. These formulas for Helen and Athena are the only ones in this division of the ἠϋκόμοιο sub-series. It is notable, to return to the comparison of Helen and Thetis, that the latter appears in a formula referring to her as mother of Achilles that corresponds exactly to Helen's in the series under discussion: Θέτιδος πάϊς ἠϋκόμοιο (*Il.* 4.512; 16.860).

This similarity between Helen and Thetis at the level of formula is non-functional in the narrative. As in the case of the same formula (δῖα γυναικῶν) used of Helen and Penelope (ch. 5), the similarity is likely to be the result of a Homeric redistribution of inherited epithets for women (ch. 12§2).

7.4 Conclusion

For the particular semantics of ἠϋκόμοιο in the formula shared with Thetis, comparison with Ἑλένης πάρα καλλικόμοιο (*Il.* 15.57–58) is telling. Out of context, the two epithets are synonyms meaning "having beautiful hair," and from a formular analysis based in prosody, like Mureddu's, the two belong to the same sub-series of epithets. But it is precisely as formulas that the two differ in meaning. At the level of the formula καλλίκομος refers to sexual attractiveness in private contexts (ch. 9§1). ἠϋκομος refers to a woman's beauty as part of her public identity. δῖος is another and simpler example of this expressive capacity of the formular system. While by itself this epithet seems banal, in the formula in which it often appears, δῖα γυναικῶν (15x), it has a distinct significance (ch. 5). Two other epithets λευκώλενος (ch. 8) and καλλιπάρῃος (ch. 9) also have their own meanings, different from those of Helen's other epithets of beauty, in the contexts in which they appear.

The beauty of Helen does not, then, in the *Iliad* and the *Odyssey* present itself as a single focal quality that determines what happens to her or what others think of her. For the most part it is only the narrator who refers to her beauty, in the various ways surveyed in this chapter. In the *Catalogue*, her epithets do not distinguish her from the many other beautiful women of this poem. In extant Greek literature it is not until Gorgias that her "godlike beauty," linked to her having Zeus as her father, becomes a central fact (ἰσόθεον κάλλος, *Hel.* 4). Isocrates takes a further step and sees it as conferring on her a "godlike power" (δύναμιν ἰσόθεον, *Hel.* 61). Much discussion of Helen still goes on under the spell of this power.

7.5 Appendix: The semantics of the formula Ἑλένης ἕνεκ' ἠϋκόμοιο

The occurrences of ε(ἵ)νεκα + genitive referring to Helen fall into two distinguishable sets: (1) the formula Ἑλένης ἕνεκ' ἠϋκόμοιο and (2) εἵνεκα + Ἑλένης or another word in the genitive referring to her, with or without an epithet other than ἠΰκομος. The first set consists of a single example in the *Iliad* (and also a plus-verse) and two Hesiodic examples.[24] Achilles poses the question: why did Agamemnon being an army here? The answer: "Was it not on account of fair-haired Helen?" (ἦ οὐχ Ἑλένης ἕνεκ' ἠϋκόμοιο, 9.339; cf. his variation of the formula at *Il*. 19.325).[25]

The following discussion assumes the two different senses of ε(ἵ)νεκα + genitive that lexicographers have distinguished ever since Stephanus, one causal and the other corresponding to Latin *causā* or *gratiā* + genitive.[26] It also relies on the findings of Luz Conti Jiménez in her study of a set of causal expressions in Homer which use the genitive, are dependent on verbs, and refer to humans.[27] These are the genitive without a preposition, ἕνεκα + genitive, and ὑπό + genitive. (In the first of these categories, the genitive typically expresses the grief, affliction, anger or irritation of the subject.) Conti Jiménez shows that on a scale from involuntary cause to responsibility without intention to responsibility with intention, only ἕνεκα + genitive can express the zero degree of causality, and is in effect specialized in this usage, although it is sometimes used for the second degree. It never expresses the third.

Conti Jiménez' scale includes, in the middle position, responsibility without intention, a sense that it sometimes has in archaic verse other than Homeric. As for Helen, nothing excludes the possibility that this is the sense of the phrase in its use in Hesiod (*Op*. 165). In that place, it is part of a summary of the two wars

---

24 *Il*. 9.339, 23.81a; Hes. *Op*. 165, *Cat*. 200.11 M-W = 109.11 H = 154e.11 M; cf. Hereas *FGrH* 486 F 2.
25 See Hainsworth 1993: 106–108 for the argument in 9.335–43. For the translation "on account of" see below.
26 s.v. ἕνεκα: "Propter. Redditur saepe et per ablativos Causa ac Gratia: quibus similem constr. habet cum gen. ..." Note that Stephanus implicitly distinguishes between the meaning *propter* and the meaning corresponding to the two Latin ablatives (n.b. *et*). The range of meanings of *propter* has no doubt also led to confusion. Cf. *OLD*² s.v. *propter* B.3 "(in giving an explanation of a state of affairs) Owing to the fact or existence of, as a result of a consequence of, in view of, because of"; 4 "(in giving the motive for an action) Through being influenced by (a fact, etc.), because of, on account of"; 5 "As a result of the actions of (a person), through the instrumentality of, on account of, because of, thanks to."
27 Conti Jiménez 1999.

that brought the age of the heroes to an end, the one at Thebes and the one at Troy. Each war is described in two lines, which end with parallel phrases: μήλων ἕνεκ' Οἰδιπόδαο (163) ~ Ἑλένης ἕνεκ' ἠϋκόμοιο (165). It would be impossible to say that Helen is subjectively to blame for the Trojan War any more than the sheep are to blame for the war at Thebes, although it might be possible that Hesiod has in mind a causal scheme like the one in the *Cypria*, in which Helen is one of Zeus' agents, having been begotten by him, in his plan to lighten the earth of mortals (*Cypria* fr. 1 B = fr. 1 D = F 1 W; schol. D *Il.* 1.5). The other agent is Achilles (cf. n. 18 above).

In Homer, no other character besides Achilles uses ἠϋκόμος of Helen. Six times the narrator uses, also in line-final position, what could be called a cognate formula: Ἑλένης πόσις ἠϋκόμοιο (§1 above). In this position it is used also of several other women and goddesses but only in the case of Helen can one speak of the deliberate avoidance of the metrically equivalent "on account of" formula (Ἑλένης ἕνεκ' ἠϋκόμοιο), which the composer(s) would have known. In this way, the Iliadic Helen is distinguished from the Hesiodic one, as the plan of Zeus is distinguished from the one in the *Cypria*.[28] This differentiation will have long since begun in hexameter verse on the Trojan War.[29] To return to Achilles, his use of the formula is a unique Iliadic allusion to the non-Iliadic conception of the Trojan War (again cf. n. 18).

The other set, i.e., of occurrences of ε(ἵ)νεκα + genitive referring to Helen, consists of seven Homeric examples (*Il.* 4x, *Od.* 3x). Again the narrator and the characters are distinguished. Hera (2.161 = 2.177), Athena (2.177), Achilles (*Il.* 19.325), Agamemnon (*Od.* 11.438), and Telemachus (*Od.* 17.118) are the characters besides Helen who use the phrase as defined at the beginning of this section (i.e., εἵνεκα + Ἑλένης or another word in the genitive referring to her, with or without an epithet other than ἠϋκόμος).

Whereas the narrator uses the metrically equivalent formula Ἑλένης πόσις/ν ἠϋκόμοιο of Paris six times (§1), he never uses Ἑλένης ἕνεκ' ἠϋκόμοιο,

---

28 Cf. Davies 1995: 3: The poet "avoids mentioning some of the *aitia* for the Trojan War which provides the background to his poem: no all-encompassing Διὸς βουλή...such as featured in the *Cypria* (F1) and remarkably little in the way of allusion to the Judgement of Paris."
29 Nannini 1995: 41 argues that 19. 273b–74 (Achilles) "introducono un elemento nuovo nel piano di Zeus..., ne modificano completamente il significato col ricondurne lo scopo primario ad una volontà di causare la morte di molti eroi..." (1995: 41). But Achilles at 1.407–12 hoped for the deaths of Achaeans when he asked Thetis to go to Zeus on his behalf. Achilles' words must be understood in the context of his awkward reconciliation with Agamemnon (note that he implicitly blames the *atē* of Agamemnon) and in the immediate context of this speech, in which his blaming Zeus is the usual *transfert du mal*.

which Hesiod uses apropos of the Trojan War (*Op.* 165). In the *Iliad* it is only Achilles who knows this formula. When the narrator says that Helen is weaving "the struggles of horse-taming Trojans and bronze-clad Achaeans which they suffered on account of her" (ἀέθλους / Τρώων θ' ἱπποδάμων καὶ Ἀχαιῶν χαλκοχιτώνων, / οὓς ἕθεν εἵνεκ' ἔπασχον, 3.126–28), his "on account of" speaks not for himself but for Helen. It is secondary focalization or, more precisely, "implicit embedded focalization," which is "embedded focalization *not* marked by a verb of perceiving, thinking/feeling or speaking."[30] Unless Helen has completely misunderstood her legal status in Troy (for which again see ch. 1), it is impossible to argue that "on account of her" (ἕθεν εἵνεκ') expresses her sense that she is the cause of the war.[31] She is the prize of the martial "contests" (ἀέθλους, 126) that she is depicting but the conflict between Achaeans and Trojans in which these contests are taking place was caused by her abduction (ch. 1§§6–7; ch. 2§8 *sub fin*.; ch. 4 *init*.).

To say that Helen is not the cause is not to say that most of the Trojans do not see her as such. In fact, most of them do see her as the cause. As she says, πάντες δέ με πεφρίκασιν "everyone shudders at me" (24.775; ch. 2§2). It is a view of her that Achilles comes to take, when he says εἵνεκα ῥιγεδανῆς Ἑλένης Τρωσὶν πολεμίζω ("am fighting the Trojans on account of Helen, at whom we shudder," 19.329–31; ch. 2§3). The two perspectives are established as soon as Helen appears in the *Iliad*. The old men (quoted above in the introduction to this ch.) say τοιῇδ' ἀμφὶ γυναικί ("over such a woman"), which might imply that she is to blame. Priam says at the beginning of his speech to her (it can be heard also as a reply to the old men): οὔ τί μοι αἰτίη ἐσσί ("For me you are not at all to blame," 3.164).[32]

Helen uses ἕνεκα twice of herself, once in the *Iliad* (6.355–57) and once in the *Odyssey* (4.145). In the *Iliad*, Helen invites Hector into her house and invites him to sit down (6.355–56),

ἐπεί σε μάλιστα πόνος φρένας ἀμφιβέβηκεν
εἵνεκ' ἐμεῖο κυνὸς καὶ Ἀλεξάνδρου ἕνεκ' ἄτης,

---

30 de Jong 2001b: 71; de Jong 2004: 118 (on secondary focalization: ch. 4).
31 In Pape 1888 s.v. the first meaning is: "wegen; zur Bezeichnung einer Absicht, eines Zweckes, zur Angabe einer Veranlassung od. Ursache." Pape has made the same distinction as Stephanus did but in reverse order. In Bailly 1994 s.v. the first meaning is: "a cause de, en raison de, pour (*au sens du lat*. propter)"; the second "a cause de, en faveur de, pour l'amour de (*au sens du lat*. causā *ou* gratiā), with examples from Theocr. and Pl. but none from archaic verse. In *DGE*² s.v. I 1 "c. valor causal, *a causa de, por*"; 2 "c. valor final, *para, con objecto de*." In Montanari 2013 s.v. the first two meanings are causal ("per, a causa di") and final ("per, allo scopo di").
32 Lowe 2000: 109 n. 8: "...Priam's speech to Helen at III.162–70 is anything but an innocent request for information: it is a delicate rejection of the hostile judgement passed in the elders' speech (cf. especially 164–5 with 159–60)."

> since it is especially you whose mind the trouble (of the war) surrounds,
> on account of me, a bitch, and on account of the blindness of Alexander.

Even if ἀρχῆς were read in this place in the *Iliad* and ἕνεκ' ἀρχῆς were taken as a parallel to Helen's "on account of," her expression could still be understood as the non-causal "on account of."[33]

In short, it is always a matter of the suffering that the war has brought, the war that is being fought "on account of," "over" Helen. Thus Achilles: εἵνεκα ῥιγεδανῆς Ἑλένης Τρωσὶν πολεμίζω "I am fighting the Trojans on account of Helen, at whom we shudder" (19.331)–an instance of the blame of Helen from the Achaean side which she earlier surmised was hers (αἴσχεα δειδιότες καὶ ὀνείδεα πόλλ' ἅ μοί ἐστιν, 3.242).[34]

The ἕνεκα phrase occurs only twice in the lyric poets, who use ἀμφί or περί + Ἑλένῃ or another word in the dative referring to her (5x).[35] In its fullest form, what could be called the lyric "on account of motif" includes, in addition to the prepositional phrase, two other elements. One is Troy and its destruction and/or Priam and the Trojans. The other is an Achaean hero or heroes and/or Achaean suffering. Either of these two elements may occur without the other. The motif can be elaborated into a whole strophe, as by Ibycus,[36] or even into what is apparently a whole poem (Alcaeus 42 V). Of course ἀμφί or περί + Ἑλένῃ occurs also in the *Iliad* and the *Odyssey* (5x). In the exchange between Helen and Menelaus in the *Odyssey* in which she says that the Achaeans came to Troy "on account of me the dog-faced one" (ἐμεῖο κυνώπιδος εἵνεκ', *Od.* 4.145) Menelaus in his reply implicitly corrects her, saying that he has just been telling Telemachus of how Odysseus toiled "on his account" (ἀμφ' ἐμοί, 153).

---

[33] West 2001: 197–98 on the variation ἄτης / ἀρχῆς at *Il.* 3.100, 6.356, and 24.28.
[34] Van Leeuwen 1912: 118: *Non dubitabat Helena quin Thersitae illi, qui aerumnas bellicas aegre ferrent, de se quamvis immerenti iactarent verba criminosa.*
[35] For the extended spatial sense of ἀμφί: "Die örtliche Auffassung blickt tw. auch noch durch im übertragenen Gebrauch, so bei 'um etwas kämpfen u.ä.'; wobei zunächst der Kampfpreis oder der Gegenstand des Streites als Mittlepunkt gedacht war" (Schwyzer 2.501).
[36] 282a.1–9 *PMG* = S151.1–9 (pp. 242–44) *PMGF*), i.e., the antistrophe and epode with which the fr. begins.

8 Other Epithets for Beauty (2): λευκώλενος

Helen has the epithet λευκώλενος in both the *Iliad* and the *Odyssey*, once in each epic. The other characters in the *Iliad* who have this epithet are Hera (24x) and Andromache (3x); in the *Odyssey* Nausicaa (4x), Arētē (3x), and servants, Nausicaa's (1x) and Penelope's (2x). The disjunction between the two epics in the use of this epithet is in the first place a matter of their different plots. Hera never appears as a character in the *Odyssey*; others refer to her in speeches (7x) but never with this epithet. Of human women it is mostly those on Phaeacia, a place unknown to the *Iliad*, who are "white-armed" (8/11x).

It is often said that women who are "white-armed" have this characteristic because they do not have to work outdoors.[1] For this reason, the servants of prosperous owners are "white-armed": Nausicaa's (6.239) and Penelope's (18.198; 19.60). Further, in both the *Iliad* and the *Odyssey*, when a woman is called "white-armed" she is usually in the *megaron* (see §2 below and fig. 5). The two human women in the *Iliad* who are "white-armed," Helen (3.121) and Andromache (6.371, 377; 24.723), both conform to this implicit rule. The exception is Nausicaa (*Od.* 6.101, 186, 251) but she is "white-armed" because she was raised in the *megaron* (*Od.* 7.12). This characteristic, once acquired, becomes permanent.

Parry commented on λευκώλενος: it "serves…to fill the space between the penthemimeral caesura and the bucolic diaeresis when versification is thereby made easier for the poet."[2] This comment applies, of course, to both places in which the epithet is used of Helen and implicitly denies the possibility of contextual meaning (cf. Introduction p. 1 n. 2). It is usually said that λευκώλενος is a "generic" epithet of women, i.e., of women of a certain social rank.[3] There is more to be said about this epithet. Its uses of Helen in the *Iliad* and the *Odyssey* differ in the first place with respect to speaker. When Athena calls Helen "white-armed," it is part of the rhetoric of her speech to Odysseus (§1).

8.1 λευκώλενος of Helen in the *Odyssey*

Athena says to Odysseus, in a lull in the slaying of the Suitors (*Od.* 22.226–29),

---

[1] Stoevesandt 6.371n; L-N-S 1.55n.
[2] Parry 1971a[1928]: 98.
[3] Krieter-Spiro 121n: "…[K]ennzeichnet den hohen sozialen Stand…; generischen Epitheton…"

οὐκέτι σοί γ', Ὀδυσεῦ, μένος ἔμπεδον οὐδέ τις ἀλκή,
οἵη ὅτ' ἀμφ' Ἑλένῃ λευκωλένῳ εὐπατερείῃ
εἰνάετες Τρώεσσιν ἐμάρναο νωλεμὲς αἰεί,
πολλοὺς δ' ἄνδρας ἔπεφνες ἐν αἰνῇ δηϊοτῆτι,

No longer, Odysseus, do you have force and strength
such as when you fought over white-armed Helen of noble father
nine years against the Trojans always unceasingly,
and killed many men in dread battle.

The epithet with which λευκώλενος is paired, εὐπατέρεια, occurs only here and at *Od.* 11.235, of Tyro, and once, of Helen, in the *Iliad* (for εὐπατέρεια see ch. 11), and each of these epithets appears with another only here.[4] Athena's epithets for Helen already seem to be extemporaneous and ad hoc.

Further, the asyndetical pairing of two epithets for Helen occurs only in the passage in the *Odyssey* under discussion and in her own self-rebuking voice (κακομηχάνου ὀκρυοέσσης, *Il.* 6.343).[5] It is what J.D. Denniston called "half asyndeton," i.e., between words, not between sentences.[6] As Demetrius said, the figure is dramatic (*Eloc.* 194).[7] It expresses feeling—quite obviously in Helen's voice, in the example just given, but also in Athena's.[8] Athena wishes to convey disesteem of Helen, in order to stir up Odysseus, for reasons to be explained. This pairing of two epithets is to be distinguished from the occurrence of two epithets for Helen in the formular lines κλαῖε μὲν Ἀργείη Ἑλένη, Διὸς ἐκγεγαυῖα / οὐδέ κεν Ἀργείη Ἑλένη, Διὸς ἐκγεγαυῖα (4.184; 23.218). The line-final formula in these places is clearly in apposition to Ἀργείη Ἑλένη. Likewise, the line-final δῖα γυναικῶν in πὰρ δ' Ἑλένη τανύπεπλος ἐλέξατο, δῖα γυναικῶν (*Il.* 3.228; *Od.* 4.305).[9]

---

[4] The phrase Ἑλένη λευκωλένῳ occurs in the same place in the line as in the *Il.*, with the same hiatus and shortening of the final vowel of the adjective. The shortening is an instance of *correptio epica*. Discussion of this phenomenon: Wachter 2000: 74.
[5] La Roche 1897: 172 lists pairs of asyndetic epithets preceding the noun that they modify, e.g., ποδάρκης δῖος Ἀχιλλεύς (*Il.* 21x). He does not cite pairs of the kind represented by *Od.* 22.227. For the text: ch. 2 n. 6.
[6] Denniston 1952: 99.
[7] See Russell 1964: 136 on this passage in Demetrius.
[8] Emotional effect: Denniston 1966: xlv. Cf. Achilles' νήστιας ἀκμήνους, as he hurls Odysseus' words back at him (*Il.* 19.207); Richardson 1993: 110 on *Il.* 22.41–43: the asyndeton in these verses "indicates urgency."
[9] In the Hesiodic *Catalogue* Helen is three times Ἀργείη and ἠϋκόμος in the same line (fr. 200.2 M-W = 156e.2 M (not in H); fr. 204.43, 55 M-W = 110.43, 55 H = 155.43, 55 M). In a line in an anonymous lyric fragment Helen is δῖα and πολυνεικής (fr. adesp. 96 *PMG*).

The phrase ἀμφ' Ἑλένῃ in the line in the *Odyssey* is a clue to the interpretation of the epithet in this passage.¹⁰ (For the "on account of" motif see ch. 7§5) The phrase appears twice in the *Iliad*. In Book 3, Paris says to Hector (3.69–70)

αὐτὰρ ἔμ' ἐν μέσσῳ καὶ ἀρηΐφιλον Μενέλαον
συμβάλετ' <u>ἀμφ' Ἑλένῃ</u> καὶ κτήμασι πᾶσι μάχεσθαι·

But put me and Menelaus dear to Zeus together in the middle
to fight over Helen and all the possessions.

Later in Book 3 Hector reports Paris' challenge before the opposing armies of Trojans and Achaeans (3.88–91):

ἄλλους μὲν κέλεται Τρῶας καὶ πάντας Ἀχαιοὺς
τεύχεα κάλ' ἀποθέσθαι ἐπὶ χθονὶ πουλυβοτείρῃ,
αὐτὸν δ' ἐν μέσσῳ καὶ ἀρηΐφιλον Μενέλαον
οἴους ἀμφ' Ἑλένῃ καὶ κτήμασι πᾶσι μάχεσθαι.

He bids the rest of the Trojans and all the Achaeans
set their fair armor on the much-nourishing earth
and that he and Menelaus dear to Ares alone in the middle
fight over Helen and all the possessions.

The phrase ἀμφ' Ἑλένῃ is formular in the metrical slot in which it occurs in these places and in the *Odyssey* (App. 3), and in all three it is a matter of fighting over Helen, although in the *Iliad* its application is restricted to the single combat of Menelaus and Paris. The difference between the place in the *Odyssey*, i.e., in Athena's speech, and the places in the *Iliad* just cited is that in the former the speaker is looking to the past and using the motif in a more general sense than it has in the *Iliad*. Athena, who has appeared in Book 22 disguised as Mentor during a pause in the fight with the suitors, tries to inspire Odysseus by taunting him.¹¹ She uses what de Jong calls "the typical rebuke technique of contrasting positive 'then' with negative 'now'."¹²

Athena says in effect: you are not now, when you are fighting over your own wife in your own palace, the man you were when you fought over Helen at Troy. The epithet that Athena uses of Helen can be explained by this then-now logic.

---

10 Fernández-Galiano in Russo *et al.* 1992: 22.227n: "the phrase is taken from *Il.* iii.70, 91." This kind of explanation assumes with great confidence that the *Il.* is a fixed text when the *Od.* is still in the process of composition.
11 Cf. Fernández-Galiano in Russo *et al.* 1992: 22.226n: "strong rebuke."
12 de Jong 2001: 534 (on *Od.* 22.226–32).

She uses the epithet, in an improvisational phrase, dismissively, as the "generic" epithet that it is often said to be. Helen was just another beautiful woman.[13] Athena is saying: you were a better man then when you were fighting for a less valuable prize than the one you are fighting for now. The comparison between Penelope and Helen that is implicit here is made explicit by Penelope herself in her speech to Odysseus in Book 23 of the *Odyssey*, though without denigration of Helen.[14] Alfred Heubeck said of this speech: "Penelope's analysis of the actions of Helen is calculated to draw the listener's (Odysseus') attention to a comparison with her own behavior, although this is not directly stated. For many years Penelope has withstood all temptation (215–17)...This self-control...was in fact rooted in her incomparable prudence and intelligence..."[15]

8.2 "White-armed" Helen in the *Iliad*

In the *Iliad* Iris, disguised as Laodicē, sister-in-law of Helen, comes to Helen to summon her to the wall (*Il.* 3.121):

Ἶρις δ' αὖθ' Ἑλένῃ λευκωλένῳ ἄγγελος ἦλθεν,

Iris, again, came as a messenger to white-armed Helen.[16]

Iris finds Helen weaving in the *megaron* (τὴν δ' εὗρ' ἐν μεγάρῳ, 125).[17] Iris tells Helen of the duel that is about to take place, and Helen rushes to the Scaean gate, where Priam and his counselors are gathered (the real Laodicē appears at 6.251–52). The reason for Iris' summoning of Helen poses a large interpretive question, opened already in the scholia.[18] Did Zeus send Iris or did she go of her own accord to Helen? The discussion of the epithet's significance can go on, however, without an answer to this larger question.

---

[13] Fernández-Galiano in Russo *et al.* 1992: 22.227n: "λευκωλένῳ also has the flavor of Iliadic imitation." Cf. n. 10 above.
[14] Comparison of Helen and Penelope: de Jong 2001a: 289; Blondell 2013: 89–92.
[15] Heubeck in Russo, Fernández-Galiano and Heubeck 1992: 336–37.
[16] "Again" in this translation because Iris came to the Trojans at *Il.* 2.786.
[17] *LfgrE* s.v. μέγαρον 2bα (with references to scholarship); 3aα: "difficult" to determine sense here.
[18] Kirk 1985: 279 cites the part of the scholium on this line which is relevant to this question: δηλονότι παρὰ τοῦ Διός· οὐ γὰρ αὐτάγγελος. He does not cite two other scholia on *Il.* 11.715: T, which says the opposite: οὐ πεμφθεῖσα ὑπό τινος, ἀλλ' ἀφ' ἑαυτῆς ("not sent by anyone but from herself") and bT for the phrase beginning ὡς: ὡς Ἶρις δ' αὖθ' Ἑλένῃ ("as Iris, again, to Helen").

The T scholiast on *Il.* 3.121 says apropos of λευκώλενος: ἐν ἀρχαῖς τῷ τῆς Ἥρας αὐτὴν ἐπιθέτῳ κοσμεῖ, Ἀργείας τε ἄμφω καλεῖ ("At the beginning [of the *Iliad*] he ornaments her with the epithet of Hera, and he calls both Argive"). It is true that λευκώλενος is Hera's epithet in the *Iliad* (24x, as against 3x of Andromache and 1x of Helen, the only others of whom it is used).[19] As for "Argive," it is used exclusively of Helen and Hera but only twice of the latter (*Il.* 4.9; 5.908) as against thirteen times of the former (*Il.* 9x, *Od.* 4x). It is in fact Helen's commonest epithet (ch. 3).[20] Even if "white-armed" is not properly Helen's epithet and "Argive" is not properly Hera's in the *Iliad*, the scholiast is right that both are used of Helen "at the beginning." The first three epithets of Helen are:
- *Il.* 2.161 Ἀργείην (Hera to Athena)
- *Il.* 2.177 Ἀργείην (Athena to Odysseus, repeating Hera)
- *Il.* 3.121 λευκώλενος (narrator)

But, for the implication of "white-armed" in the context in which it is used of Helen in the *Iliad*, other considerations will be found to be more relevant.

First, the scholiast on *Iliad* 6.377, where the epithet λευκώλενος is used of Andromache, makes a distinction that is relevant to the understanding of this epithet as used of Helen: τοῦ ποιητοῦ τὸ ἐπίθετον, οὐ τοῦ προσώπου (bT) ("the epithet is the poet's, not the character's"). At *Il.* 3.121, too, where λευκώλενος is used of Helen, it represents the narrator's perspective, not Iris'. In fact, it is nearly always the narrator who uses epithets referring to Helen's beauty (fig. 4).

Tab. 4: Helen: epithets of beauty, with speakers

Il. 3.121	Ἶρις δ' αὖθ' Ἑλένῃ λευκωλένῳ ἄγγελος ἦλθεν	narrator
Il. 3.329	δῖος Ἀλέξανδρος, Ἑλένης πόσις ἠϋκόμοιο	narrator
Il. 7.355	δῖος Ἀλέξανδρος, Ἑλένης πόσις ἠϋκόμοιο	narrator
Il. 8.82	δῖος Ἀλέξανδρος, Ἑλένης πόσις ἠϋκόμοιο	narrator
Il. 9.339	Ἀτρεΐδης; ἦ οὐχ Ἑλένης ἕνεκ' ἠϋκόμοιο	Achilles
Il. 11.369	αὐτὰρ Ἀλέξανδρος, Ἑλένης πόσις ἠϋκόμοιο	narrator
Il. 11.505	εἰ μὴ Ἀλέξανδρος, Ἑλένης πόσις ἠϋκόμοιο	narrator
Il. 13.766	δῖον Ἀλέξανδρον, Ἑλένης πόσιν ἠϋκόμοιο	narrator
Il. 23.81a	μαρνάμενον δηΐοις Ἑλένης ἕνεκ' ἠϋκόμοιο	Patroclus

---

19 These statistics from L-N-S 1.55n.
20 Cf. Ἀργείης Ἑλένης (line-initial) in Hes. *Cat.* 204.55 M-W = 110.55 H = 155.55 M; line-initial and acc. case in 204.62 M-W = 110.62 H = 155.62 M.

Od. 15.58	ἀνστὰς ἐξ εὐνῆς, Ἑλένης πάρα καλλικόμοιο	narrator
Od. 15.123	ἀργύρεον· Ἑλένη δὲ παρίστατο καλλιπάρῃος	narrator
Od. 22.227	οἵη ὅτ' ἀμφ' Ἑλένῃ λευκωλένῳ εὐπατερείῃ	Athena

Second, for understanding the narrator's point of view, comparison of the epithet as used of another human character, as in the discussions of δῖα γυναικῶν (ch. 5) and ἠΰκομος (ch. 7), helps to define its implication as used of Helen. This time two other characters are relevant. One is Andromache, the other is Arētē.

When Hector returns to the city from the battlefield in Book 6, one of those whom he goes to find is Andromache (6.370–71):

αἶψα δ' ἔπειθ' ἵκανε δόμους εὖ ναιετάοντας,
οὐδ' εὗρ' Ἀνδρομάχην λευκώλενον ἐν μεγάροισιν,

And quickly then he came to his well-built house
and he did not find white-armed Andromache at home.

The plural in the phrase ἐν μεγάροισιν is the "poetic plural." As Hector's question to the servant shows, he expected to find Andromache at home. He asks: "Where did white-armed Andromache go from the house?" (πῇ ἔβη Ἀνδρομάχη λευκώλενος ἐκ μεγάροιο, 377).[21] In Book 7 of the *Odyssey*, when Arētē converses with Odysseus in the *megaron* (ἐν μεγάρωι, 230), she is called "white-armed" (233).[22] (She questions Odysseus about the clothes he is wearing, which she perceives as having been woven by herself and her servants. See fig. 5.) Later "white-armed" Arētē bids her servants prepare a bed for Odysseus in the portico (335–38) and they leave the *megaron* to do so (ἐκ μεγάροιο, 339). In Book 11, at the end of Odysseus' account of the heroines whom he encountered in the underworld, the narrator describes his effect on those in the hall (κατὰ μέγαρα, 334) and then "white-armed" Arētē speaks (335). In general, when women, including serving women, are "white-armed" they are in, or coming from, or unexpectedly not in, the *megaron*. Further, if it is the mistress of the household, she is likely to be engaged in weaving. Nausicaa tells Odysseus that he will find her mother, Arētē, who is thrice called "white-armed," "sitting at the hearth, in the light of the fire, turning her purple spindle" (i.e., spinning purple thread). Putting together a majority of the places in the *Iliad* and the *Odyssey* in which human characters are

---

21 *LfgrE* s.v. μέγαρον B 3aα under 3 "house, dwelling, compound," citing this place.
22 *LfgrE* s.v. μέγαρον B 1aα: "*hall*, main room (where male guests are entertained)."

called "white-armed," one discerns a context for what could be called the normative use of this epithet. This context includes nearly always the *megaron* and sometimes references to fabric in some sense or other (fig. 5).[23]

Tab. 5: "White-armed"

Character	"White-armed"	Megaron	Reference to fabric
Helen	*Il.* 3.121	√	3.125, weaving
Andromache	*Il.* 6.371	explicitly not in, 371, 377	ø
Nausicaa	*Od.* 6.251	ø	6.252, places garments on cart
Nausicaa	*Od.* 7.12	√	ø
Arētē	*Od.* 7.233	√ 230	234, recognizes Odysseus' garments
Arētē	*Od.* 7.335	√ 339	336, bids servants prepare bed
Arētē	*Od.* 11.335	√ 334	ø
Servants of Penelope	*Od.* 18.198 ≈ 19.60	√ √	ø

The narrator's perspective

The distinction between the narrator's and the characters' points of views is borne out by the rest of the epithets used by the narrator in Book 3:
- *Il.* 3.171 δῖα γυναικῶν
- *Il.* 3.199 Διὸς ἐκγεγαυῖα
- *Il.* 3.228 τανύπεπλος
- *Il.* 3.228 δῖα γυναικῶν
- *Il.* 3.329 ἠυκόμοιο
- *Il.* 3.418 Διὸς ἐκγεγαυῖα
- *Il.* 3.423 δῖα γυναικῶν
- *Il.* 3.426 κούρη Διὸς αἰγιόχοιο

---

23 Tsagalis 2009: 43–44 has pointed out status as wife and weaver as the common characteristic of Helen and Andromache, who share the epithet λευκώλενος.

All of these epithets except δῖα γυναικῶν implicitly associate her with goddesses.[24] The characters and Helen herself take the pragmatic and otherwise down-to-earth perspective already observed in earlier chapters:
- *Il.* 3.48 γυναῖκ' εὐειδέ' (Hector to Paris)
- *Il.* 3.70 ἀμφ' Ἑλένῃ καὶ κτήμασι πᾶσι (Paris to Hector)
- *Il.* 3.72 κτήμαθ' ἑλὼν εὖ πάντα γυναῖκά τε (Paris to Hector)
- *Il.* 3.91 ἀμφ' Ἑλένῃ καὶ κτήμασι πᾶσι (Hector to Trojans and Achaeans)
- *Il.* 3.93 κτήμαθ' ἑλὼν εὖ πάντα γυναῖκά τε (Hector to Trojans and Achaeans)
- *Il.* 3.130 νύμφα (Iris to Helen)
- *Il.* 3.162, 192 φίλον τέκος (Priam to Helen)
- *Il.* 3.157 τοιῇδ' ἀμφὶ γυναικὶ (old men)
- *Il.* 3.180 κυνῶπις (Helen of herself)
- *Il.* 3.204 γύναι (Antenor to Helen)
- *Il.* 3.254 γυναικί (heralds to Priam)
- *Il.* 3.255 γυνὴ καὶ κτήμαθ' (heralds to Priam)
- *Il.* 3.282 Ἑλένην ἐχέτω καὶ κτήματα πάντα (Agamemnon in prayer to Zeus)
- *Il.* 3.285 Ἑλένην καὶ κτήματα πάντ' (Agamemnon in prayer to Zeus)
- *Il.* 3.396 κυνῶπις (Helen of herself)
- *Il.* 3.404 στυγερή (Helen of herself)
- *Il.* 3.414 σχετλίη (Aphrodite to Helen)

The *Iliad* is thus able to maintain two different perspectives. In one, Helen is the exceptional woman for whom the Trojan War is worth fighting. In the other, she is the pragmatic goal of the fighting ("Helen and all the possessions": ch. 3§1; ch. 4 §1.1). She is part of the royal family of Troy ("dear child"; cf. ch. 1). She says, in effect, that she is reprehensible ("dog-eyed"; cf. ch. 2). The point at which the perspectives of the narrator and of the characters sometimes overlap is the beauty of Helen. In the first of the two lists just presented, there were two epithets indicating her beauty (τανύπεπλος, ἠΰκομος). In the second, besides the epithet that Hector uses (3.48), there was the old men's "such a woman," i.e., "such a beautiful woman," as the context of this phrase clearly shows. For the most part, however, those who speak to or of Helen in the *Iliad* and the *Odyssey* do not refer to her beauty, nor does the narrator refer to it often.

---

24 Including τανύπεπλος, of Thetis (the only other character in the poems to receive the epithet) and ἠΰκομος, three times of Athena, once of Hera, three times of Leto, and once of Themis. On Thetis and Helen see ch. 7§2.

8.3 Athena again

With this context in mind, one returns to Athena's use of "white-armed" of Helen in her speech to Odysseus (§1). The epithet is de-contextualized and it is *as such* that Athena uses it, i.e., without any of its normative connotations. What makes it possible for Athena to speak as she does is the lapse of time since the Trojan War, or, to put it another way, the difference in temporal perspective between Athena and the narrator as users of the epithet in question. When the narrator calls Helen λευκώλενος in Book 3 of the *Iliad* the war is still going on and apparently reaching a climax. When Athena speaks, the war is long since over. The narrator's use, furthermore, belongs to a rather full characterization of Helen, including other epithets all in play in Book 3 of the *Iliad*; Athena's use is isolated. Her use, in comparison with the narrator's, is a passing, ad hoc reduction of the over-all Iliadic characterization. Corroboration of this point can be found in Athena's asyndetic juxtaposition of λευκώλενος and εὐπατερείη (ch. 11). It reduces to two single terms the two sets of terms that appear in the epithets that the narrator (i.e., as distinguished from characters in the narrative) uses of Helen in the rest of Book 3 after he has called her λευκώλενος (321). These, beginning at line 171, are epithets for her beauty and epithets referring to her as daughter of Zeus.

8.4 Conclusion

The survey of λευκώλενος in its contexts in the *Iliad* and the *Odyssey* shows that its main significance is social rank. Among the goddesses it is Hera who is "white-armed," presumably because she is preeminent as both wife and sister of Zeus, as she herself avers (*Il.* 4.59–61; 18.364–67). Human serving women have this epithet by association with their mistresses. Further, women who have this epithet are typically in the *megaron*, and their activity is wool-working of one kind or another, as the examples of Helen and Arētē show. While it is often said that λευκώλενος indicates beauty, this meaning, if it is operative, must be secondary.[25] Are the serving women who are called "white-armed" in the same class as their mistresses with respect to beauty? It is difficult to believe that Nausicaa's "white-armed" serving women are as beautiful as she is.

---

25 Krieter-Spiro 3.121n: "zur Charakterisierung weibl. Schönheit"; other elements of Krieter-Spiro's definition were quoted in n. 3 above.

The narrator's and Athena's uses of the epithet λευκώλενος of Helen differ markedly, because the former's is part of the context that gives the epithet its normative value and the latter's is decontextualized. Further, Athena's asyndetic pairing of this epithet with εὐπατερείη produces a caricature of Helen. (It is argued in chapter 11 that the latter is the least honorific of the kinship epithets of Helen.) Athena's use of λευκώλενος implicitly contrasts Helen with Penelope, whereas, in certain situations, and from another point of view, the narrator's, these two women are similar (ch. 5 on δῖα γυναικῶν).

Finally, for the effectiveness of the decontextualized λευκώλενος its third use of Andromache is illustrative. At the prothesis of Hector (24.723–74)

τῇσιν δ' Ἀνδρομάχη λευκώλενος ἦρχε γόοιο
Ἕκτορος ἀνδροφόνοιο κάρη μετὰ χερσὶν ἔχουσα

For them (the other women) white-armed Andromache began the lament
holding the head of man-slaying Hector in her hands.

The epithet calls attention to itself because the narrator could have said ἀδινοῦ ἐξῆρχε γόοιο (4x, including Hecabe at 24.747).[26] Andromache is not in the *megaron* where as "white-armed" she could have been expected to be found when Hector goes to find her (6.371, 377).[27] When he finds her on the wall of Troy, she is "richly dowered" (πολύδωρος. 6.394) and "the daughter of great-hearted Eëtion" (θυγάτηρ μεγαλήτορος Ἠετίωνος, 6.395). The epithet is effective here precisely because it is out of context. Andromache is outdoors, not in the *megaron*. She is using her arms and hands not for wool-working (cf. when she received the news of Hector's death) but to hold the head of her husband as he lies on his bier. Christos Tsagalis has pointed out the parallelism of Ἀνδρομάχη (724) and ἀνδροφόνοιο (725) and the resemblance in sound of νέος ὤλεο (725) to λευκώλενος (723). These are means by which the narrator couples Andromache with her husband's doom.[28]

---

26 Richardson 1993: 352 on lines 723–24 on this formula. Richardson says: "This could be a...sign that he [i.e., the poet] has in mind the meeting of Hektor and Andromakhe in Book 6."
27 Cf. Andromache in Eur. *Tro.* 647–50: "Putting aside the desire for staying outdoors, which attracts blame to a woman, I stayed at home" (ἔμιμνον ἐν δόμοις). Euripides is remembering Hector's injunction to Andromache: ἀλλ' εἰς οἶκον ἰοῦσα τὰ σ' αὐτῆς ἔργα κόμιζε / ἱστόν τ' ἠλακάτην τε, καὶ ἀμφιπόλοισι κέλευε / ἔργον ἐποίχεσθαι· πόλεμος δ' ἄνδρεσσι μελήσει / πᾶσι, μάλιστα δ' ἐμοί, τοὶ Ἰλίῳ ἐγγεγάασιν ("But go into the house and take care of your own work, the loom and the spindle, and bid your servants to go about their work. War will be the concern of the men, all men, and especially me, of all those who live in Troy," 6.490–93).
28 Tsagalis 2004: 61–63.

9 Epithets for Beauty (3): καλλίκομος, καλλιπάρηος

Two epithets of Helen are compounds formed on the geminated stem of καλός with a noun indicating a physical feature: καλλιπάρηος, "fair-cheeked" and καλλίκομος, "fair-haired." They have in common also the fact that each is used of her once, in Book 15 of the *Odyssey* on the day of Telemachus' departure from Sparta. Although both of these epithets refer to an aspect of her beauty, the first of them certainly does not distinguish her as more beautiful than other women. Indeed, καλλιπάρηος is used in the *Iliad* of Chryseïs (3x), Briseïs (5x), Theano (3x), and Diomedē (1x). Two goddesses also have this epithet: Leto (1x) and Themis (1x). Far less frequent in the *Odyssey*, it is used only once of another woman, Melantho, the consort of Eurymachus, who is hanged by Odysseus along with the other serving women (18.321). As for καλλίκομος, in its only other appearance in Homer beside the place in the *Odyssey*, Phoenix uses it to describe his father's concubine (*Il.* 9.449).

9.1 καλλίκομος

Καλλίκομος is not the only epithet of Helen that refers to her hair. ἠΰκομος is used of Helen seven times, all in the *Iliad*, with the significance discussed earlier (ch. 7). The connotation of καλλίκομος is different from that of ἠΰκομος, as appears from its rather consistent usage in various kinds of verse. In Hesiod *Works and Days* it is used of the Seasons, who crown Pandora with spring flowers (75); in Pindar, of the daughter of Antaeus, whose suitors hoped "to pluck the fruit of Hebe" (*P.* 9.106). In three places it describes women whom Zeus lusted after and slept with.[1] In four places it describes either Aphrodite (Epimenides fr. 19.1 D-K) or her attendants the Charites, who, like Aphrodite, inspire eros.[2] In the *Cypria*, it describes Nemesis, the mother of Helen, as a conquest of Zeus (fr. 9.2 B = fr. 7.2 D = F. 10.2 (p. 80) W). In short, καλλίκομος suggests sexual desirability.

---

1 Hes. *Theog.* 915 (Mnemosynē); Hes. *Cat.* fr. 141.10 M-W = 56.10 H = 90.10 M (Europa); *Cypria* fr. 9.2 B = fr. 7.2 D = F 10.2 W (pp. 80–82) (Nemesis).
2 Charites: Ibycus fr. 288.1–2 *PMG* / *PMGF*; Sappho fr. 128 V; Ar. *Pax* 798; *IG* 1³ 983 = *CEG* 312 = *AP* 6.144 (Anacreon) = Anacreon 15 Page = 119 Friedländer.

This epithet is thus appropriately used by Phoenix of his father's concubine. He refers to an event from his youth, when he was forced to flee his home because he had angered his father (9.448–49):

φεύγων νείκεα πατρός Ἀμύντορος Ὀρμενίδαο,
ὅς μοι παλλακίδος περιχώσατο καλλικόμοιο,

Fleeing the wrath of my father, Amyntor son of Ormenus,
who hated me because of his fair-haired concubine.

He had angered his father by sleeping with his father's concubine, at his mother's urging. The same kind of story is found in the Bible.[3] When, at the urging of his first wife Rachel, Jacob takes the handmaiden Bilhah as a concubine, he offends his second wife, Leah. Leah's son Reuben sleeps with Bilhah. Jacob confronts Reuben, takes away his birthright, and prophesies that he will not prosper in life. The story looks like a type: a man takes a lover and in doing so offends his wife. The wife appeals to her son to intervene, and the son sleeps with his father's lover. The father grows angry with his son and punishes him. Each story is in a sense driven by the presence of the concubine, whose sexual desirability threatens the wife and leads to the rebellion of the son, who is loyal to his mother. Xenophon tells a simpler form of the story. The king of the Assyrians castrated Gadatas when the king's concubine praised the young man's beauty and felicitated his future wife. The king later maintained that Gadatas had made advances toward his concubine (*Cyr.* 5.2.28). The mother of the young man has no role.

The epithet καλλίκομος refers, then, to sexual attractiveness and its consequences in private contexts and hardly, as with ἠΰκομος, to beauty as marking a public identity. To turn to its use of Helen in the *Odyssey*, she is called καλλίκομος when she is lying in bed. It is the morning of the day on which Telemachus and Peisistratus take their leave from Sparta (15.57–58).

ἀγχίμολον δέ σφ' ἦλθε βοὴν ἀγαθὸς Μενέλαος,
ἀνστὰς ἐξ εὐνῆς, Ἑλένης πάρα καλλικόμοιο.

Menelaus, good at the war-cry, came up near to them,
rising from his bed from beside fair-haired Helen.

---

3 *Genesis* 35.22, 49.4. Cited by Hainsworth 1993: 9.447–52n.

Bed seems to be exactly the right place for this epithet, whereas when Helen and Menelaus retired the evening before, Helen's epithets were the same ones that described her on the wall of Troy (4.304–305):[4]

Ἀτρεΐδης δὲ καθεῦδε μυχῷ δόμου ὑψηλοῖο,
πὰρ δ' Ἑλένη τανύπεπλος ἐλέξατο, δῖα γυναικῶν.

And the son of Atreus was sleeping in an inner recess of the lofty house
and beside him long-robed Helen, noble among women, lay.

Helen's epithets in the first of these two lines are discussed elsewhere (chs. 5–6), where it is suggested that the change from them to καλλίκομος is pointed.

9.2 καλλιπάρῃος

The two main uses of καλλιπάρῃος are of concubines, in the *Iliad*, and, in Hesiod and in the Hesiodic *Catalogue*, of marriageable young women. What all of these women have in common is sexual attractiveness. For this reason, it is not surprising that the Charites, who are "fair-haired" (cf. §1 above), are also "fair-cheeked" (Hes. *Theog.* 907).

The connection between having fair cheeks and having sexual intercourse is close. In Hesiod, the fair-cheeked Molionē (Hes. fr. 17a.3 M-W = 11.3 H = 13.3 M) "mingled in desire and bed" with her husband (5). Xuthus' wife was the fair-cheeked Creusa (Hes. fr. 10a.21 M-W = 5.21 H = 10.21 M), with whom he "commingled in love" (24). Helius married fair-cheeked Idyia (Hes. *Theog.* 960), who was "overpowered in love because of golden Aphrodite..." (963). In the *Iliad*, fair-cheeked Diomedē lay beside Achilles (9.664–65). Sometimes, however, the fair-cheeked woman simply becomes a wife, without reference to sex. There are an unidentified woman (Hes. fr. 85.6 = 120.6 H [not in M]; ἄκ[οι]τιν in preceding line) and Mestra (Hes. fr. 43a.19 = 37.19 H = 69.19 M; ἄλοχον in the next line).[5]

Like καλλίκομος as used by Phoenix of his father's concubine, καλλιπάρῃος is a way, indeed the preferred way, to describe a concubine in the *Iliad*: thus of Brisēïs (1.184, 323, 346, 19.246, 24.676), Chrysēïs (1.143, 310, 369) and Diomedē

---

4 Cf. τὸν δ' Ἑλένη τανύπεπλος ἀμείβετο, δῖα γυναικῶν, *Il.* 3.228.
5 At Hes. *Theog.* 976, Agave, one of the four daughters of Cadmus and Harmonia, all of them named, is "fair-cheeked," but it is Autonoē who is specified as having married. Places in *Cat.* not discussed because too fragmentary: fr. 129.13 = 46.13 H = 77.13 M (Eurydice mother of Danaë); fr. 180.13 = 111.13 H = 182.13 M, where, however, note marriage bed in line 11 (if reference is to the same person as in line 13).

(9.665). The T scholiast, having in mind the sexual connotation, says of the epithet's use of Briseïs that it is "opportune, indicating the disposition of the lover, by showing what sort of woman he loves."[6]

The use of this epithet of Theano, the Trojan priestess of Athena, seems anomalous. She was once, of course, the fair-cheeked young woman and potential bride. The narrator puts Theano in this perspective when he refers to her, apropos of the lineage of her son Iphidamas. This boy was raised by his maternal grandfather, Kissēs, and this fact prompts the narrator to add, apropos of Kissēs, that it was he "who begot fair-cheeked Theano" (Il. 11.224). From her birth until the moment she is married, she is in the category of the fair-cheeked maiden, the potential bride. As the wife of Antenor, she is curiously seen in the same perspective: "fair-cheeked Theano, daughter of Kissēs, wife of horse-taming Antenor" (Θεανὼ καλλιπάρῃος / Κισσηῒς ἄλοχος Ἀντήνορος ἱπποδάμοιο, Il. 6.298–99). So also in her role as priestess of Athena (cf. Il. 6.300). When at Hector's bidding the Trojan women take a *peplos* as an offering to Athena, Theano receives it: "fair-cheeked Theano took the robe and placed it on the knees of fair-haired Athena" (Il. 6.302–303).[7] (In a dithyramb of Bacchylides on the embassy of Menelaus and Odysseus into Troy to demand the return of Helen and the possessions, Theano is βαθύ]ζωνος.[8])

Goddesses are sexually attractive by definition, including the goddesses who are chaste. On this premise one can explain the remaining Iliadic uses of καλλιπάρῃος. Themis is "fair-cheeked" (Il. 15.87; cf. αἰδοίη, Hes. *Theog.* 15; λιπαρή, 901). So is Leto in Achilles' account of Niobe's rash comparison of herself with the goddess (Il. 24.607). In Hesiod, Ceto is "fair-cheeked (*Theog.* 238) and likewise, unexpectedly, her daughters the Graeae (*Theog.* 270).[9] So is the anthropo-

---

6 Schol. T on 1.346: εὔκαιρον τὸ ἐπίθετον, τὴν τοῦ ἐρῶντος διάθεσιν ἐμφαῖνον τῷ δηλοῦν οἵας ἐρᾶται. Cf. Irwin 2005: 49 of the Hesiodic *Catalogue*: "While women are praised for their beauty, this certainly does not necessarily imply this praise to be an end in itself: the praise of the beauty of a sexual partner is as easily, or *more* easily, construed as praise of the male who penetrates her, rather than the passive female, beautiful or no" (her emphasis).
7 An analytical explanation for the reason for Theano's anomalous epithet would be that Theano and the whole scene in which she appears in Book 6 are a later and imperfectly integrated addition to the *Il.*, as Espermann 1980: 35–49 has argued. (She does not discuss the epithet.)
8 Bacch. 15(14).7 S-M. The embassy: Hom. *Il.* 3.204–207 (cf. 11.140); *Cypria* Arg. 55–57 B = 72–74 D = 10c W (pp. 116–17).
9 The epithet seems paradoxical but is in effect explained in the next line. Only their hair is old. See West 1966: 270n.

morphic side of Echidna (*Theog.* 298). Finally, even Hera has this epithet, although this example is more complex than the others (Hes. fr. 343.5 M-W = 294.5 M (not in H)):

αὐτὰρ ὅ γ' Ὠκεανοῦ καὶ Τηθύος ἠυκόμοιο
κούρηι νόσφ' Ἥρης παρελέξατο καλλιπαρήου
ἐξαπαφὼν Μῆτιν καίπερ πολύιδριν ἐοῦσαν[10]

But he (Zeus) beside the maiden (daughter) of Ocean and fair-haired Tethys,
lay in bed, apart from fair-cheeked Hera,
deceiving Mētis, shrewd though she is.

Hera has the epithet that would normally belong to the maiden (κούρη), here Mētis. But Hera is still seductive, as in the deception of Zeus, even if she no longer possesses the seductiveness of youth. Further, the Iliadic Hera has the status of Zeus' consort, as appears when she asks Aphrodite for love and desire (φιλότητα καὶ ἵμερον, 14.198) on the pretext that she wishes to use this gift in reconciling Oceanus and Tethys. (The gift takes the form of a κεστὸν ἱμάντα, "embroidered strap," 214.) Aphrodite cannot refuse, she explains, "for you sleep in the arms of greatest Zeus" (Ζηνὸς γὰρ τοῦ ἀρίστου ἐν ἀγκοίνησιν ἰαύεις, 213). Hera is by definition, as it were, the sexual partner of Zeus.[11]

To turn to the *Odyssey*, against the background of the passages in the *Iliad* and in Hesiod that have been discussed, that Melantho is "fair-cheeked" is no surprise. Melantho scolds Odysseus, who is disguised as a beggar (18.321–25):

τὸν δ' αἰσχρῶς ἐνένιπε Μελανθὼ καλλιπάρηος,
τὴν Δολίος μὲν ἔτικτε, κόμισσε δὲ Πηνελόπεια,
παῖδα δὲ ὣς ἀτίταλλε, δίδου δ' ἄρ' ἀθύρματα θυμῷ·
ἀλλ' οὐδ' ὣς εἶχε πένθος ἐνὶ φρεσὶ Πηνελοπείης,
ἀλλ' ἥ γ' Εὐρυμάχῳ μισγέσκετο καὶ φιλέεσκεν.
ἥ ῥ' Ὀδυσῆ' ἐνένιπεν ὀνειδείοισ' ἐπέεσσι·

And fair-cheeked Melantho scolded him shamefully,
she, whom Dolius begot, and Penelope provided for her
and cherished her as her own child, and gave her playthings to please her heart.
Yet even so she could feel no sorrow for Penelope,

---

10 For ἠυκόμοιος and καλλιπάρηος in line-final position in successive lines: *Il.* 6.302–303.
11 The name Hera may be a derivative of PGk *$ı̯ēr$- "year, good season, youth" and thus connected with ὥρα. This connection would underlie two of her attributes, "(1) *youth and related matters like weddings and fertility*" and "(2) a *period of the year*," the period of bloom (García Ramón 2016: 45–46; his emphasis). These are not her attributes in the *Il.*, however.

> but she loved Eurymachus and slept with him.
> So she scolded Odysseus with shameful words.

Here the formular expression for fair-cheeked maiden or nymph whom so-and-so begot or bore does not have its usual broader context of her marriage and offspring. Melantho is having sexual relations, as "fair-cheeked" would predict,– and frequently to judge by the verb forms–, but illicit and non-productive ones, which are doubly reprehensible because they entail ingratitude and disloyalty to her mistress.

In the farewell scene in *Odyssey* Book 15 at the beginning of which Helen is καλλίκομος (§1 above), she is also called καλλιπάρῃος, as she and Menelaus offer Telemachus parting gifts (15.123–30):

> Ἑλένη δὲ παρίστατο καλλιπάρῃος
> πέπλον ἔχουσ' ἐν χερσίν, ἔπος τ' ἔφατ' ἔκ τ' ὀνόμαζε·
> "δῶρόν τοι καὶ ἐγώ, τέκνον φίλε, τοῦτο δίδωμι,
> μνῆμ' Ἑλένης χειρῶν, πολυηράτου ἐς γάμου ὥρην,
> σῇ ἀλόχῳ φορέειν· τεῖος δὲ φίλῃ παρὰ μητρὶ
> κεῖσθαι ἐνὶ μεγάρῳ. σὺ δέ μοι χαίρων ἀφίκοιο
> οἶκον ἐϋκτίμενον καὶ σὴν ἐς πατρίδα γαῖαν."
> ὣς εἰποῦσ' ἐν χερσὶ τίθει, ὁ δ' ἐδέξατο χαίρων.

> Fair-cheeked Helen stood by him
> holding a robe in her hands, and spoke and addressed him.
> "I, too, dear child, give you a gift, this one,
> a memorial of the hands of Helen, for the time of your much-loved marriage,
> for your wife to wear. In the meantime, in your mother's keeping
> let it lie in your hall. May it be with joy that you reach
> your well-built house and your native land."
> So speaking she puts it in his hands and he received it with joy.

"Fair-cheeked" at first seems to be one of those incongruous epithets of which "blameless" as used of Aegisthus is probably the most famous example.[12] It is obvious that the narrator could have said δῖα γυναικῶν, which would have been appropriate in the context (ch. 5).[13] She is past the age at which she could be

---

[12] *Od.* 1.29. See Elmer 2015 for an interpretation of this and other incongruous epithets in the *Il.* and the *Od.* as a self-conscious feature of oral formulaic style, employed deliberately in accordance with the contrasting "ethics of language use" in the two epics, which correspond to the straight-speaking Achilles and the wily indirectness of Odysseus.

[13] Cf. Page 1959: 286–87 n. 90: καλλιπάρῃος is "antitraditional for δῖα γυναικῶν."

called "fair-cheeked" and, even if she were younger, the epithet would make no sense in this context.¹⁴

The epithet occurs in lines introducing a speech and can be understood in relation to this speech. Helen is presenting Telemachus with a gift for his future bride, "a memorial of the hand of Helen." Who is the Helen of this memorial? Helen in the Hesiodic *Catalogue* is the bride par excellence, for whom every hero of any note competed. Hers was not the only bride contest–there was Danaüs' for his forty-eight daughters and the foot-races organized by Antaeus for his daughter and by Icarius for his–but it was the most important. This Helen, the young "fair-cheeked" one, is the one who is passed on symbolically in the gift for the hypothetical bride, who can be expected to be fair-cheeked herself.¹⁵ Helen looks to the predictable event in Telemachus' future with which she can link herself, even if the prospect of his marriage is otherwise irrelevant in the *Odyssey*.¹⁶

What Gregory Nagy said of Helen's second speech in the farewell scene, when she interprets the bird omen, is even truer of the speech under discussion: "This meaning of the *Odyssey* is intended not for Menelaus and Helen, characters who are left over from the old world of the tale of Troy; rather, the outcome of the *Odyssey* is meant for the characters of the new world as represented by Telemachus and his companion."¹⁷ There has already been occasion to point out epithets in the *Odyssey* that look to Helen's old world, Iliadic identity (ch. 3§2). καλλιπάρῃος uniquely looks to her pre-Iliadic identity as the object of a bride contest. Richard Martin takes a further step: "By preposing the Telemachy and thus foregrounding the whole problem of father-son relations, the poet of the *Odyssey* made a conscious attempt to perform a poem about the *end* of tradition."¹⁸ In fact, the bride of Telemachus, contrary to Helen's expectation, will not be one who is likely to wear the *peplos* that she has woven. According to the *Telegony*, Telegonus, the son of Odysseus by Circe, having killed his father by mistake, takes Telemachus, still unmarried, and Penelope, to Circe. Telemachus then marries Circe, Telegonus Penelope, and they live on in Aiaia.¹⁹ It is the end of Odysseus' line.

---

14 How old she was when she was abducted by Paris is uncertain. She was at Troy for ten years and her return to Sparta with Menelaus took eight years (Apollod. *Epit.* 6.29).
15 This Helen has nothing to do with Helen the "virtuous housewife" to whom de Jong 2001a: 15.109–32n refers in her discussion of the gifts of Menelaus and Helen to Telemachus.
16 West 2014: 241 n.160.
17 Nagy 2002: 146.
18 Martin 1993: 240 (his emphasis).
19 *Teleg.* Arg. 17–20 B = Arg. 22–25 D = Args. 4a–4b (incl. testimonia) W (pp. 304–306); fr. 5 B = F 6 W (p. 306).

9.2.1 μνῆμ' Ἑλένης χειρῶν, πολυηράτου ἐς γάμου ὥρην

In the second line of her speech to Telemachus Helen shifts from the first to the third person, referring to herself as "Helen." In this way Helen adopts the perspective of the future, when the robe will be a μνῆμα "memorial" of her. In the two other occurrences of this word in Homer, it refers to the *phialē* presented to Nestor as a memorial of Patroclus' funeral (*Il.* 23.619) and to the bow given Odysseus by his guest-friend Iphitus, which Odysseus left behind in Ithaca when he sailed to Troy (*Od.* 21.38–41). The robe will in the future have, Helen expects, this high status of an object attached to the memory of a particular person.

The referent of the adjective πολυήρατος in the line under discussion has sometimes been thought to be ambiguous as between Helen and the marriage to which she refers. So Eustathius thought ("It is uncertain whether one should say 'much-beloved Helen' or 'much-beloved marriage'," ἄδηλον γὰρ εἴτε πολυηράτου Ἑλένης ῥητέον, εἴτε γάμου πολυηράτου, II.94.24 Stalbaum).[20] It is unlikely that an ancient audience would have heard the adjective as referring to Helen. In its seventeen occurrences in archaic verse it refers to a human or god only once, to Linus (Hes. fr. 305.1 M-W = *11.1 H = 255.1 M). It refers preponderantly to the beauty (εἶδος) of a woman (5x) and, directly or indirectly, to youth (5x).[21] It refers thrice to marriage or the marriage bed (*Od.* 15.126, 23.354, Hes. *Theog.* 404); once to water (Hes. *Op.* 739).

9.3 Comparison of formular behavior of καλλίκομος and καλλιπάρηος

While καλλίκομος and καλλιπάρηος are not synonyms, the fact remains that both, as the preceding discussion in this chapter has shown, signify sexual attractiveness, and in the genitive they have the same metrical value, i.e., in the genitive καλλίκομος belongs to the same system of line-final adonean-shaped epithets as καλλιπάρηος /-ωι /-ον and ἠϋκόμοιο (ch. 7§3). The preceding discussion also, however, suggested a distinction between καλλίκομος and καλλιπάρηος, viz., that the latter refers specifically to young women.

---

20 The idea is pursued by Goldhill 1994: 62–63.
21 Beauty of a woman: *Hymn. Hom. Cer.* 315; Hes. *Theog.* 908; Hes. fr. 10(a).32, 45 M-W = 5.32, 45 H = 10.32, 45 M; fr. 17a.7 M-W = 11.7 H = 13.7 M. Youth: *Od.* 15.366; *Hymn. Hom. Ven.* 225, 274; Hes. fr. 30.31 M-W = 20.31 H = 27.31 M; fr. 205.2 M-W = 95.2 H = 145.2 M; Theognis 1305.

An analysis of the formular behavior of καλλιπάρηος bears out the distinction. The same kind of division made in the discussion of ἠΰκομος can be made in the formula in which καλλιπάρηος/-ῳι /-ον/-ους appears in line-final position. Usually this epithet is preceded immediately by the name of a woman or goddess (16x = 4x in Hes. and 12x in Homer) or by ἑλικώπιδα (2x).[22] In a smaller set of examples, καλλιπάρηος appears in line-final position preceded by a word (with one exception always a verb) other than a woman's or a goddess' name:

– ᴗ Βρισηῒς παρελέξατο καλλιπάρηος Hom. *Il.* 24.676
– – – Ἥρης παρελέξατο καλλιπαρήου Hes. fr. 343.5 = 294.5 M (not in H)
– ᴗ ᴗ – Ἑλένη δὲ παρίστατο καλλιπάρηος Hom. *Od.* 15.123
– ᴗ ᴗ – Κητὼ γραίας τέκε καλλιπαρήους Hes. *Theog.* 907
– ᴗ ᴗ – Λητοῖ ἰσάσκετο καλλιπαρήῳ Hom. *Il.* 24.607
– ᴗ ᴗ – ᴗ ᴗ – Χάριτας τέκε καλλιπαρήους Hes. *Theog.* 907
– – – ᴗ ᴗ – ᴗ Θέμιστι δὲ καλλιπαρήῳ Hom. *Il.* 15.87

Both the grammatical case of the epithet and the metrical shape of the formula, or perhaps one should say formulas, vary much more widely than in the larger set (epithet preceded immediately by the name of a woman or goddess).[23] In this smaller set, Helen and Briseïs are the only two mortal women and the only two in the nominative case. The verbs distinguish them: "Briseïs lay beside (him)" and "Helen stood beside (them)," or, if one thinks of the verbs not semantically but as παρα- compounds in the same metrical slot, the verbs associate them (cf. the Hera example, also a παρα- compound).[24] If καλλιπάρηος is the preferred way to describe a concubine in the *Iliad*, then epithet and verb go together in the example of Briseïs. A woman would not have to be καλλιπάρηος, however, to *stand* beside other persons. The verb that is used of Helen takes her, so described, out of the usual semantic range of the epithet. It seems that in the particular smaller set under discussion, the formula has a semantic openness that it does not have in the larger set.

As it happens, καλλίκομος, which occurs twice in Homer, is used once of a concubine and once of Helen. Phoenix, in the passage discussed above (§1), says of his father Amyntor (*Il.* 9.449):

---

22 Hes. *Theog.* 298; fr. 43a.19 M-W = 37.19 H = 69.19 M.
23 There is also a set of five examples in which καλλιπάρηος appears in positions other than line-final. All of these lines are fragmentary: Hes. frs. 10(a).21 = 5.21 H = 10.21 M, 17a.3 M-W = 11.3 H = 13.3 M, 85.6 = 120.6 H (not in M), 129.13 = 46.13 H = 77.13 M, 180.13 = 111.13 H = 182.13 M.
24 Tsagalis 2004: 162–65, with reference to six earlier studies (n. 435), elucidates a structural parallelism of Helen and Briseïs in the *Iliad*. In the earlier studies he singles out Suzuki 1989: 21–29, 55.

– – παλλακίδος περιχώσατο καλλικόμοιο

he was enraged with me because of his fair-haired concubine.

Homer describes Menelaus rising from his bed (*Od*. 15.58),

– – – – – Ἑλένης πάρα καλλικόμοιο

from beside fair-haired Helen.

In these two examples, the epithet is used correctly, so to speak, each time, while the verb that Phoenix uses is unexpected. As in the smaller set of καλλιπάρῃος examples, the formula appears to be both metrically and semantically adaptable to the needs of the narrative.

9.4 Conclusion

The two epithets discussed in this chapter both have clearly definable meanings in archaic hexameter verse. They differ, however, in their susceptibility to contextual interpretation when they refer to Helen. καλλίκομος has a particular relevance to the physical setting, i.e., the bed that she shares with Menelaus, in which she is called "fair-haired." καλλιπάρῃος seems anomalous as used of her (and also as used of Hera and Theano).

For the interpretation of καλλίκομος two kinds of comparison proved to be possible. Its contextual meaning comes first from the contrast between its standard connotation of sexual attractiveness, and the other epithet referring to her hair, ἠΰκομος, which consistently refers to Helen in her role as the wife of Paris. While the lexical meanings are the same, in the formulas in which they appear the meanings are different. Second, the standard connotation of καλλίκομος contrasts with the two other epithets used of Helen in the same setting, which refer to her in her social identity.

καλλιπάρῃος, an epithet appropriate to sexually attractive young women, seems anomalous when it is used of Helen because she is now far beyond the age of marriage and in any case nothing in the scene of Telemachus' departure prompts indication of sexual attractiveness, even if she might be assumed not to have lost it. The epithet can, however, be understood in relation to the speech that she gives when she presents the *peplos* to him for his future wife to wear at their wedding. As with other epithets in speech introductions, it can be understood in relation to the speech in which Helen presents the gift. The anachronistic epithet recalls an earlier aspect of Helen. The gift goes from the bride par excellence of the past to a bride of the future. By this interpretation, the anomaly of the use of καλλιπάρῃος can be reduced. As used of Theano and Hera, however, this epithet is more difficult to explain.

10 Kinship Epithets

Besides εὐπατέρεια (ch. 11), Helen has three other kinship epithets. Each of these three explicitly describes her as the daughter of Zeus: Διὸς θυγάτηρ, κούρη Διὸς αἰγιόχοιο, and Διὸς ἐκγεγαυῖα.¹ The instances of these epithets are divided almost evenly between the *Iliad* and the *Odyssey* –three in the former (all in Book 3), four in the latter (three in Book 4, and one in Book 24). With the exception of the example in Book 24 of the *Odyssey*, the narrator is the speaker. That the narrator should nearly always be the speaker is unsurprising. The contrast between his transcendent perspective on Helen and the more limited perspectives of the characters has already been discussed (ch. 8§2). Helen's birth and beauty make her worth the effort of the Achaeans and Trojans, even if they are completely oblivious of her parentage or indifferent to her beauty and have other motives for seeking to recover her or wishing to keep her (ch. 1).

Because of their semantic similarity, and because they cluster in the ways just indicated, these three kinship epithets are studied as a group in this chapter. The one that comes first in the *Iliad* is Διὸς ἐκγεγαυῖα, which occurs in a verse introducing a reply of Helen to Priam in the Teichoscopia. It is one of three reply-verses in this scene.

10.1 Ἑλένη Διὸς ἐκγεγαυῖα (*Iliad* 3.199)

The line in which this epithet occurs happens to be an example of the τὸν δ' ἠμείβετ' ἔπειτα "type-verses," as Parry called them, in which an epithet invariably occurs and is, according to him, "purely ornamental."² The epithet here, however, has a contrastive function in its context. After Helen has appeared on the wall, in longing for her former husband, her home town, and her parents (139–45), Priam summons her (161).³ The narrator uses her name without an epithet in this line. Priam addresses her, calling her "dear child" (162), and asks a question

---
1 Others also have these epithets. See ch. 12 for their distribution.
2 Parry 1971[1930]: 305 n. 2.
3 When Priam asks her to sit "in front of me" (162), he means: with her back toward him, so that both can see the Achaean army. See Krieter-Spiro 2009: 3.162n.

about an Achaean who will turn out to be Agamemnon (cf. ch. 1 on Priam's appellative).[4] When Priam asks her a second question about another Achaean, he again addresses her as "dear child" (192). When Helen replies to Priam she has the epithet Διὸς ἐκγεγαυῖα (199), which contrasts implicitly with Tyndareus as her father, who was surely implied in the reference to her parents (140), and contrasts explicitly with Priam's "dear child."[5] The sequence of the different modes of reference and address is as follows:

Tab. 6: Helen at the beginning the Teichoscopia

3.121	Ἶρις δ' αὖθ' Ἑλένῃ λευκωλένῳ ἄγγελος ἦλθεν	(narrator)
3.154	οἳ δ' ὡς οὖν εἴδονθ' Ἑλένην ἐπὶ πύργον ἰο	(narrator of old men)
3.162	δεῦρο πάροιθ' ἐλθοῦσα φίλον τέκος ἵζευ ἐμεῖο	(Priam)
3.161	Ὣς ἄρ' ἔφαν, Πρίαμος δ' Ἑλένην ἐκαλέσσατο φωνῇ	(narrator)
3.171	Τὸν δ' Ἑλένη μύθοισιν ἀμείβετο δῖα γυναικῶν	(narrator)
3.192	εἴπ' ἄγε μοι καὶ τόνδε φίλον τέκος ὅς τις ὅδ' ἐστί	(Priam)
3.199	Τὸν δ' ἠμείβετ' ἔπειθ' Ἑλένη Διὸς ἐκγεγαυῖα	(narrator)

The contrast between the narrator's perspective and the pragmatic and otherwise down-to-earth perspective of the characters discussed earlier (again ch. 8§2) is evident. The epithet Ἑλένη Διὸς ἐκγεγαυῖα is thus part of the review of the cause of the war that Book 3 provides and it implies a validation of Helen's role (as does the laudatory epithet at 3.121). The narrator and his audience know, even if the characters do not know, that Helen is the daughter of Zeus.[6]

---

4 Lowe 2000: 109 n. 8: "…Priam's speech to Helen at III.162–70 is anything but an innocent request for information: it is a delicate rejection of the hostile judgement passed in the elders' speech (cf. especially 164–5 with 159–60)."
5 Tyndareus as her father in this passage: see Kirk 1985: 281 on lines 139–40; Krieter-Spiro 2009: 3.140n.
6 On οὐ νέμεσις, which appears only here in the *Il.* and in the *Od.* only at 1.350, see Pucci 1987: 205 n. 30.

10.2 Ἑλένη Διὸς ἐκγεγαυῖα (*Iliad* 3.418), κούρη Διὸς αἰγιόχοιο (426)

After Aphrodite has snatched Paris from the battlefield to his bedroom (313–82), she goes to Helen on the wall of Troy, disguised as the old spinning woman whom Helen brought from Sparta, and summons her to the bedroom (383–94).[7] Helen sees through the disguise and delivers a powerful rebuke of Aphrodite (395–412). She says, amongst other things, "Go and sit beside him...until he makes you his wife or his slave" (406–409). Aphrodite, enraged, threatens Helen, who immediately complies and goes with Aphrodite to Paris. Aphrodite sits her down on a chair in front of her husband (424–27), putting her in the position which she had proposed for Aphrodite. It has been said that Aphrodite "is still acting the part of the old servant."[8] She is in any case backing up in action the rebuke of Helen that she has just delivered. To seat her in front of Paris is to put her in the role of wife that she has resisted, although Helen continues to resist by turning her eyes away and scolding Paris (427). The conjugal significance of sitting in this passage can be compared with the places in which Odysseus and Penelope sit opposite one another (*Od.* 23.89, 165; cf. 5.198, where Calypso sits opposite Odysseus, whom she wishes to keep with her).[9]

In this brief passage in which Aphrodite brings Helen and Paris face to face, a dense clustering of epithets and denominations (δαίμων and θεά in the following list) occurs:

- 413 δῖ' Ἀφροδίτη
- 418 Ἑλένη Διὸς ἐκγεγαυῖα
- 420 δαίμων (Aphrodite)[10]
- 423 δῖα γυναικῶν (Helen)
- 424 φιλομμειδὴς Ἀφροδίτη[11]

---

[7] This paragraph has been adapted from Edmunds 2016a: 194.
[8] West 2011a: 137 n. on 3.424. The old servant was last mentioned in line 386.
[9] These places and others are discussed by Neuberger-Donath 1977, who interprets Sappho 31.1–2 V as showing that the two persons referred to by Sappho are man and wife.
[10] Leaf 1900.1: 3.420n: this noun only here of a goddess. Wilamowitz-Moellendorff 1931–1932.1: 357 n. 1: "Wenn Helene von Aphrodite gezwungen zu Paris gehen muß,...und der Dichter zufügt ἦρχε δὲ δαίμων so geht eben Aphrodite als der Zuteiler voran, der Helene ihr Schicksal gegeben hat."
[11] Boedeker 1974: 24 "The epithet φιλομμειδής is regularly associated with Aphrodite's role as goddess of love." Boedeker discusses the use of this epithet in the scene in *Il.* 3 as an example of a context "where she inflicts ἵμερος on others" (34). See Kirk 1985: 3.424n, where the metrically possible alternative Διὸς θυγάτηρ is discussed. Kirk observes that the difference between the two

- 425 θεά (Aphrodite)
- 426 κούρη Διὸς αἰγιόχοιο[12] (Helen)

A contrast between Helen and Aphrodite, precisely with respect to divine status, is at work.[13] After Aphrodite threatens her, Helen "sprung of Zeus" is afraid (418). Helen "the daughter of Zeus" (426) obediently sits down on the chair that Aphrodite has placed in front of Paris. The epithets seem to have concessive force: although Helen is the daughter of Zeus, she is intimidated by another, more powerful daughter of Zeus.[14] In the list just given, Helen and Aphrodite share one adjective, δῖα. In Helen's case, it is part of the epithet δῖα γυναικῶν (423; cf. ch. 5). In Aphrodite's case, it is more difficult to say what the epithet means.[15] In this match-up, however, Aphrodite, is the goddess (δαίμων, 420 and θεά, 425) and Helen is a mortal, even if she is the daughter of Zeus. Her rebuke of Aphrodite has already ended in what has been called a human *cri de coeur*.[16]

Helen sits down opposite Paris (3.426):

ἔνθα κάθιζ' Ἑλένη, κούρη Διὸς αἰγιόχοιο,

Then Helen, the daughter of aegis-bearing Zeus, sat down.

"is well exemplified in book 14, where Aphrodite is Διὸς θυγάτηρ at 193 while Here is making her request to her but φιλομμειδής at 211 when she grants it and hands over her belt with its erotic properties."

12 Both parts of this word are etymologically uncertain (see *LfgrE* s.v. E) but the first is usually understood as coming from αἰγίς, the goatskin shield of Zeus. The fatherhood of Zeus when he bears this epithet is elsewhere referred to in the *Il.* apropos of Athena (1.202, 222; 2.157; 5.115, 714, 733, 815; 8.352, 384, 427; 10.278, 553; 21.429 = 13x); the Muses (2.491, 598); nymphs (6.420); Heracles (5.396); Sarpedon (5.635); hypothetically (13.825: "if Zeus were my father"); of Zeus the father in general (22.221).

13 On the intervention of Aphrodite see Fränkel 1951: 74–75, who, in support of his assertion that "whoever has been endowed with such charm by Aphrodite, must play the role of beloved and lover to the end," well refers to "the lovely gifts of golden Aphrodite," of which Paris earlier said: "one cannot cast away the glorious gifts of the gods, as many as they give, but one would not willingly choose them" (3.64–66).

14 Reckford 1964: 12. "[A]lthough she is a daughter of Zeus, the epithet κούρη Διὸς αἰγιόχοιο (3.426) becomes in its context a kind of mockery of her state."

15 *LfrgE* s.v. δῖος, after a list of the many goddesses to whom this epithet is applied: "In the face of this list, one has concluded that δ. has been reduced to a heroic adj. with vague sem. character…"

16 Kirk 1985: 324 on lines 410–12.

The kinship epithet again suggests Helen's status in relation to another character, in this case Paris, and her status seems to give her the right to an insulting speech, but again she acquiesces to the wishes of her interlocutor.[17] She follows Paris to bed and the narrator refers to her as his wife (ἄκοιτις, 447). Paris in his reply had already addressed her as "lady" (γύναι, 437). In keeping with the action, the middle-level view of Helen replaces the higher one.

10.3 Διὸς ἐκγεγαυῖα (*Odyssey* 4.184)

Menelaus, Helen, and Telemachus weep over Odysseus (4.184–187):

> κλαῖε μὲν Ἀργείη Ἑλένη, Διὸς ἐκγεγαυῖα,
> κλαῖε δὲ Τηλέμαχός τε καὶ Ἀτρεΐδης Μενέλαος,
> οὐδ' ἄρα Νέστορος υἱὸς ἀδακρύτω ἔχεν ὄσσε·
> μνήσατο γὰρ κατὰ θυμὸν ἀμύμονος Ἀντιλόχοιο,

> Argive Helen, descended of Zeus, wept,
> And Telemachus wept, and Menelaus, son of Atreus,
> Nor did the son of Nestor keep his eyes without tears;
> For he thought in his heart of noble Antilochus.

The characters here are recalling the Trojan War, and the narrator gives Helen and Menelaus their Iliadic identities (cf. ch. 3 *sub fin.*).[18] Ἀργείη makes sense when it is used of Helen in the *Iliad*, as it often is (see ch. 5), but now that she is in her native Argos (cf. 4.174 for Argos as including Sparta), the epithet, like Menelaus', looks back to her Iliadic identity.

The kinship epithet in the same line has, however, a precise contrastive function. Helen has called herself "dog-faced" (145) and no other epithet for her has intervened until she is called "descended of Zeus." It is exactly the same sequence, with the same two epithets, and with an intervening appellative, as in Book 3 of the *Iliad* (180, 199):

---

17 Krieter-Spiro 2009: 3.426n: "hier weist die Wendung wohl auf Helenas hohen Rang, der ihr die zynische Beschimpfung eines Königssohnes erlaubt." Di Benedetto 1998: 7 n. 1 speaks of Helen's use of ἀρηϊφίλου Μενελάου (430) and ἀρηΐφιλον Μενέλαον (432) as "sarcastic iteration" of Paris' use of this formula, also in line-final position, in line 69. But Hector has used the same formula at 3.90 and the narrator uses it in line 452.
18 The formula used of Menelaus here occurs 6x in *Il.*, 2x in *Od.*

Tab. 7: Sequences of epithets and appellatives in *Iliad* Book 3 and *Odyssey* Book 4

Iliad Book 3	*Odyssey* Book 4
180 δαὴρ αὖτ' ἐμὸς ἔσκε κυνώπιδος	145 ἐμεῖο κυνώπιδος εἵνεκ'
192 φίλον τέκος	148 γύναι
199 Διὸς ἐκγεγαυῖα	184 Διὸς ἐκγεγαυῖα

With the kinship epithet in the passage under discussion the narrator restores the higher perspective on Helen, after she has spoken of herself in a self-denigrating way.

10.4 Διὸς ἐκγεγαυῖα (*Odyssey* 4.219), Διὸς θυγάτηρ (227)

Soon after the company stops their weeping, Menelaus calls for dinner.[19] The passage begins (4.219):

> ἔνθ' αὖτ' ἄλλ' ἐνόησ' Ἑλένη Διὸς ἐκγεγαυῖα·
>
> Then Helen, descended of Zeus, thought of another thing.

Of Helen's kinship epithets this one comes closest to being hers exclusively. She has it five times, Athena once.[20] The verb ἐνόησ' / ἐνόησε is one of those that Bakker lists as introducing "epiphanic" formulas.[21] Here, however, Helen, who is already a commanding presence, needs no such introduction. To understand the epithet it is helpful to consider the other formula in the line, ἄλλ' ἐνόησ'. While this verb is very common in both the *Iliad* and the *Odyssey*, with many different subjects, the formula ἄλλ' ἐνόησ' / ἐνόησε is used in the *Iliad* only of Achilles (*Il.* 23.140, 193) and in the *Odyssey* seven times of Athena and once of Penelope.[22]

---

[19] Line 213. A second dinner? At line 68 Telemachus and Pisistratus had finished eating.
[20] Higbie 1995: 143 says that aside from this epithet, used only of Helen and Athena, the two "seem to have little in common." But Higbie herself observes that Helen "can see through Odysseus just as Athena can do" (182 n. 39), i.e., as Helen reports of herself in her speech at *Od.* 4.235–64. Even if they in fact have little in common, it is still possible for Helen to adopt briefly an Athena-like role, as it will be suggested that she does in *Od.* 4.
[21] Bakker 1997: 163.
[22] Athena: 2.382, 393; 4.795; 6.112; 18.187; 23.242, 344. Penelope: 16.409. In the *Il.*, it is one of the formular peculiarities of Book 23 that seem to bring this book into relation with the *Od.* See Bozzone 2015: 81–83.

Irene de Jong comments: "The 'X thought of something else' motif highlights a sudden or unexpected turn in the story...The X usually...is Athena in her role of 'director' of the story of the *Odyssey*."²³ What Helen has thought of is, of course, the drug. After the narrator has described the potency of the drug at some length (220–26), he says (4.227)

> τοῖα Διὸς θυγάτηρ ἔχε φάρμακα μητιόεντα,
>
> Such wise drugs the daughter of Zeus had.

This epithet is one that Helen has only here, while Aphrodite and Athena each has it ten times. It can be suggested that the association with Athena prevails, not only because of what has just said about line 219 but also because Athena has already twice been called Διὸς θυγάτηρ in the preceding book of the *Odyssey* (3.337, 378), where Athena, as Mentor, takes her departure from Pylos in the form of a vulture and Nestor immediately perceives that it is she, who honored Telemachus' father amongst the Achaeans (371–79). It can be suggested, in short, that the formulas in line 219 characterize Helen as Athena-like.

Helen becomes at this point the director of the recollection of Odysseus that has been going on, in one way or another, ever since Menelaus referred to Odysseus as the one, of those who fought at Troy, for whom he grieves the most (104–12).²⁴ These recollections bring grief to everyone and grief is also the subject of some reflections of Pisistratus (190–202). The drug now makes it possible to remember Odysseus without pain and Helen exploits this possibility to tell a self-serving story about an encounter with Odysseus that she had at Troy (cf. *Ilias parva* frs. 6–7 B = fr. 8 D = FF 8–9 W (pp. 195–97)). Her speech is introduced as an answer: ἐξαῦτις μύθοισιν ἀμειβομένη προσέειπεν, "Again she spoke answering words and said" (4.234). But, as Edwards observed, "Helen 'answers' to nothing, but is restarting a dropped conversation; perhaps the meaning is something like 'took up the conversation'." He adds: "[B]ut one wonders why the poet did not choose to end the verse with the simple προσηύδα δῖα γυναικῶν."²⁵ The answer to Edwards' question would be the association with Athena that has been proposed. At this point δῖα γυναικῶν would undercut the stature that the kinship epithet Διὸς θυγάτηρ (4.227) has given her.

---

23 de Jong 2001a: *Od*. 2.382n.
24 S. West 1988: 4.107n: "With an irony very characteristic of the *Odyssey*, Menelaus speaks spontaneously of what most concerns Telemachus..."
25 Edwards 1970: 29.

In this "actorial analepsis," she plays the role of Athena, seeing immediately through Odysseus' disguise and parrying his evasive cunning (κερδοσύνη) (242–59). Athena is in this role on Ithaca at the time of Odysseus' return, when Odysseus tells a tall tale about why he is there.[26] She is disguised as a shepherd boy. She then takes the form of a beautiful woman and affectionately reproaches him for his deviousness (13.291–99): The one who could surpass you would be cunning (κερδαλέος, 13.291; cf. κέρδεα, 297). But Helen's speech in Book 4 also cleverly uses her recollection of Odysseus as a way of exonerating herself. Helen's story ends with his killing Trojans as he left Troy and the cries of the Trojan women: "But my heart rejoiced, because now my heart had changed, to returning back home, and I lamented the blindness that Aphrodite gave me, when she brought me thither from my dear native land, abandoning my daughter, my bedchamber, and my husband, a man lacking nothing in either intelligence or looks" (4.259–64). Helen's directorship of the recollection of Odysseus ends in a redefining of the recollection of herself, with a final line of flattery of her husband (but, as far as his looks are concerned, not quite so flattering as the epithet, θεοειδής, that Helen uses of Paris [*Il.* 24.763]).[27]

Her strategy in her speech is to stage herself as a bard (thus assuming what we think was a male role) in performance (4.238–40):

ἦ τοι νῦν δαίνυσθε καθήμενοι ἐν μεγάροισι
καὶ μύθοις τέρπεσθε· ἐοικότα γὰρ καταλέξω.
πάντα μὲν οὐκ ἂν ἐγὼ μυθήσομαι οὐδ' ὀνομήνω,

Indeed feast now sitting in the hall
and delight yourself with speeches, for I shall tell appropriate things.[28]
I shall not tell or enumerate everything.

Playing on the formula ἀληθείην καταλέξω, Helen recalls the self-declaration of Hesiod's Muses (*Theog.* 26–28).[29] She proceeds to imitate one of the lines in the prologue to the Catalogue of Ships (*Il.* 2.488; cf. Odysseus at *Od.* 11.328).[30] One

---

26 Cf. Higbie *loc. cit.* in n. 20 above.
27 Menelaus was *kalos.* See schol. bT *Il.* 17.49 (ξανθός, εὔμηρος, καλλίσφυρος).
28 Scholars debate the meaning of ἐοικότα here but Helen's self-characterization as a poet is not in doubt (see next n.).
29 Finkelberg 2012: 80–81. With *Theog.* 27 (ἴδμεν ψεύδεα πολλὰ λέγειν ἐτύμοισιν ὁμοῖα) compare *Od.* 19.203, of Odysseus (ἴσκε ψεύδεα πολλὰ λέγων ἐτύμοισιν ὁμοῖα).
30 Ford 1992: 72–74; Higbie 1995: 181 n. 21. Nagy 1999[1979]: 271 compares *Il.* 20.203–205 (Aeneas to Achilles) with *Il.* 2.485–86 (the poet to the Muses). Aeneas adopts a conceit of the poet.

can observe in passing that, if Helen can imitate a bard and if bards could imitate the tones of voice appropriate to the various *muthoi* and *epē* in their performances, then it is no surprise that Helen could imitate the wives of the heroes concealed inside the Trojan Horse, as, in Menelaus' account, she did (277–79). She would not have to have known, in fact she could not have known, each of the wives in person but she could call to each of the heroes by name in the mode of lament as if it was his wife lamenting.[31] Helen displays her characteristic skill as a speaker.[32]

To return now to the kinship epithets that introduced Helen in this scene (219, 227), they bear on her taking charge, or her directorship of the situation. They also of course bear on her capacity for shrewd rhetoric, which is displayed whenever she speaks. When, however, Menelaus replies to Helen at the end of her speech, he addresses her as γύναι "lady" (266), returning her to her conventional social role.[33] Menelaus' form of address represents the alternation in the levels of Helen's epithets and denominations that we encounter again and again (cf. chart in §4 above). He knows that Helen is the daughter of Zeus and that as her husband and Zeus' son-in-law he will go to Elysium when he dies (*Od.* 4.569: Proteus' prophecy to him), but this knowledge has no effect on his relations with Helen as presented in the *Odyssey*.

With the immediate context in *Od.* (4.239–242), Ramersdorfer 1981: 154–55 compares *Od.* 11.326–30 and *Od.* 11.516–19, arguing that the Iliadic verse (2.488) is secondary.

31 For Helen as a lamenter in this scene: Martin 2003: 120–23.

32 Danek 1998: 105 argues that there are two Helens in Book 4. The first is the matronly Helen who is introduced by the Artemis simile and the second is the Helen who mixes the drug in the wine. The second is "demonic." In particular, the second Helen has the power to change others or herself (Menelaus' story about Helen at Troy, in which she imitates the voices of the wives of the Achaean heroes) into something else. Further, "[d]er Charakter des εἴδωλον im Sinne eines Etwas-Anderes-Seins ist in beiden Szenen unverkennbar." The Egyptian elements in the story of Menelaus and Helen are a signal that the Helen figures in previous contrasting versions of her story have been unified in a single figure.

33 It has often been pointed out that the Trojan War story that Menelaus is about to tell (in which Helen and her then husband Deïphobus circle the Trojan Horse three times and Helen calls out to the Argive heroes imitating their wives' voices) presents, contrary to what Helen has just said about herself, a pro-Trojan Helen. Scafoglio 2015 argues that the poet is also juxtaposing two different earlier versions of Helen at Troy, both identifiable in Cyclic Epic.

10.5 Διὸς ἐκγεγαυῖα (*Odyssey* 23.218)

This instance differs from the others that have been discussed in two main respects: the speaker is not the narrator but Penelope, and Helen is not present but rather the subject of discussion (23.218–221).³⁴

> οὐδέ κεν Ἀργείη Ἑλένη, Διὸς ἐκγεγαυῖα,
> ἀνδρὶ παρ' ἀλλοδαπῷ ἐμίγη φιλότητι καὶ εὐνῇ,
> εἰ ᾔδη, ὅ μιν αὖτις ἀρήιοι υἷες Ἀχαιῶν
> ἀξέμεναι οἶκόνδε φίλην ἐς πατρίδ' ἔμελλον.

> Argive Helen, descended of Zeus, would not
> have lain with a foreign man in bed,
> if she had known that the warlike sons of the Achaeans
> intended to lead her home to her dear native land.

In this passage, Penelope explains to Odysseus that she was hesitant to accept that he was her long-lost husband because she always feared a man would try to trick her into being unfaithful by claiming to be Odysseus. She then turns to Helen and both defends and condemns her. Helen, Penelope claims, would have refused Paris if she had known her actions would lead to war. There is an implicit comparison with Penelope who, like her cousin, had to deal with men and their advances. The comparison is complex, however.³⁵ As noted in chapter 3, the epithet Ἀργείη signifies in the *Iliad* Helen's place of origin and is used in contexts in which the Achaean claim to her is asserted. When Penelope calls Helen "Argive," she looks back to the Helen of the Trojan War, the one whom the Achaeans came to recover. Διὸς ἐκγεγαυῖα takes the narratorial view of the worth of the Achaeans' object (cf. *Il.* 3.199, discussed above in §1).

---

34 There is in fact debate as to whether these lines belong in the poem at all. Aristarchus athetized the lines. Many modern scholars side with Aristarchus on the grounds that Helen and Penelope are not suitable figures for comparison, as their circumstances were different: both dealt with suitors, but Helen gave in to hers and Penelope did not. Stanford 1958–1959.2: 401 on lines 218–24 argues that the difficulty lies with Penelope's dual desires to show Helen as an example of the problem of trusting strangers and to defend her (or at least, not to condemn her). In other comparisons of heroines in Homer, moreover, the comparisons are made by a third party; here Penelope compares herself to Helen. For a list of those scholars who reject the lines and those who accept them, see Heubeck in Russo *et al.* 1992: 336–37 on lines 218–24.
35 For discussion of and bibliography on this difficult comparison see Danek 1998: 450–51.

10.6 Conclusion

The first three kinship epithets discussed in this chapter serve to contrast two points of view. One is the narrator's. The narrator is the only one who knows that Helen is the daughter of Zeus and the only one besides Penelope to speak of her as such.[36] The other is the down-to-earth point of view, expressed in various ways, of the characters in the *Iliad* and the *Odyssey*. The two poems consistently maintain this division (Penelope, for reasons given above, is not really an exception).

The narrator is of course right that Helen is the daughter of Zeus, and at least one character knows this fact, although it does not figure in his thinking about Helen (cf. §4 above *sub fin.* on Menelaus). It does not follow that the characters are wrong in thinking of Helen as a mortal woman. In the account of her confrontation with Aphrodite, even though Helen has two of her kinship epithets (§2 above), she is subservient to the goddess. Her kinship with Zeus counts for nothing. In the narrator's narrative, the mortal status of Helen is writ large. When she makes her first appearance, on the wall of Troy, the narrator calls her, amongst other things, the daughter of Zeus (§1 above); when she follows Paris to bed at the end of Book 3 the narrator refers to her as the "wife" of Paris.

---

36 It is odd, then, to hear that "although Helen appears to be a woman and not a goddess in the *Iliad*, she is still a goddess" and that "despite appearances as poetically created in the *Iliad*, Helen is recognized even there as a goddess" (Nagy 2016c).

11 εὐπατέρεια

This epithet occurs in a line already discussed (*Od.* 22.227):

οἵη ὅτ' ἀμφ' Ἑλένῃ λευκωλένῳ εὐπατερείῃ

as when (you fought) over white-armed Helen of noble father.

The epithet λευκώλενος in this line was interpreted as part of Athena's rebuke of Odysseus (ch. 8). (For the unusual asyndetic pairing of epithets: ch. 8§1.) She is disparaging Helen, for whom Odysseus once fought bravely, in implicit comparison with Penelope, for whom he ought to be fighting just as, or more, bravely now. The epithet εὐπατέρεια might be expected to be part of the same strategy. Its particular connotation in this context remains to be defined. εὐπατέρεια is used in one other place of Helen (*Il.* 6.288–92 [the narrator is the speaker]) (§1) and once of Tyro (*Od.* 11.235 [Odysseus is the speaker]). The passage concerning Tyro helps to explain the narrator's use of this epithet of Helen (§2).

11.1 Helen as εὐπατέρεια in *Iliad* Book 6

As with λευκώλενος, so with εὐπατέρεια, Athena's use of the word differs from the narrator's. He calls Helen εὐπατέρεια in the passage in which he describes Hecuba reacting to Hector's behest that she take her finest mantle and place it on the lap of Athena (6.288–92):[1]

αὐτὴ δ' ἐς θάλαμον κατεβήσετο κηώεντα,
ἔνθ' ἔσάν οἱ πέπλοι παμποίκιλα ἔργα γυναικῶν
Σιδονίων, τὰς αὐτὸς Ἀλέξανδρος θεοειδὴς
ἤγαγε Σιδονίηθεν, ἐπιπλὼς εὐρέα πόντον,
τὴν ὁδὸν ἣν Ἑλένην περ ἀνήγαγεν εὐπατέρειαν·

She went down into her fragrant storeroom,
where there were *peploi*, the all-variegated work of women
of Sidon, whom god-like Alexander himself

---

[1] Kirk 1990: 198 (on line 288) suggests that the scene is modelled on the one in *Od.* 15.99–110 in which Helen, Megapenthes and Menelaus take gifts to the departing Telemachus. But a one-to-one correspondence between the two passages is unlikely. Cf. de Jong 2001a: App. F "The 'Storeroom' Type-Scene." On the plus-verses 6.288a–b see ch. 5§2.

brought from Sidonia, sailing the broad the sea,
on the journey on which he brought back Helen, daughter of a noble father.²

With αὐτή (288) the narrator distinguishes between Hecuba and her servants, whom she has sent to summon the older Trojan women. The task of choosing the *peplos* is entirely hers.³ The storeroom is hers (n.b. οἱ, 289). Everything that is now said of her *peploi* could be understood as "implicit embedded focalization" (defined in ch. 7§5), i.e., as her view of the matter at hand. On this interpretation, εὐπατέρεια will refer not to Zeus as Helen's father but to Tyndareus. Hecuba is thinking of Helen as having been brought back from Sparta, as "daughter of a noble (Spartan) father." (At *Od.* 11.298–99, Tyndareus is mentioned apropos of Leda and her sons, the Dioscouroi, and at 24.199, as the father of Clytemnestra.)

The narrator has already explicitly identified Helen as the daughter of Zeus— as Διὸς ἐκγεγαυῖα ("born of Zeus," *Il.* 3.199, 418) and κούρη Διὸς αἰγιόχοιο ("child of aegis-bearing Zeus," *Il.* 3.426). But Hecuba does not know what the narrator knows (see ch. 8§2 and ch. 10§1 for the difference between the narrator's and the characters' points of view).

11.2 Helen as εὐπατέρεια in *Odyssey* Book 22

As for her status as daughter of Zeus, although Helen could be called κούρη Διὸς αἰγιόχοιο in the *Iliad* (3.426), this epithet is Athena's in the *Odyssey*.⁴ Athena is also Διὸς κούρη μεγάλοιο, αἰγιόχοιο Διὸς τέκος, and Διὸς θυγάτηρ.⁵ In short, Athena is the daughter of Zeus. When, in the line quoted at the beginning of this chapter, she calls Helen εὐπατέρεια she is hardly equating Helen's status with

---

2 Wathelet 1995: 167 n. 4: "Mal inspirée, Hécube a choisi un voile 'oeuvre des Sidoniennes, qu'Alexandre pareil aux dieux a ramené de Sidon,...au cours du même voyage dont il a ramené aussi Hélène'...Rappel indiscret du jugement de Pâris dont Athéna ne doit pas avoir gardé un très bon souvenir."
3 Cf. Stoevesandt 2008: 288–95n *init*.
4 2.296, 3.394, 4.752, 5.382, 13.190, 252, 318, 371, and, after the place in *Od.* 22 under discussion, also 24.529, 547; *Il.* 5.733, 8.384.
5 Διὸς κούρη μεγάλοιο: *Od.* 6.323, 24.521; *Il.* 6.304, 312, 9.536, 10.296. The epithet is used of Artemis at 6.151. αἰγιόχοιο Διὸς τέκος: *Od.* 4.762, 6.324. In *Il.* 1.202, 2.157, 5.115, 5.714, 8.352, 8.427, 10.278, 21.420. The Muses are once Διὸς αἰγιόχοιο / θυγατέρες (*Il.* 2.484–85; cf. θυγατὲρ Διὸς of the Muse at *Od.* 1.10) and once κοῦραι Διὸς αἰγιόχοιο (*Il.* 2.594). Nymphs are κοῦραι Διὸς αἰγιόχοιο (*Il.* 6.420, *Od.* 6.105, 9.154). Heracles is υἱὸς Διὸς αἰγιόχοιο at *Il.* 5.396. Διὸς θυγάτηρ: *Od.* 3.337, 3.378, 13.359, 22.205, 24.502. In *Il.* 2.548, 4.128, 4.515, 7.24. Aphrodite (8.308), Artemis (20.61), and Persephone (11.217) each have this epithet once in *Od.*; Aphrodite nine times in *Il.* (3.374, 5.131, 312, 348, 820, 14.193, 224, 21.416, 23.185). Atē once (*Il.* 19.91).

her own. Although both she and Helen are by definition daughters of Zeus, Athena is functionally a goddess, and "more than any other deity Athena is always near her protégés," as here she tries to stir up Odysseus in the fight with the Suitors.⁶

In the *Odyssey*, after Book 4, Helen is called "daughter of Zeus" only once, by Penelope, who refers to her as Ἀργείη Ἑλένη, Διὸς ἐκγεγαυῖα (23.218). Again, as with Ἀργείη, so with the kinship epithet one can say that it is a matter of Helen's Iliadic identity, and in fact Penelope gives, in effect, a summary of the Trojan War. In the implicit comparison of the two heroines here, the human Penelope is the superior one.

11.3 Tyro in *Odyssey* Book 11

Besides εὐπατέρεια in the places already discussed, one in the *Iliad* and one in the *Odyssey*, this epithet occurs a third time in Book 11 of the *Odyssey*, of Tyro. She is the first in the succession of heroines encountered by Odysseus in the underworld (11.235–36):

ἔνθ' ἦ τοι πρώτην Τυρὼ ἴδον εὐπατέρειαν,
ἥ φάτο Σαλμωνῆος ἀμύμονος ἔκγονος εἶναι,

There I saw first Tyro, daughter of a noble father,
who said she was the off-spring of blameless Salmoneus.

Tyro is a central figure in Greek myth, the mother of Peleus, who led the Argonauts, and of Neleus, the father of Nestor. She comes first in Odysseus' catalogue in the *Odyssey*. She is the first woman whom Antinous mentions when he lists women of earlier times surpassed by Penelope (2.116–19).⁷

Tyro appears also in the Hesiodic *Catalogue* but not with the epithet that Odysseus uses of her. The same is true of two other women who appear in Odysseus' catalogue: Chloris, the daughter of Tyro (11.281) and Pero, the daughter of Chloris (11.287). With these three women none of the formulas coincides as between the *Odyssey* and the *Catalogue*.⁸ (How this differentiation came about is a

---

6 Burkert 1985: 141–42.
7 The women named by Antinous: Tyro, Alcmene, and Mycene. Di Benedetto 2010: 212–13 on lines 2.115ff. observes that when Antinous names Athena as the source of Penelope's mental qualities, including κέρδεα (116–18), he associates Penelope with an Athena "odisseizzata" who prides herself on exactly this trait (13.298–99).
8 As observed by Osborne 2005: 16.

separate question.) Odysseus' Tyro is clearly a catalogue heroine and the fact that she has the epithet εὐπατέρεια in the *Odyssey* suggests an explanation for the Homeric uses of this epithet of Helen.

11.4 εὐπατέρεια as a catalogue epithet

To return to the passage in the *Iliad*, the mantles that Hecuba has are ones "which god-like Alexander himself brought from Sidonia, sailing the broad sea, on the journey on which he brought back (ἀνήγαγεν) Helen, daughter of a noble father." The simplex ἤγαγε / ἠγάγετο is the normal word in the *Catalogue* for bringing home a bride (ch. 1§§6–7). Paris in this respect is the typical catalogue hero and Helen is, in Hecuba's recollection of Paris' return with her to Troy, for a moment the typical catalogue woman. These women enact the same story again and again in the *Catalogue*: "What drives the *Catalogue* along is men's inability to resist an attractive woman."[9] Helen's epithet εὐπατέρεια in the *Iliad* becomes possible to explain as a momentary, retrospective way of thinking of her. A striking example of an epithet used in this way is καλλιπάρῃος, of the middle-aged Helen at the time of the departure of Telemachus and Peisistratus (*Od.* 15.123; ch. 9§2). In the Hesiodic *Catalogue*, it is used of marriageable young women.

As a catalogue epithet, εὐπατέρεια also makes Helen human. The other women in the *Catalogue* may have a god somewhere in their family tree but not in their parents' generation. Tyro, unlike Helen, is the granddaughter, not the daughter, of a god (and the god is Aeolus, not Zeus) and the daughter of a mortal hero. It is this mortal hero to whom Odysseus implicitly refers when he calls Tyro εὐπατέρεια, and his use of this epithet would thus correspond to the narrator's at *Il.* 6.292, if, as in the interpretation of that place suggested earlier, the narrator is thinking of Tyndareus as Helen's father. If εὐπατέρεια is a poetic formation that presupposes εὐπάτωρ (attested first in Aesch. *Pers.* 970), then the word is likely to have the capacity for reference to humans, as distinguished from gods, from the beginning.[10] In *Od.* 22.227, part of Athena's rhetoric may be an implicit contrast between herself and Helen precisely with respect to divinity.

Another question concerns the appropriateness of the epithet of Salmoneus that Odysseus attributes to him, "blameless" ("who said she was the off-spring of

---

[9] Osborne 2005: 14.
[10] On this idea about the formation of εὐπατέρεια: Bader 1969: 28 n. 80 cited in *LfgrE* s.v. εὐπατέρεια. Fernández-Galiano in Russo *et al.* 1992: 22.227n says "a rare and much-discussed formation" but does not give any references.

blameless Salmoneus," 11.236). First in the Hesiodic *Catalogue of Women* and then in the later mythographic tradition Salmoneus called himself the equal of Zeus, attempted to counterfeit thunder and lightning, and received condign punishment.[11] The scholiast (H) on *Od.* 11.236 reports that some write ἀτασθάλου for ἀμύμονος:

> ἣ φάτο Σαλμωνῆος ἀτασθάλου ἔκγονος εἶναι
>
> who said she was the off-spring of presumptuous Salmoneus.

But would Tyro describe her father thus? If the reading of the received text is retained, "blameless" would be another instance of the incongruous use of this epithet, which is notoriously used of Aegisthus (*Od.* 1.29), and εὐπατέρειαν would be ironic (thus schol. ZM)–unexpectedly in the context. Another scholiastic solution, perhaps the correct one, was to say that Salmoneus became blameworthy only in later poets (QT). It happens that in the passage on Tyro in the *Catalogue of Women*, the earliest place in which Salmoneus is culpable, Tyro does not have the epithet that she has in Homer. She is here (Hes. *Cat.* fr. 30.25 M-W = 20.25 H = 27.25 M (P. Oxy. 2485)

> Τυρὼ ἐυπ]λόκαμος ἰκέλη χ[ρυσῆι Ἀφρο[δ]ίτηι
>
> fair-haired Tyro, like to golden Aphrodite.

Or she is (Hes. *Cat.* fr. 20.25 M-W (P. Oxy. 2481) = 17.25 M (not in H):

> Τυρὼ ἐυπ]λόκαμος ἰκέλη [φα]έ[εσ]σι σελήνης
>
> fair-haired Tyro, like to moon-light.

The *Catalogue* is thus, by excluding εὐπατέρεια, consistent with its account of the impiety of Salmoneus earlier in the same passage.

11.5 Another example in Odysseus' catalogue and a parallel in the *Cypria*

Earlier, Odysseus' catalogue of women in the *Odyssey* was said to differentiate itself from catalogue hexameter in the epithets for Tyro, Chloris and Pero (§2). In

---

11 For a summary of the tradition: Apollod. 1.9.7.

another place in his catalogue, however, Odysseus seems to be taking a phrase (θαῦμα βροτοῖσι) from this kind of hexameter (not necessarily from the Hesiodic *Catalogue*) and Pero is the one to whom the phrase refers. The immediate context clearly indicates the particular sphere in which she is located (11.287–88):

> τοῖσι δ' ἐπ' ἰφθίμην Πηρὼ τέκε, θαῦμα βροτοῖσι,
> τὴν πάντες μνώοντο περικτίται·
>
> After them she (Chloris) bore Pero, a wonder to mortals,
> whom all the dwellers around wooed.

Wooing is the principle activity of heroes in the *Catalogue* (μνάσθαι 10x; μνηστεύειν 3x; μνηστήρ 3x). The more important the heroine the more suitors she has. The suitors of Helen constitute a catalogue within the Hesiodic *Catalogue*.[12] Pero was not Helen but she was a woman "whom all the dwellers around wooed." (The context in the *Odyssey* is the story of Melampus' courtship of Pero on behalf of his brother.)

The phrase used by Odysseus of Pero is found in archaic hexameter elsewhere only in the *Cypria*, where it is used of Helen. (It is attested in only two other places before the Sibylline Oracles and Quintus of Smyrna.[13]) The line in the *Cypria* (fr. 9.1 B = fr. 7.1 D = fr. 10.1 W (p. 80)):[14]

> τοὺς δὲ μέτα τριτάτην Ἑλένην τέκε, θαῦμα βροτοῖσι
>
> Third after them he (or she) bore Helen, a wonder for mortals.[15]

---

12 Thus the title of Cingano 2005.
13 One is the parodos of Euripides' *Iphigeneia at Aulis*, of the hero Meriones (201–202). This place is not mentioned by Jouan 1966: 293–98 in his useful discussion of the parodos.
14 The subject of τέκε is taken to be Leda (Currie 2015: 299) or Nemesis (Parlato 2010: 292–95, following Eustathius on *Il.* 23.639; opposed by West 2013: 80 n. 22). On Eustathius: Bernabé app. crit. (second register) on fr. 9.1: "at τέκε legit Eust., qui ea de causa confudit rem...; immo subiectum Iuppiter est, quamquam tantum Pollucis pater est..., sed auctor usum formularem sequens errat, dicere volens 'post eorum ortum Iuppiter tertiam Helenam procreavit, quam Nemesis peperit', ergo nihil necesse est lacunam statuere post vers. 1..." Cf. Debiasi 2004: 113 n. 16.
15 "Them" probably refers to the Dioscouroi. The subject of τέκε is unclear.

This line bears a very close compositional resemblance to the one describing Pero in the *Odyssey* quoted above. It also bears, in meter and diction, a resemblance to the line introducing Helen's lament for Hector (24.761):[16]

τῇσι δ ἔπειθ' Ἑλένη τριτάτη ἐξῆρχε γόοιο·

Then Helen was the third to lead the women's lament.

The line in the *Cypria* can now be seen to combine two formulas:

```
     τριτάτη / -ην        τέκε, θαῦμα βροτοῖσι
       /       \            /         \
  Il. 24.761    Cypria fr. 9.1 B    Od. 11.287
```

It seems improbable that the resemblance is a matter of reference by one place to the other. Arie Hoekstra's discussion of the form Πηρώ points to an explanation.[17]

In the conclusion of his study of Homeric modifications of formular prototypes, in which he concentrated on changes made possible by quantitative metathesis and by loss of digamma, Hoekstra referred to some other sources of change. One was contraction. He took as an example –οα > –ω and he gave examples in Homer that showed a distinction between change in the history of the Greek language and the creation of look-alike's within the formular system. An example of the former is ἣ δ' ἄρα πέπλον ἑλοῦσα Θεανὼ καλλιπάρῃος ("and fair-cheeked Theano taking the robe," *Il.* 6.302), where the uncontracted *Θεανόα would scan. Πηρώ in the line quoted above is an example of the latter. This pseudo-contracted form of the name might, Hoekstra suggested, have come from a formula in which Πηρώ was once the subject. In the Hesiodic *Catalogue* Pero is in fact the subject of a sentence (she bears Talaus), although her name comes first in the line and thus fails to correspond to the formula at *Odyssey* 11.287.[18]

Hoekstra compares the formula comprising the second hemistich of this line in the *Odyssey* and of the line in the *Cypria* fragment to ἣ δὲ Διώνυσον Σεμέλη τέκε χάρμα βροτοῖσιν· ("and Semele bore Dionysus, a joy to mortals," Hom. *Il.* 14.325) and ἣ ὥς σε πρῶτον Λητὼ τέκε χάρμα βροτοῖσι ("how at first Leto bore you as a joy to mortals," *Hymn. Hom. Ap.* 25). (In the nominative Λητώ, –ω is not

---

16 Tsagalis 2004: 55–56 discusses the six single-verse introductions to lament speeches in the *Il.* and shows that, in this Iliadic context of usage, τριτάτη (24.761) replaces ἀδινοῦ. He takes the adjective to mean "third and last."
17 Hoekstra 1965: 132–33.
18 Πηρὼ δ' [ἠ]ύκομος Ταλα[ὸν... / γείνατο παῖδα Βίαντο[ς... (Hes. *Cat.* fr. 37.8–9 M-W = fr. 27.8–9 H = fr. 35.8–9 M), not cited by Hoekstra.

a contraction but a very widespread suffix used especially in the formation of women's names and still productive in Modern Greek.) Hoekstra's examples are of additional interest here because of χάρμα βροτοῖσιν. The similarity of Λητώ τέκε χάρμα βροτοῖσι to Πηρώ τέκε θαῦμα βροτοῖσι is obvious. (Hoekstra also referred to the possible associations of the formula for Leto's bearing Apollo: ὅν / τὸν ἠΰκομος τέκε Λητώ.[19]) In Hoekstra's two examples one notes that the name of the woman in the metrical slot after the masculine caesura is in the nominative. Pero could appear in either the nominative or the accusative–as the one who bore or as the one born.[20] The contrast in grammatical case between these examples and the line in the *Cypria* fragment points to the main conclusion to be drawn from Hoekstra's observations.

For those who composed these poems the grammatical ambiguity of the name was an asset. In Odysseus' catalogue Pero is the object. Likewise, in the *Cypria*, Helen is the one begotten, and for a reason.[21] The *Cypria*, for its own purposes, avails itself of a phrase and a construction with catalogue affiliations and thus offers an example of the capacity of those composing in one kind of hexameter verse to draw upon the resources of another.

11.6 Conclusion

Outside of Homer εὐπατέρεια occurs only once in archaic poetry, in Ibycus fr. S174 SLG / PMGF, which is too meager to allow identification of the subject or of the person to whom the epithet applies. It appears next in Euripides, anomalously applied to an inanimate object, the courtyard of Zeus, in the hymn to Artemis sung by Hippolytus and his followers (*Hipp.* 68).[22] But thereafter it will continue as the epithet of women divine or mortal. In the third century, Apollonius of Rhodes uses it of Artemis herself (1.570). In a fragment of Apollonius, from a poem on the founding of Naucratis, it belongs to Chesias, who was impregnated by a river and bore the beautiful Ocyroē (fr. 7 Powell, from Athenaeus 7.283e). Apollo fell in love with her–and the story goes on. Rhianus begins a poem, the subject of which is unknown, by invoking Athena as Ἀρακυνθιὰς εὐπατέρεια ("Aracynthian," after the mountain Aracynthus in Boeotia, "of noble sire," fr. 56

---

19 Hom. *Il.* 1.36, 19.413, *Od.* 11.318, *Hymn. Hom. Ap.* 178.
20 For Pero as the one who bears off-spring cf. also Ap. Rhod. *Argon.* 1.122: ἴφθιμός τε Λεώδοκος, οὓς τέκε Πηρώ.
21 I.e., because she will be part of Zeus' plan to lighten the earth of mortals. Cf. Edmunds 2016b; Sammons 2017: 35, 60, 188. See also Sammons' reconstruction of the *Cypria*: 211.
22 Barrett 1964 is silent on this word.

Powell). The Athena of the *Odyssey* would not be pleased. In the mid-second century, Moschus in the "pocket epic" *Europa* uses it of the companions of Europa, whom she gathers to accompany her to the seashore to pick flowers (29). There Zeus sees her–and the story goes on. Menander uses it of Nike (in the form εὐπάτειρα).²³ The range of those who receive the epithet, humans and goddesses, continues to expand in the Greek Anthology and in the Orphic Hymns.

In these later places women called εὐπατέρεια may be either human or divine, contrary to what seemed to be its usage in the archaic examples of Tyro, Pero, and Chloris. These archaic women are human, as are most of the women in the *Catalogue*. Of course, as between the *Odyssey* and the *Catalogue* there is also the apparently deliberate differentiation in the formulas of Tyro, Pero, and Chloris that has been noticed, an explanation for which might be multiple parallel epic traditions, in the mode of on-going composition and re-composition in performance.²⁴ Under these conditions the poets of the *Odyssey* and the *Catalogue* are neither of them drawing upon the other; both are drawing upon a preceding or contemporary body of catalogue poetry. At the same time, to try to answer the question of differentiation, they are clearly using the means at their disposal to present women in general in different lights.²⁵ They do so perhaps partly to meet expectations that come from the context of performance.²⁶ In any case, they are deliberately distinguishing themselves from each other within a shared kind of epic hexameter. It is a phenomenon seen again in the proems of the *Iliad* and of the *Cypria*, where mutual awareness can take the more precise form of allusion.²⁷

---

23 Austin 1973: frag. 151.465. This form is also found in a papyrus fragment of Euripides: Austin 1968: frag. 81.8.
24 Heubeck in Heubeck and Hoekstra 1989: 11.235–59n: "The poet of the *Ehoiai*, like the poet of the *Odyssey*, drew his material from old epic tradition, but also had 235–59 before him." (Heubeck thus partly combines an oralist and a "scripsist" view of the matter.) The question of the authenticity of the catalogue passage in the *Odyssey*, on which see Heubeck 225–332n, is a separate one.
25 Irwin 2005: 49.
26 Irwin 2005 argues for the symposium as a performance context for the *Catalogue*.
27 Edmunds 2016b.

12 Reflections on Kinship Epithets and Epithets of Beauty

The approach to Helen's epithets taken in this monograph has been synchronic, for reasons given in the Introduction. For the most part, synchronic, i.e., contextual, meaning has emerged, more or less specific to a single context. To repeat, from the Preface, Hainsworth's dictum: "relevance and redundancy [of formulas] are the ends of a spectrum." At the same time, the synchronic approach has shown some oddities, in particular when Helen shares an epithet with another woman or goddess with whom she has nothing else in common. These non-functional similarities escape synchronic explanation. At this point, what Joshua Katz has called "the mantra of the historical linguist" applies: "if you encounter a synchronic oddity, search for a diachronic explanation."[1] The second half of this chapter (§2) undertakes an explanation of this kind.

12.1 The synchronic dimension

Brief surveys of Helen's epithets of beauty (§1.1; cf. also conclusion to ch. 7) and of her kinship epithets follow (§1.2). Her epithets of beauty are compared with those in the Hesiodic *Catalogue* (§1.1.1) Some conclusions follow each of these discussions.

12.1.1 Epithets of beauty

Helen has four epithets of beauty (ἠΰκομος, καλλίκομος, καλλιπάρῃος, λευκώλενος), not including Hector's oblique reference to her as εὐειδής (3.48).[2] Their connotations differ considerably and for the most part it is possible to explain how they are relevant in the contexts in which they occur. But the characters do not do or saying anything that reflects their sense of her as beautiful. The old men's reaction to the sight of Helen is not an exception to this rule. When they say that Helen is "terribly like the immortal goddesses to look upon" (αἰνῶς ἀθανάτῃσι θεῇς εἰς ὦπα ἔοικεν 3.158; cf. ch. 7 intro.), they are only saying somewhat more

---

[1] Katz 2010: 360; Katz 2013a: 173; Katz 2013b: 90.
[2] It is a catalogue epithet and is not intended in this context as praise of Helen. Catalogic: Krieter-Spiro 2009: 32 on line 48.

copiously what is said of Briseïs (ἐϊκυῖα θεῇσι, 19.286) and of other women.³ (Briseïs and other women are also "like to golden Aphrodite.")⁴ Only once is Helen said or implied to be the most beautiful woman: the reparation offered to Achilles by Agamemnon includes twenty Trojan women who are "most beautiful after Helen" (9.140 = 282).

Tab. 8: Helen's epithets of beauty

Helen	Frequency	Speaker(s)
εὐειδής	1x *Il.*	Hector
ἠΰκομος	7x *Il.*	narrator 6x, Achilles 1x
καλλίκομος	1x *Od.*	narrator
καλλιπάρῃος	1x *Od.*	narrator
λευκώλενος	1x *Il.*, 1x *Od.*	narrator, Athena
τανύπεπλος	1x *Il.*, 2x *Od.*	narrator

As for Helen's beauty as the cause of the war, in the story presupposed by the *Iliad* she was promised, as the most beautiful woman in the world, to Paris by Aphrodite at the time of the Judgment. The war is going on, however, because Helen has been abducted and is in Troy, not because she is beautiful. The old truism that "[l]a beauté d'Hélène est la cause de la guerre" should be abandoned.⁵ Thus Menelaus prays to Zeus for vengeance, which will be an example to men in the future of what happens to those who violate guest-friendship (3.351–54).⁶ He rebukes the Trojans for their defiance of Zeus Xenios in their stealing of his wedded wife and many possessions (13.622–27). In other words, the one who has caused the war that the Achaeans are fighting is Paris. It is not Helen. From Achilles' point of view it is a

---

3 E.g., of Castianeira (8.305); of Hecamede (11.638). For a survey of instances: Kelly 2007: Lexicon #152 ("Goddess similes"). For the relation of the comparison to πῆμα (3.161) and for the contrast with other places in which a woman is compared to a goddess or a named goddess: Ready 2011: 110–13.
4 ἰκέλη χρυσέῃ Ἀφροδίτῃ, 19.282; also of Cassandra (24.699); of Tyro (fr. 30.25 M-W = 20.25 H = 27.25 M).
5 Monsacré 1984: 132.
6 Even in his version of the Trojan War (Helen not at Troy) Herodotus finds that the destruction of Troy (in spite of the fact that the Trojans did not have Helen) was a lesson for mankind that great punishments come from the gods for great crimes (such as the violation of hospitality) (2.120.5).

matter of honor. Achilles says that the Achaeans are at Troy to oblige Agamemnon "and to win honor for you and Menelaus" (τιμή, 1.159).[7] In Book 17, Menelaus says that Patroclus died for his honor (τιμή, 17.92; cf. 5.550–53).[8]

Comparison of the two epithets referring to Helen's hair shows the different function of epithets that are apparently semantically synonymous, "having beautiful hair," but in the formulas in which they appear have different meanings. καλλίκομος refers to sexual attractiveness in private contexts (ch. 9§1). ἠΰκομος refers to a woman's beauty as part of her public identity. Two other epithets λευκώλενος (ch. 8) and καλλιπάρῃος (ch. 9) also have in their formulaic usage what might be called a second-order semantics which could not be predicted from their lexical definitions. The second of these epithets is, however, difficult to explain as applied to Theano and to Helen.

Epithets of beauty in the Hesiodic *Catalogue*

The following brief comparison of Helen's epithets for beauty with those in the Hesiodic catalogue proceeds on the assumption that, even if this poem post-dates the Homeric poems, its diction continues a catalogue tradition that would have been known to those who composed the Homeric poems.

In the generally accepted sequence of the papyrus fragments in which it survives, the *Catalogue* ends with the wooing of Helen and a vision of the end of the heroes.[9] Helen is not, then, just another sexually attractive woman whom men desire, like the women in the rest of the poem.[10] Two of her six epithets are readily understood as belonging to a larger epochal plan, ἠΰκομος (5x) and Ἀργείη (4x), both of them also Homeric but with differing implications. These two epithets

---

[7] Cf. 10.27–28, of Menelaus: Ἀργεῖοι, τοὶ δὴ ἕθεν εἵνεκα πουλὺν ἐφ' ὑγρὴν / ἤλυθον ἐς Τροίην πόλεμον θρασὺν ὁρμαίνοντες "The Argives, who, on account of him, came over much water to Troy, rushing on fierce war."

[8] In these places honor might mean either material recompense (in the first place Helen and all the possessions stolen by Paris: cf. 3.67–70) or the standing that Menelaus in particular has lost (cf. *LfgrE* s.v. τιμή B1b) or both (cf. L-N-S 2000: 79–80 on lines 159–60).

[9] It is the arrangement of M-W, which is explained by West 1985: 31–50; cf. Cingano 2005: 120–21; Cingano 2009: 112–116; Ormand 2014: 182–84. Cingano 2009: 120–21 discusses doubts concerning the Merkelbach and West arrangement. Fragments published after their edition of 1967 are integrated in Merkelbach and West 1990³.

[10] For this plot: Osborne 2005: 13–14: "What drives the *Catalogue* along is men's inability to resist an attractive woman. Women appear and gods and men fall for them...That is the basic narrative without which there would be nothing to hold the *Catalogue* together..." Cf. Tsagalis 2012: 164 for the formulas related to the themes of marriage and lovemaking; Aguirre Castro 2005.

make Helen already, *before* she has married Menelaus, the Helen of the Trojan War. In Hesiod's *Works and Days*, the first of these epithets attaches to her implicitly in her role in the end of the heroes (165). As for the *Catalogue*, her suitors do not know that they are doomed by their attraction to the fair-haired Helen and by the oath that they swear.[11] The other four epithets used of Helen in the *Catalogue* are used of her nowhere else: καλλίσφυρος (2x), τανίσφυρος (1x), κυανῶπις (1x), and εὐώλενος (1x). She also bears the name Ἀργειώνη (2x), not attested of her elsewhere.[12] But the epithets just mentioned are used of other women besides Helen both in the *Catalogue* and elsewhere. They make Helen a typical *Catalogue* heroine, characterized above all by beauty and sexual attractiveness, at the same time that she has her ominous role in the history of the heroes.[13]

Tab. 9: Helen's epithets of beauty in Homer compared with those in Hesiod, *Cypria* and lyric (App. 4). Double parentheses indicate dubious fragments.

Homer	Hes. *OD*	Hes. *Cat.*	*Cypria*	Lyric
ἠΰκομος	v	v	((of Demeter))	
καλλιπάρῃος		(of other women)		
καλλίκομος		(of another woman)	(of Nemesis)	
λευκώλενος		(of other women)		
τανύπεπλος				
(of other women)		καλλίσφυρος		
		τανίσφυρος		
		κυανῶπις	((of Electra))	
		εὐώλενος		
(of Pero)		cf. θαῦμα ἰδέσθαι, ἰδ[εῖν] (of other women)	θαῦμα βροτοῖσι	
		(of other women)		ἑλικῶπις
		(of other women)		καλλιπλόκαμος
		(of another woman)		ξανθά / ξάνθα
				ὑψίκομος

---

11 Cingano 2005: 126 and n.30.
12 To whom it refers at Hes. *Cat.* fr. 217.6 M-W = 102.6 H = 160.6 M is unclear but it is not Helen.
13 Koning 2017: 105: "As the catalyst for the Trojan War, she is an agent of Zeus' will, playing a role that is rather unique in terms of divine determination: no other heroines in the poem seem to be specifically conceived to fulfill some kind of destiny."

These observations on Helen's epithets of beauty in the Hesiodic *Catalogue* lead to the conclusion that the Homeric poems have differentiated their Helen from the Hesiodic one.

12.1.2 Kinship epithets

The epithets that refer to Helen as the daughter of Zeus characterize her in the same way as the epithets of beauty, outside the cognizance of the other characters. It is striking that in the *Iliad* only the narrator knows that Helen is the daughter of Zeus. No other character betrays any knowledge of this fact nor, for that matter, does Helen herself. In the *Odyssey*, Penelope uses Διὸς ἐκγεγαυῖα of Helen. At this point, Helen is a "historical" figure and the epithet looks to her old-time identity (ch. 10§5). Again in the *Odyssey*, Menelaus has learned, if he did not already know, of Helen's parentage. Proteus tells him (*Od.* 4.561–69):

> σοὶ δ' οὐ θέσφατόν ἐστι, διοτρεφὲς ὦ Μενέλαε,
> Ἄργει ἐν ἱπποβότῳ θανέειν καὶ πότμον ἐπισπεῖν,
> ἀλλά σ' ἐς Ἠλύσιον πεδίον καὶ πείρατα γαίης
> ἀθάνατοι πέμψουσιν, ὅθι ξανθὸς Ῥαδάμανθυς,–
> τῇ περ ῥηΐστη βιοτὴ πέλει ἀνθρώποισιν·
> οὐ νιφετός, οὔτ' ἂρ χειμὼν πολὺς οὔτε ποτ' ὄμβρος,
> ἀλλ' αἰεὶ ζεφύροιο λιγὺ πνείοντος ἀήτας
> Ὠκεανὸς ἀνίησιν ἀναψύχειν ἀνθρώπους,–
> οὕνεκ' ἔχεις Ἑλένην καί σφιν γαμβρὸς Διὸς ἐσσι.

> For you, Zeus-fostered Menelaus, it is not ordained
> that you die in horse-raising Argos and meet your fate,
> but the immortals will send you to the Elysian plain and ends of the earth,
> where yellow-haired Rhadamanthys is–
> there life is very easy for mortals.
> There is no snow, nor heavy storm, nor rain ever,
> but the breezes of the sharp-blowing west wind
> Ocean continually sends to revive men–
> because you have Helen and in their eyes you are the son-in-law of Zeus.

Thus Menelaus to Telemachus in the course of his long reply to Telemachus' request for news of his father. It is the morning after the day of the visitor's arrival and the feast in his and Peisistratus' honor. At no point in the narrative, however, does Menelaus show any recognition of Helen as the daughter of Zeus. From his point of view she is simply his wife (4.148, 266; 15.93).

In calling Helen the daughter of Zeus, the narrator brings out something that is a given of the archaic vulgate, but in the system of epithets inherited by the

Iliad and the *Odyssey* something to be sorted out. The same can be said concerning the blame of Helen, as in the "on account of" phrase that encapsulates the archaic vulgate. For the narrator of the *Iliad* and the *Odyssey*, the blame can be assumed to be a given but he puts it in Helen's own words in impressive speeches that undoubtedly characterize her more fully than ever before.

Probably most scholars would agree with the view expressed by Wolfgang Kullmann, who contrasted characterization in Cyclic Epic and in Homer, minimal in one, fuller in the other.[14] Further, in the *Iliad*, he said, there is extraordinary differentiation in the depiction of persons, who have a new inwardness (*Verinnerlichung*).[15] He gives Helen as an example. "Homer describes...what is going on with the abducted Helen of the [pre-Iliadic] saga. The recklessness of the woman, who lets herself be seduced, is transformed into disappointment, but disappointment leads in turn to the consolidation of personality. In suffering, Helen has a new life."[16] He points to direct speech in particular as a means of transposing the fact into the psychological (*Psychische*).

Tab. 10: Helen's kinship epithets: frequency, distribution and speaker(s)

Helen	Frequency	Speaker(s)
Διὸς ἐκγεγαυῖα	2x *Il.*, 3x *Od.*	narrator, Penelope (1x)
Διὸς θυγάτηρ	1x *Od.*	narrator
εὐπατέρεια	1x *Il.*, 1x *Od.*	narrator (1x), Athena (1x)
κούρη Διός	1x *Il.*	narrator

Zeus as father of Helen in the Hesiodic *Catalogue*

Zeus is not said in any undisputed fragment of the *Catalogue* to be Helen's father nor does she have a kinship epithet in this poem. He can be assumed to be her father, however, and to have sired her for the same reason as in the *Cypria*.[17] So the juxtaposition of her marriage to Menelaus and Zeus' disruption of life on earth

---

14 Kullmann 1960: 382–88.
15 Taplin 1992: 11 reckons that there are over thirty characters in Homer who are "recognizably individualized...with consistent attributes and life-stories."
16 "Homer schildert...was mit der geraubten Helena der [pre-Iliadic] Sage vor sich geht: Der Leichtsinn der Frau, die sich verführen ließ, schlägt in Enttäuschung um, die Enttäuschung führt aber wieder zur Festigung der Persönlichkeit; im Leid wächst Helena wieder."
17 See ch. 11§5 and n. 14.

indicates (see §1.1.1 *init.* above). As for her mother, in a scholium on Pindar *Nemean* 10 she is said to be the daughter of Zeus and an Oceanid. West regarded this scholium as untrustworthy.[18] As it happens, there is a fragment of the *Catalogue* that lists three daughters of Leda and Tyndareus, Timandra, Clytemestra, and Phylonoe and does not include Helen.[19] Hirschberger combined this fragment with the scholium on the Oceanid, although she did not count the latter as a fragment of the *Catalogue*, taking the scholium as the explanation for Leda's having three, not four, daughters. She observed that the capacity for shape-changing shown by Nemesis, the eventual mother of Helen in the *Cypria*, would fit well with an Oceanid. Other sea creatures, Thetis and Proteus, have this capacity. If Nemesis bore an egg that later came into the possession of, and was hatched by, Leda, the Oceanid might also have borne an egg from which Helen emerged.[20] Leda would then be only the nominal mother of Helen (and Tyndareus would of course be her nominal father). But whoever Helen's mother in the *Catalogue* is, Helen has the role that she has because she is the daughter of Zeus, even if she has no kinship epithets in this poem.

12.2 The diachronic dimension

Some of Helen's epithets of beauty suggest similarities between her and other women who have the same epithets, similarities that are in fact non-functional. These pseudo-resemblances can be explained on the hypothesis of a Homeric redistribution of an inherited stock of epithets for women. Likewise, the kinship epithets that Helen shares with goddesses point not to her similarity to them but to her difference.[21] These epithets, too, can be assumed to have been inherited and again a synchronic redistribution, which can be shown to be quite deliberate, has taken place.

---

18 West 1985: 123 and n. 211 on fr. 24 M-W = fr. 21 M (not in H): "We cannot regard this isolated testimonium as trustworthy."
19 fr. 23a.7–10 M-W = fr. 15.7–10 H = 19.7–10 M.
20 H: 207–208 (on her fr. 15).
21 Nagy 2016a: §2: "...[T]he dominant gene in the genetic code of ancient Greek mythmaking is mortality while the recessive gene is immortality,...In other words, if the family tree that produced you includes even one solitary mortal ancestor, that will be enough to make you mortal as well—no matter how many immortal ancestors grace your genealogy..."

12.2.1 Epithets of beauty

The epithet ἠΰκομος as used of Helen in the *Iliad* has clear parallels in Hesiod, both in the *Works and Days* and in the *Catalogue*. Such correspondences have been explained in various ways.[22] Borrowing or quoting seems the least likely explanation. The Homeric epics are more plausibly seen as drawing upon a shared store of epithets, as also in the case of καλλιπάρῃος (ch. 9), where, however, specifically catalogic verse may lie in the background. The epithet καλλίκομος (ch. 9) might have suggested the same background but it is used of Helen's mother in the *Cypria*. If λευκώλενος was once a "generic epithet of women," as it might have been, it has been pointedly distributed among women in the *Iliad* and as between the *Iliad* and the *Odyssey* (ch. 8).

12.2.2 Kinship epithets

Helen has four kinship epithets, one of which is εὐπατέρεια (see intro. to this chapter). None of the other three (Διὸς ἐκγεγαυῖα, Διὸς θυγάτηρ, κούρη Διός) is used exclusively of Helen.[23] The principle of differentiation is less obvious than with the epithets of beauty, but Διὸς ἐκγεγαυῖα, used of Helen five times, is almost uniquely hers. It is the first kinship epithet that she has in the *Iliad* (2x) and the first in the *Odyssey* (2x). Penelope's use of this epithet of Helen (*Od.* 23.218) can be considered "historical," as suggested above. Athena has this epithet once and she is the only one besides Helen who has it. The kinship epithets show several minimal overlaps of this kind, as between goddesses and Helen and as between goddesses.

Differentiation between Aphrodite and Athena is clear. The former goddess is Διὸς θυγάτηρ in the *Iliad* (8x *Il.*, 1x *Od.*). The latter is κούρη Διὸς αἰγιόχοιο in the *Odyssey* (10x and exclusively of Athena). By an implicit principle of exclusion concerning these epithets, Helen can receive the principal epithet of Aphrodite

---
22 See Edmunds 2016b: 1–2.
23 Their distribution is as follows. (1) Διὸς θυγάτηρ: Aphrodite (8x *Il.*, 1x *Od.*); Athena (3x *Il.*, 3x *Od.*); Persephone (1x *Od.*); the Muses (1x *Il.*); Ἄτη (1x *Il.*); Helen (1x *Od.*). (2) κούρη Διὸς αἰγιόχοιο: Athena (2x *Il.*, 10x *Od.* [exclusively of Athena]), Helen (1x *Il.*). The Muses (1x *Il.*) and nymphs (1x *Il.*, 4x *Od.*) are called κοῦραι Διὸς αἰγιόχοιο. Cf. other kinship epithets entailing Zeus' epithet: (2a) θυγάτηρ Διὸς αἰγιόχοιο: Athena (1x); a Muse (1x). The Muses (1x *Il.*) are called Διὸς αἰγιόχοιο / θυγατέρες. (2b) αἰγιόχοιο Διὸς τέκος: Athena (8x *Il.*, 2x *Od.* [4.762 = 6.324, a formulaic line]); Apollo (1x). There is also θυγάτηρ Διός without Zeus' epithet: Athena (2x *Od.* 22.205 =24.502, a formulaic line). (3) Διὸς ἐκγεγαυῖα: Helen (2x *Il.*, 3x *Od.*); Athena (1x *Od.*).

or Athena only in the poem in which this epithet is not used of the goddess. Thus Διὸς θυγάτηρ (Aphrodite in the *Iliad*) is used of Helen once in the *Odyssey*, and κούρη Διὸς αἰγιόχοιο (Athena in the *Odyssey*) is used of Helen once in the *Iliad*. There are some overlaps as between the two goddesses but the main difference stands. The two epithets just mentioned are, with Helen, nominative expedients in a predominantly nominative system, the first bringing the first hemistich to the penthemimeral caesura, the second comprising the second hemistich after that caesura.

With the two epithets just discussed, Helen seems to be a borrower. To return to Διὸς ἐκγεγαυῖα, one can add that the form ἐκγεγαυῖα does not occur in Homer outside this formula and for this reason it looks as if, in its nonce use of Athena, the goddess has borrowed it from Helen. From the distribution of Διὸς θυγάτηρ and of κούρη Διὸς αἰγιόχοιο in Homer, however, it looks as if Helen has borrowed one from Aphrodite and the other from Athena and one has to ask if also in the case of Διὸς ἐκγεγαυῖα Helen is really the borrower, the *Iliad* and the *Odyssey* happening to conceal the fact. ἐκγεγαυῖα is unique only in these epics, not in the wider ambit of archaic hexameter. Hesiod calls the Muses "nine daughters born from great Zeus" (ἐννέα θυγατέρες μεγάλου Διὸς ἐκγεγαυῖαι, *Theog.* 76) and Dikē has the epithet "born from Zeus" (Διὸς ἐκγεγαυῖα, *Op.* 256). These places suggest a wider diffusion of the epithet that the Homeric poems happen not to attest.

A more likely hypothesis is that all of these kinship epithets have already been neutralized or rather indifferently distributed in the tradition from which the Homeric poems draw and have then been somewhat systematically redistributed. It has been suggested, with reference to the epic comparanda, that Διὸς θυγάτηρ in Alcaeus fr. 206.1 V (the referent is unclear) is the trace of Indo-European poetic language.[24] If so, it is all the more likely that this epithet in its many centuries of use would have attached itself to more than one goddess. Olav Hackstein offers a picture of "a cumulation of (quasi) synonymous formulae" that "attests to the semantic bleaching of formulae, which over the course of time underwent routinization, generalization, and automatization, a natural process observable already in the *Iliad* and the *Odyssey*."[25] (His chronological assumption concerning the date of the Homeric epics is beside the point here.) To Hackstein's picture must be added the notion of these epics as new, even if not completely perfect, instantiations of the formulas as a differential system.

Helen can be seen as needy and the borrower on the hypothesis that she has an importance in the Homeric epics that she did not have in Cyclic Epic. One can

---

24 Naafs-Wilstra 1987: item 7.
25 Hackstein 2010: 418.

compare Patroclus. Observing the inappropriateness of the apostrophes to him (*Il.* 16.20, 744) and the fact that he has no formular expression in the nominative, Hoekstra surmised that in "a stage not much anterior to the composition of the *Iliad*, Menoitios' son was only a character of secondary importance, known not for what he did but for his friendship with Achilles and his death."[26] One can also compare Heracles. If there was a Heracles epic, then it must have been important that Zeus was his father. If a fully declinable periphrasis for his name (βίη + adj. form of Heracles) survives in archaic epic, as in fact it does, then one might have expected, when he is called the son of Zeus, that he would have his own epithet.[27] In the *Iliad*, however, he is "the son of aegis-bearing Zeus" (υἱὸς Διὸς αἰγιόχοιο, *Il.* 5.396). It is a masculine variant of Athena's κούρη Διὸς αἰγιόχοιο: Athena (2x *Il.*, 10x *Od.* [exclusively of Athena]). Helen, to repeat, has the same epithet once. Both Helen and Heracles seem to be borrowers.

To discuss one further example, Memnon, the son of Tithonus and Eos, is mentioned for the first time in the *Odyssey* with a matronymic (4.188), as Patroclus is mentioned for the first time in the *Iliad* with a patronymic (*Il.* 1.307)—Memnon more plausibly than Patroclus (if Hoekstra is right about Patroclus' history), because Memnon was one of the main heroes of the *Aethiopis*—and the second time with his name (*Od.* 11.522).[28] Memnon has the epithet ἀγλαός. He is the "glorious son" of Eos, as Peisistratus is the "glorious son" of Nestor (*Od.* 4.21, 103; 15.144). This adonean-shaped line-final epithet is used in the *Iliad* also of Eurypylus (5x), Pandarus (7x), Sthenelus (1x), and Antilochus (2x). The epithet is, then, a very convenient one for someone who is referred to as someone's son. The fact that both Antilochus, who was slain by Memnon, and Antilochus' brother Peisistratus have this epithet might suggest a deliberate use of the Iliadic and Odyssean system of epithets, a pointed reminder, when it is used of Memnon, of his connection to the family of Nestor. In any case, no matter what his prominence in the *Aethiopis*, Memnon has not, any more than Heracles, brought any distinctive epithet with him.

Whether or not Helen is in fact the borrower of ἐκγεγαυῖα, it is clear that her kinship epithets are a way of accommodating her to the new version of the Trojan

---

26 Hoekstra 1965: 139.
27 The periphrasis: Nagy 1999[1979]: 318.
28 An example not discussed here is Menelaus, whose various martial epithets emphasize a quality for which he is not conspicuous except in Book 17. For a survey of his epithets: Rousseau 1990: 325–27. For his single combat with Paris in Book 3, which, as a formal trial of arms, is to be distinguished from other instances of single combat, see Rousseau 1990: 346–47. These epithets could be explained (*pace* Rousseau) as attaching to Menelaus in other hexameter verse on the Trojan War and somewhat inconsistently continued in the *Il.*

War story in the *Iliad* and the *Odyssey*. While she was already the daughter of Zeus in the archaic vulgate, from which the narrator of the *Iliad* distances himself already in the prooemium, she was only Zeus' means to a further end and apparently the diction neither of the specific Iliadic tradition nor of the broader hexameter tradition provided the composer of the *Iliad* with good resources for his purposes.[29] To the "realism" of the other characters in their attitude toward Helen he had to oppose her particular eminent status, for which he had to find the appropriate epithets. To repeat, the narrator never uses the "on account of" motif that appears again and again in versions of the archaic vulgate, and through Priam he introduces immediately the question of Helen's culpability. Her own view of the matter can be inferred– indeed has to be inferred–from her use of epithets of opprobrium of herself.

12.3 Conclusion

In both the *Iliad* and the *Catalogue* Helen has five epithets of beauty. The one that the two poems have in common is ἠΰκομος, used of her also in *Works and Days*. It refers to Helen as the one over whom the war is fought, with implications that differ according to context and, in the case of Achilles in the *Iliad*, according to speaker. Ἀργείη, in both the *Iliad* and the *Catalogue*, looks to Helen in the same sense. The four epithets of beauty used of her only in the *Catalogue* (but not exclusively of her in this poem), καλλίσφυρος, τανίσφυρος, κυανῶπις, and εὐώλενος, make her a typical heroine and at the same time look to her larger role in the archaic vulgate.

Helen's epithets of beauty seem, as lexical items, to be synonyms but they are differentiated in Homer and have different meanings according to their contexts. Likewise, her kinship epithets seem to be synonyms but have been shown to observe a differentiation between her and the goddesses with whom she shares these epithets. For both of these sets of epithets their meaning comes from their use in the *Iliad* and the *Odyssey* and is not determined by their undoubted origin in earlier hexameter. Thus the point made in the Introduction to this monograph concerning the diachronic as a signifier, not a signified, is borne out. In fact, as

---

29 On the archaic vulgate and the prooemium to the *Il.*: Edmunds 2016b.

the similarities between Helen and other women sometimes created by the epithets of beauty have shown, the diachronic can be the source of an apparent but misleading signification.³⁰

Neither of these sets of epithets is functional in the narratives of the two epics. No character in the *Iliad* or the *Odyssey* does or says anything because Helen is beautiful.³¹ (For the old men on the wall see §1.1 above. For Achilles' statement that he is fighting Ἑλένης ἕνεκ' ἠϋκόμοιο (9.339): Ch.7§7. For λευκώλενος in Athena's rhetoric: ch. 8§1.) No character in the *Iliad* or the *Odyssey* does or says anything because Helen is the daughter of Zeus. (For Penelope, an apparent exception to this rule, see §1.2 above). The inspired narrator, however, provides a higher perspective on events and characters, as indicated in the Introduction (p. 2). The narrator tells the audience something about Helen that the characters do not know.³² In this perspective, to be discussed in the Conclusion, the epithets of Helen have a function in the narrative.

---

30 To this extent, i.e., to the extent that the epithets of Helen are relevant to the question of the diachronic, one must agree with Jahn 1987: 225 n. 21: "jeder Schritt über die synchrone Ebene hinaus einem Schritt ins Leere gleichkommt."
31 Neither of the epic sources for the Judgment of Paris refers to the beauty of Helen: *Il.* 24.29–30; *Cypria* Arg. 4–9 B = 5–12 D = Arg. 1d; F 8 W (pp. 83–85).
32 In narratological terms, the narrator is the primary focalizer. See Nünlist and de Jong 2000: 163 s.v. "Fokalisator."

13 Conclusion

In *Epistles* 1.2 Horace writes from Praeneste to Maximus Lollius, a young man practicing oratory in Rome. Themes drawn from Homer are apparently Lollius' subject matter.[1] At the same time, Horace is rereading Homer, who provides more useful moral lessons, he says, than do the philosophers Chrysippus and Crantor. The lesson of the *Iliad* is negative:[2]

> Fabula, qua Paridis propter narratur amorem
> Graecia barbariae lento conlisa duello,
> stultorum regum et populorum continet aestum.
> Antenor censet belli praecidere causam:
> quid Paris? ut saluus regnet uiuatque beatus
> cogi posse negat. Nestor componere lites
> inter Pelidem festinat et inter Atriden;
> hunc amor, ira quidem communiter urit utrumque.
> quidquid delirant reges, plectuntur Achiui.
> seditione, dolis, scelere atque libidine et ira
> Iliacos intra muros peccatur et extra.
>
> *Epist.* 1.2.6–16

> The story in which, on account of Paris's love, it is told that Greece is wasted in a tedious war with the barbarians, contains the tumult of foolish kings and peoples. Antenor gives his opinion for cutting off the cause of the war. What does Paris do? He cannot be brought to comply, even if he may reign safely and live happily. Nestor strives to bring to an end the quarrel between Achilles and Agamemnon. Love inflames the first, anger both of them equally. Whatever the derangement of their kings, the Achaeans take the punishment. Because of sedition, guile, wickedness and lust and anger—inside and outside the walls of Troy wrong is done.

To the *Iliad* so conceived Horace opposes the positive moral teaching of the *Odyssey* (17–31). Helen is not mentioned but the war is taking place *Paridis propter amorem* (1) and Helen is the reason for Paris' refusal to end it (7.362–64; ch. 1§5).[3] No doubt *libido* refers to the passion that Aphrodite inspired in her and that she inspired in Paris.

---

[1] Kiessling-Heinze 1957: 24 *ad loc.*
[2] The text given here follows that of Mayer 1994.
[3] At the Trojan assembly in book 7, in response to Antenor's proposal that Helen and the possessions be returned to the Achaeans (347–53), Paris offers to return the possessions but not "the woman" (354–64), without explanation, and Priam supports Paris, without explanation (368–78).

The *Iliad*, in the figure of Thersites, contains its own awareness of the possibility of a Horatian reception and, in Odysseus' chastisement of him, a defense of the leaders, especially Agamemnon, Achilles, and Odysseus himself, against his blame (2.212–77).⁴ It is unlikely, further, that a Greek audience of the *Iliad* would agree with Horace that both sides in the conflict were equally reprehensible. Menelaus expects divine sanction. As he faces Paris in combat in Book 3, he prays to Zeus for vengeance: it would be an example to men in the future of what happens to those who violate guest-friendship (3.351–54). Again, Menelaus rebukes the Trojans for their defiance of Zeus Xenios in their stealing of his wedded wife and many possessions (13.622–27). Even in his version of the Trojan War (Helen not at Troy) Herodotus finds that the destruction of Troy (in spite of the fact that the Trojans did not have Helen) was a lesson for mankind that great punishments come from the gods for great crimes (such as the violation of hospitality) (2.120.5). The Achaean cause is also principled. Achilles says that the Achaeans are at Troy to oblige Agamemnon and "to win honor for you and Menelaus" (τιμή, 1.159).⁵ Menelaus says that Patroclus died for his honor (τιμή, 17.92; cf. 5.550–53).⁶

Helen, too, is the object of blame and again the *Iliad* countenances, but does not grant, a Horatian interpretation of the action. She says that all the Trojans shudder at her (24.775) and it is clear that vilification is what she means (cf. 767–71). When Aphrodite summons her to return from the wall of Troy to Paris, she fears blame (Τρῳαὶ δέ μ' ὀπίσσω / πᾶσαι μωμήσονται, "all the Trojan women will blame me hereafter," 3.411–12). The self-blame heard in her speeches can be interpreted as a pre-emption of the blame that she fears and suffers from the Trojans (ch. 2 *init*.).⁷ She also expects blame from the Achaeans. When she does not see her brothers, the Dioscouroi, from the wall of Troy, she imagines that they have not entered the battle because they fear (to hear) the vilification and reproaches that are hers (αἴσχεα δειδιότες καὶ ὀνείδεα πόλλ' ἅ μοί ἐστιν, 3.242). In fact the only Achaean who uses a term of opprobrium of her is Achilles (ῥιγεδανή, 19.325; ch. 2§3).

---

4 See B-S-V 2003: 2.211–24n.
5 Cf. 10.27–28, of Menelaus: Ἀργεῖοι, τοὶ δὴ ἔθεν εἵνεκα πουλὺν ἐφ' ὑγρὴν / ἤλυθον ἐς Τροίην πόλεμον θρασὺν ὁρμαίνοντες "The Argives, who, on account of him, came over much water to Troy, rushing on fierce war."
6 In these places honor might mean either material recompense (in the first place Helen and all the possessions stolen by Paris: cf. 3.67–70) or the standing that Menelaus in particular has lost (cf. *LfgrE* s.v. τιμή B1b) or both (cf. L-N-S 2000: 79–80 on lines 159–60).
7 Ebbott 1999: 20 concludes: "Thus, the blame that Helen speaks is not just an internal one–shame–but, more importantly, she gives voice to the external blame, the nemesis, that her deeds provoke but that is otherwise unspoken in the *Iliad*."

Against Helen as an object of blame must be set the narrator's epithets for her. The narrator is the source of almost all of her epithets of beauty and her kinship epithets. They often occur in places in which they contrast his and the characters' points of view. Theirs often originate in various familial, social, or pragmatic conceptions of her. The narrator knows more than the characters do and in effect corrects them. While Parry evoked the "principle that the epithet adorns all epic poetry rather than a single line," Helen's epithets have particular functions in the places in which they occur.[8] Parry's words seem to anticipate "traditional referentiality" (Introduction, p. 11), a concept that blurs these functions.

Helen in the narrator's, and thus the audience's, perspective is a worthy object of the struggles of the heroes. She herself looks forward to fame in the future when she says to Hector that Zeus has sent an evil destiny upon her and Paris in order that they might be sung of by men in the future (*Il.* 6.344–58). She has something like this stature already in her lifetime, as can be seen in Telemachus' report to his mother concerning his visit to Sparta (*Od.* 17.118) and in Penelope's reflections on Helen (*Od.* 23.218–221; ch. 10§5). Hélène Monsacré concluded a survey of the subordinate position of women in the *Iliad* with a speculation on the special status of Helen:

> While it is fair to suggest that the close relationship and consubstantial status of Andromache and Penelope with their husbands allow for a certain circulation of masculine values, Helen is the only heroine who does not owe her renown to her husband. In the *Iliad*, Helen is situated beyond the conjugal relationship, and this is, perhaps, what makes her a heroic figure.[9]

While Helen in the narratives of the two epics is at any moment pragmatically a wife and nothing else (ch. 1), she has twice been able to leave and enter (or in the case of Menelaus reenter) the marital relationship and to this extent is "beyond" it. Paris' name is amplified by the formula "husband of fair-haired Helen" (ch.7§1); his prestige is increased by his marriage to her. Her special status is seen also in her motherhood. She has no child by Paris. Further, her relationship with her only child, Hermione, fails to characterize her as mother. In the *Iliad* Helen refers to her once (3.175; but cf. 139–40, where Hermione could have been mentioned but is not). In the *Odyssey*, at the beginning of Book 4, Menelaus is holding a feast to celebrate the marriages of his daughter and his bastard son Megapenthes. It is explained that Helen had no children after Hermione, who is named for

---

8 Parry 1971[1928]: 138. Parry 1971[1928b]: 249 "only…an added quality of epic nobility."
9 Monsacré 2018: concl. of II.3 = Monsacré 1984: 133.

the first and last time (4.12b–14). The wedding feast is then forgotten in the account of the arrival of Telemachus and Peisistratus and replaced by a feast in their honor.[10] Hermione is forgotten, except that Helen refers to her, without naming her, at the end of her speech about Odysseus in Troy (4.263). Although in the *Odyssey* they have been living under the same roof, the relationship between Helen and Hermione is a blank. Helen stands outside both the marital and the parental relationships. Monsacré's speculation applies to both.

While Helen, unlike Penelope (*Od.* 24.196–97), cannot expect *kleos* and to this extent cannot be a "heroic figure," to use Monsacré's term, she can expect that she and Paris will be remembered in song in the future, as she says to Hector (6.357–58). She is right, as we know, and as the original audiences knew, whose hearing these lines was an immediate and indeed simultaneous confirmation of the truth of what she says. The Helen of this song, of the *Iliad*, or of the *Odyssey*, is not only the Helen who has begun her speech to Hector in the mode of lament and with self-reproach, but also the Helen of the narrator's epithets. Coming from the narrator they are authoritative and they counter the self-presentation of Helen (which has its own reasons, as this monograph has argued) and they elevate her above her familial and social identities. They make her a worthy counterpart of the heroes.

---

10 See de Jong 2001: 90 on lines 3–19.

Appendix 1: Helen's Epithets in Homer in Order of Occurrence

Il. 2.161	Ἀργείην Ἑλένην, ἧς εἵνεκα πολλοὶ Ἀχαιῶν	Hera
Il. 2.177	Ἀργείην Ἑλένην, ἧς εἵνεκα πολλοὶ Ἀχαιῶν	Athena
Il. 3.121	Ἶρις δ' αὖθ' Ἑλένῃ λευκωλένῳ ἄγγελος ἦλθεν	Homer
Il. 3.171	τὸν δ' Ἑλένη μύθοισιν ἀμείβετο, δῖα γυναικῶν	Homer
Il. 3.180	δαὴρ αὖτ' ἐμὸς ἔσκε κυνώπιδος, εἴ ποτ' ἔην γε	Helen
Il. 3.199	τὸν δ' ἠμείβετ' ἔπειθ' Ἑλένη Διὸς ἐκγεγαυῖα	Homer
Il. 3.228	τὸν δ' Ἑλένη τανύπεπλος ἀμείβετο δῖα γυναικῶν	Homer
Il. 3.329	δῖος Ἀλέξανδρος, Ἑλένης πόσις ἠυκόμοιο	Homer
Il. 3.404	νικήσας ἐθέλει στυγερὴν ἐμὲ οἴκαδ' ἄγεσθαι	Helen
Il. 3.414	μή μ' ἔρεθε, σχετλίη, μὴ χωσαμένη σε μεθείω	Aphrodite
Il. 3.418	ὣς ἔφατ', ἔδεισεν δ' Ἑλένη Διὸς ἐκγεγαυῖα	Homer
Il. 3.423	ἡ δ' εἰς ὑψόροφον θάλαμον κίε δῖα γυναικῶν	Homer
Il. 3.426	ἔνθα κάθιζ' Ἑλένη, κούρη Διὸς αἰγιόχοιο	Homer
Il. 3.458	ὑμεῖς δ' Ἀργείην Ἑλένην καὶ κτήμαθ' ἅμ' αὐτῇ	Agamemnon
Il. 4.19	αὖτις δ' Ἀργείην Ἑλένην Μενέλαος ἄγοιτο	Zeus
Il. 4.174	Ἀργείην Ἑλένην, σέο δ' ὀστέα πύσει ἄρουρα	Agamemnon
Il. 6.292	τὴν ὁδὸν ἣν Ἑλένην περ ἀνήγαγεν εὐπατέρειαν	Homer
Il. 6.323	Ἀργείη δ' Ἑλένη μετ' ἄρα δμῳῇσι γυναιξὶν	Homer
Il. 6.344	δᾶερ ἐμεῖο κυνὸς κακομηχάνου κρυοέσσης	Helen
Il. 7.350	δεῦτ' ἄγετ' Ἀργείην Ἑλένην καὶ κτήμαθ' ἅμ' αὐτῇ	Antenor
Il. 7.355	δῖος Ἀλέξανδρος, Ἑλένης πόσις ἠυκόμοιο	Homer
Il. 8.82	δῖος Ἀλέξανδρος, Ἑλένης πόσις ἠυκόμοιο	Homer
Il. 9.339	Ἀτρεΐδης; ἦ οὐχ Ἑλένης ἕνεκ' ἠυκόμοιο	Achilles
Il. 11.369	αὐτὰρ Ἀλέξανδρος, Ἑλένης πόσις ἠυκόμοιο	Homer
Il. 11.505	εἰ μὴ Ἀλέξανδρος, Ἑλένης πόσις ἠυκόμοιο	Homer
Il. 13.766	δῖον Ἀλέξανδρον, Ἑλένης πόσιν ἠυκόμοιο	Homer
Il. 19.325	εἵνεκα ῥιγεδανῆς Ἑλένης Τρωσὶν πολεμίζω	Achilles
Il. 23.81a	μαρνάμενον δηίοις Ἑλένης ἕνεκ' ἠυκόμοιο	Patroclus
Od. 4.145	ὅτ' ἐμεῖο κυνώπιδος εἵνεκ' Ἀχαιοὶ	Helen
Od. 4.184	κλαῖε μὲν Ἀργείη Ἑλένη, Διὸς ἐκγεγαυῖα	Homer
Od. 4.219	ἔνθ' αὖτ' ἄλλ' ἐνόησ' Ἑλένη Διὸς ἐκγεγαυῖα	Homer
Od. 4.227	τοῖα Διὸς θυγάτηρ ἔχε φάρμακα μητιόεντα	Homer
Od. 4.296	ὣς ἔφατ', Ἀργείη δ' Ἑλένη δμῳῇσι κέλευσεν	Homer

Od. 4.305	πὰρ δ' Ἑλένη τανύπεπλος ἐλέξατο, δῖα γυναικῶν	Homer
Od. 15.58	ἀνστὰς ἐξ εὐνῆς, Ἑλένης πάρα καλλικόμοιο	Homer
Od. 15.106	τῶν ἕν' ἀειραμένη Ἑλένη φέρε, δῖα γυναικῶν	Homer
Od. 15.123	ἀργύρεον· Ἑλένη δὲ παρίστατο καλλιπάρῃος	Homer
Od. 15.171	τὸν δ' Ἑλένη τανύπεπλος ὑποφθαμένη φάτο μῦθον	Homer
Od. 17.118	ἔνθ' ἴδον Ἀργείην Ἑλένην, ἧς εἵνεκα πολλὰ	Telemachus
Od. 22.227	οἴη ὅτ' ἀμφ' Ἑλένῃ λευκωλένῳ εὐπατερείῃ	Athena
Od. 23.218	οὐδέ κεν Ἀργείη Ἑλένη, Διὸς ἐκγεγαυῖα	Penelope

Appendix 2: The Name Helen without Epithets

Il. 2.356	τείσασθαι δ' Ἑλένης ὁρμήματά τε στοναχάς τε	Nestor
Il. 2.590	τείσασθαι δ' Ἑλένης ὁρμήματά τε στοναχάς τε	Narrator
Il. 3.70	συμβάλετ' ἀμφ' Ἑλένῃ καὶ κτήμασι πᾶσι μάχεσθαι	Paris
Il. 3.91	οἴους ἀμφ' Ἑλένῃ καὶ κτήμασι πᾶσι μάχεσθαι	Hector
Il. 3.154	οἳ δ' ὡς οὖν εἴδονθ' Ἑλένην ἐπὶ πύργον ἰοῦσαν	Narrator
Il. 3.161	ὣς ἄρ' ἔφαν· Πρίαμος δ' Ἑλένην ἐκαλέσσατο φωνῇ	Narrator
Il. 3.282	αὐτὸς ἔπειθ' Ἑλένην ἐχέτω καὶ κτήματα πάντα	Agamemnon
Il. 3.285	Τρῶας ἔπειθ' Ἑλένην καὶ κτήματα πάντ' ἀποδοῦναι	Agamemnon
Il. 3.383	αὐτὴ δ' αὖθ' Ἑλένην καλέουσ' ἴε· τὴν δ' ἐκίχανεν	Narrator
Il. 6.343	τὸν δ' Ἑλένη μύθοισι προσηύδα μειλιχίοισιν	Narrator
Il. 6.360	μή με κάθιζ', Ἑλένη, φιλέουσά περ· οὐδέ με πείσεις	Hector
Il. 7.401	μήθ' Ἑλένην. γνωτὸν δέ, καὶ ὅς μάλα νήπιός ἐστιν	Diomedes
Il. 11.125	οὐκ εἴασχ' Ἑλένην δόμεναι ξανθῷ Μενελάῳ	Narrator
Il. 22.114	καί οἱ ὑπόσχωμαι Ἑλένην καὶ κτήμαθ' ἅμ' αὐτῇ	Hector
Il. 24.761	τῇσι δ' ἔπειθ' Ἑλένη τριτάτη ἐξῆρχε γόοιο	Narrator
Od. 4.12	ἐκ δούλης· Ἑλένη δὲ θεοὶ γόνον οὐκέτ' ἔφαινον	Narrator
Od. 4.130	χωρὶς δ' αὖθ' Ἑλένῃ ἄλοχος πόρε κάλλιμα δῶρα	Narrator
Od. 4.569	οὕνεκ' ἔχεις Ἑλένην καί σφιν γαμβρὸς Διός ἐσσι	Menelaus quoting Proteus
Od. 11.438	ἐξ ἀρχῆς· Ἑλένης μὲν ἀπωλόμεθ' εἵνεκα πολλοί	Odysseus quoting himself
Od. 14.68	ἀλλ' ὄλεθ'. ὡς ὤφελλ' Ἑλένης ἀπὸ φῦλον ὀλέσθαι	Eumaeus
Od. 15.100	οὐκ οἶος, ἅμα τῷ γ' Ἑλένη κίε καὶ Μεγαπένθης	Narrator
Od. 15.104	ἀργύρεον· Ἑλένη δὲ παρίστατο φωριαμοῖσιν	Narrator
Od. 15.126	μνῆμ' Ἑλένης χειρῶν, πολυηράτου ἐς γάμου ὥρην	Helen

Appendix 3: The "On account of" Motif

1. εἵνεκα + Ἑλένης or another word in the genitive referring to her, with or without an epithet other than ἠύκομος (cf. 2. below)
- *Il.* 2.161 = 2.177 Ἀργείην Ἑλένην, ἧς εἵνεκα πολλοὶ Ἀχαιῶν
- *Il.* 3.127–28 Ἀχαιῶν χαλκοχιτώνων, / οὓς ἔθεν εἵνεκ' ἔπασχον ὑπ' Ἄρηος παλαμάων
- *Il.* 6.355–57 εἵνεκ' ἐμεῖο κυνὸς καὶ Ἀλεξάνδρου ἕνεκ' ἄτης
- *Il.* 19.325 εἵνεκα ῥιγεδανῆς Ἑλένης Τρωσὶν πολεμίζω
- *Od.* 4.145 ἐμεῖο κυνώπιδος εἵνεκ'
- *Od.* 11.438 ἐξ ἀρχῆς· Ἑλένης μὲν ἀπωλόμεθ' εἵνεκα πολλοί
- *Od.* 17.118 ἔνθ' ἴδον Ἀργείην Ἑλένην, ἧς εἵνεκα πολλὰ
- Sem. 7.118 W² γυναικὸς εἵνεκ' ἀμφιδηριωμένους
- Alcaeus 283.14 V ἔν]νεκα κήνας

2. The formula Ἑλένης ἕνεκ' ἠυκόμοιο
- *Il.* 9.339 ἦ οὐχ Ἑλένης ἕνεκ' ἠϋκόμοιο
- *Il.* 23.81a (from Aeschines 1.149) μαρνάμενον δηίοις Ἑλένης ἕνεκ' ἠυκόμοιο (cf. *Od.* 22.227–28)
- Hes. *Op.* 165 ἐς Τροίην ἀγαγὼν Ἑλένης ἕνεκ' ἠυκόμοιο
- Hes. *Cat.* 200.11 M-W = 109.11 H = 154e.11 M Ἑλένη]ς ἕνεκ' ἠυ[κόμοιο
- Fr. adesp. *SH* 1155.2 μαρνάμενον Θησεὺς Ἑλένης ἕνεκ' ἠϋκόμοιο

3. ἀμφί or περί + Ἑλένῃ or another word in the dative referring to her
- *Il.* 3.70 ≈ 3.91 συμβάλετ' ἀμφ' Ἑλένῃ καὶ κτήμασι πᾶσι μάχεσθαι·
- *Il.* 3.157 τοιῇδ' ἀμφὶ γυναικὶ πολὺν χρόνον ἄλγεα πάσχειν·
- *Il.* 3.254 μακρῇς ἐγχείῃσι μαχήσοντ' ἀμφὶ γυναικί
- Cf. *Il.* 3.137 μακρῇς ἐγχείῃσι μαχήσονται περὶ σεῖο
- *Od.* 22.227–28 οἵη ὅτ' ἀμφ' Ἑλένῃ λευκωλένῳ εὐπατερείῃ / εἰνάετες Τρώεσσιν ἐμάρναο (cf. *Il.* 23.81a)
- Hes. *Cat.* 204.81 M-W = 110.81 H = 155.81 M ἀμφὶ γάμωι κούρης εὐ[ω]λ[ένο]υ
- Alcaeus fr. 42.15–16 V οἱ δ' ἀπώλοντ' ἀμφ' Ἐ[λέναι
- Ibycus S151.5 PMG / PMGF ξα]νθᾶς Ἑλένας περὶ εἴδει <dots under letters to be added>
- fr. adesp. 71 PMG Ἴλιον ἀμφ' Ἑλένηι πεπυρωμένον ὤλετο
- Pind. *Pyth.* 11.33–34 ἀμφ' Ἑλέναι πυρωθέντας / Τρώων ἔλυσε δόμους
- Pind. *Pae.* 6.95 περὶ δ' ὑψικόμῳ [Ἑ]λένᾳ / χρῆν ἄρα Πέργαμον εὐρὺ[ν] ἀ- / ιστῶσαι σέλας αἰθομένου / πυρός

4. Cf.
- Alcaeus 42.1–3 V ὡς λόγος κάκων ἄ[/ Περράμω‹ι› καὶ παῖσ[ι / ἐκ σέθεν πίκρον, π[/ Ἴλιον ἴραν
- Hom. *Il.* 10.27–28 Ἀργεῖοι, τοὶ δὴ ἔθεν εἵνεκα πουλὺν ἐφ' ὑγρὴν / ἤλυθον ἐς Τροίην πόλεμον θρασὺν ὁρμαίνοντες
- Hes. *Cat.* fr. 196.4 = 104.4 H = 154a.4 M εἵνεκα κούρης

Appendix 4: Helen's epithets in lyric

- Ἀργεία: Alcaeus fr. 283.4 V
- δῖα: δῖ' fr. adesp. 96 PMG (from schol. A Hom. *Il.* 16.57c (cf. πολυνεικής below)
- ἑλικῶπις: ἑλικώπιδα fr. adesp. 93(a) PMG (from Priscian *inst.* I 20, on digamma) ὀψόμενος Ϝελέναν ἑλικώπιδα
- καλλιπλόκαμος: καλλιπλοκάμωι θ᾽ Ἑλέναι Pind. *O*. 3.1
- *Menelaïs* (?)[1]
- ξανθά: Stesichorus fr. 112.5 D-F = S103.5 PMGF [p. 191] = S103.5 SLG (p. 30) from POxy 2619 fr.14); Ibycus 1(a).5 PMG = S 151.5 PMGF; ξάνθα: Sappho 23.5 V
- πολυνεικής: fr. adesp. 96 PMG (one of two epithets in this line: cf. δῖ' above)
- ὑψίκομος: ὑψικόμωι Pind. *Paean* 6.95–96

---

[1] *Menelaïs Helena* in Ibycus fr. 290 PMG / PMGF: from Diomedes *Ars grammatica* 1 (*Gramm. Lat.* 1.323 Keil) in a list of examples of patronymics formed on the names of relations other than father. The last example in the list is attributed to Ibycus. *Menelaïs Helena* is the next-to-last example and may be included in the attribution.

Works Cited

Akmajian, Adrian, Richard A. Demers, Ann K. Farmer, Robert M. Harnish. 2001. *Linguistics: An Introduction to Language and Communication*. 5th ed. Cambridge, MA: MIT Press.
Andò, Valeria. 1996. "'Nymphe': La sposa e le Ninfe." *Quaderni Urbinati di Cultura Classica* NS 52.1: 47–79.
Arend, Walter. 1933. *Die typischen Szenen bei Homer*. Berlin: Weidman.
Armstrong, James. 1958. "The Arming Motif in the *Iliad*." *AJP* 79: 337–54.
Austin, Colin. 1968. *Nova fragmenta Euripidea in papyris reperta*. Berlin: De Gruyter.
Austin, Colin. 1973. *Comicorum Graecorum fragmenta in papyris reperta*. Berlin: De Gruyter.
Austin, Norman. 1966. "The Function of Digressions in the *Iliad*." *GRBS* 7: 295–312.
Austin, Norman. 1975. *Archery at the Dark of the Moon: Poetic Problems in Homer's* Odyssey. Berkeley: University of California Press.
Bader, F.B. 1969. "Alexandre et Cléopatre, ou le problème du genre grammatical dans les noms propres composés du grec." *RPh* 43: 15–38.
Bailly, Anatole. 1994. *Dictionnaire grec-français*. Rev. ed. Paris: Hachette.
Bakker, Egbert J. 1997. *Poetry in Speech: Orality and Homeric Discourse*. Ithaca, NY: Cornell University Press.
Bakker, Egbert J. 2010. *A Companion to the Ancient Greek Language*. Chichester, West Sussex, UK: Wiley-Blackwell.
Barber, Elizabeth J.W. 1991. *Prehistoric Textiles: The Development of Cloth in the Neolithic and Bronze Ages*. Princeton, NJ: Princeton University Press.
Barrett, W.S. 1964. *Euripides: Hippolytus*. Oxford: Oxford University Press.
Beck, William. 1986. "Choice and Context: Metrical Doublets for Hera." *AJP* 107: 480–88.
Benveniste, Émile. 1969. "philos." In *Le vocabulaire des institutions indo-européennes*. Vol. 1. Paris: Editions de Minuit. Pp. 335–53.
Bergold, Wolfgang. 1977. *Der Zweikampf des Paris und Menelaos: zu Ilias (Gamma) 1–(Delta) 222*. Habelts Dissertationsdrucke: Reihe klassische Philologie, 28. Bonn: Habelt.
Bettini, Maurizio. 1998. *Nascere: Storie di donne, donnole, madri ed eroi*. Turin: Einaudi.
Bierl, Anton and Joachim Latacz, eds. 2000–. *Homers Ilias, Gesamtkommentar: Basler Kommentar (BK)*. Auf der Grundlage der Ausgabe von Ameis-Hentze-Cauer (1868–1913). Munich: Saur. Berlin: de Gruyter.
Bierl, Anton. 2015. "New Trends in Homeric Scholarship." In Anton Bierl and Joachim Latacz, eds., *Homer's* Iliad: *The Basel Commentary: Prolegomena*. Trans. by Benjamin W. Millis and Sara Strack. Ed. by S. Douglas Olson. Berlin: de Gruyter. Pp. 177–203.
Bird, Graeme D. 2010. *Multitextuality in the Homeric* Iliad: *The Witness of the Ptolemaic Papyri*. Washington, DC: Center for Hellenic Studies. Distributed by Harvard University Press. Also http://chs.harvard.edu/CHS/article/display/4864
Blondell, Ruby. 2013. *Helen of Troy: Beauty, Myth, Devastation*. Oxford: Oxford University Press.
Boedeker, Deborah D. 1974. *Aphrodite's Entry into Greek Epic*. Mnemosyne Suppl., 39. Leiden: Brill.
Boedeker, Deborah D. 2012. "Helen and 'I' in Early Greek Lyric." In Marincola *et al.* 2012: 65–82.
Bouvier, David. 1997. "Mémoire et répétition dans la poésie homérique." In Létoublon and Dik 1997: 79–92.
Bouvier, David. 2003. "The Homeric Question: An Issue for the Ancients?" *Oral Tradition* 18.1: 59–61.

Bouvier, David. 2015. "Quand le concept de 'formule' devient un obstacle épistémologique: la conception du stock de formules préfabriquées (Ire partie)." *Gaia* 18: 225–43.
Bozzone, Chiara. 2015. *Constructions: A New Approach to Formularity, Discourse, and Syntax in Homer*. Diss. University of California, Los Angeles.
Brillante, Carlo. 2005. "Il controverso nostos di Agamennone nell'Odissea (IV 512–522)." *Aevum Antiquum* NS 5: 5–25.
Brillet-Dubois, Pascale. 2015. "'Hector tueur d'hommes' ou 'Hector dompteur de chevaux': L'art formulaire au service du récit de l'*Iliade*." *Gaia* 18: 261–73.
Brügger, Claude, Magdalena Stoevesandt and Edzard Visser. 2003. In Bierl and Latacz, eds. 2000–. Vol. 2 (Book 2). Fasc. 2 (Commentary). Munich: Saur.
Brunot, Ferdinand. 1922. *La pensée et la langue: méthode, principes et plan d'une théorie nouvelle du langage appliquée au français*. Paris: Masson.
Burkert, Walter. 1985. *Greek Religion*. Trans. by John Raffan. Cambridge, MA: Harvard University Press.
Burkert, Walter. 2001. "La cité d'Argos entre la tradition mycénienne, dorienne et homérique." *Kleine Schriften*. Vol. 1 (Homerica). Göttingen: Vandenhoeck & Ruprecht. Pp. 166–177. Orig. pub. in V. Pirenne-Delforge, ed., *Les Panthéons des cités des origines à la Périégèse de Pausanias*. Actes du Colloque organisé à l'Université de Liège du 15 au 17 mai 1997 (2e partie) = *Kernos* Suppl. 8 (1998) 47–59.
Cairns, Douglas L. 1993. *Aidōs: The Psychology and Ethics of Honour and Shame in Ancient Greek Literature*. Oxford: Clarendon Press.
Cairns, Douglas L. 2011. "Introduction." In Cairns, ed. 2001: 1–56.
Cairns, Douglas L. 2012. "Atē in the Homeric Poems." *Papers of the Langford Latin Seminar* 15: 1–52.
Cairns, Douglas L. 2013. "A Short History of Shudders." In Chaniotis and Ducrey 2013: 77–99.
Cairns, Douglas L., ed. 2001. *Readings in Homer's* Iliad. Oxford: Oxford University Press.
Calhoun, George. M. 1933. "Homeric Repetitions." *University of California Publications in Classical Philology* 12.1: 1–26.
Cantilena, Mario. 1979. "Le *Eoeae* e la tradizione orale." Rev. of Meier 1976. *Athenaeum* 47: 139–45.
Cantilena, Mario. 1982. *Per uno studio della formularità degli Inni Omerici*. Rome: Ateneo.
Cantilena, Mario. 2012a. "Oralità, tradizione, testo: tre dimensioni della questione omerica." In Guido Bastianini and Angelo Casanova, eds., *I papiri omerici: Atti del Convegno Internazionale di Studi, Firenze 9–10 Giugno 2011*. Florence: Istituto Papirologico «G. Vitelli». Pp. 79–95.
Cantilena, Mario. 2012b. "Intorno alla tradizione." *Seminari Romani di Cultura Greca* NS 1:147–163.
Catling, Hector W. and Helen Cavanagh. 1976. "Two Inscribed Bronzes from the Menelaion, Sparta." *Kadmos* 15.2: 144–57.
Chaniotis, Angelos and Pierre Ducrey, eds. 2013. *Unveiling Emotions II: Emotions in Greece and Rome: Texts, Images, Material Culture*. Heidelberger althistorische Beiträge und epigraphische Studien, 55. Stuttgart: Franz Steiner.
Cingano, Ettore. 2004. "Tradizioni epiche intorno ad Argo da Omero al VI sec. A.C." In Bernardini 2004: 59–78.
Cingano, Ettore. 2005. "A Catalogue within a Catalogue: Helen's Suitors in Hesiod's Catalogue of Women (frr. 196–204)." In Hunter 2005: 118–52.

Cingano, Ettore. 2009. "The Hesiodic Corpus." In Montanari, Rengakos, and Tsagalis 2012: 91–130.
Cingano, Ettore. 2010. "Differenze di età e altre peculiarità narrative in Omero e nel ciclo epico." In *id*., ed., *Tra panellenismo e tradizioni locali. Generi poetici e* storiografia. Alessandria: Edizioni dell'Orso. Pp. 77–90.
Cingano, Ettore. 2011. "Aporie, parallelismi, riprese e convergenze: la costruzione del ciclo epico." In Antonio Aloni and Massimiliano Ornaghi., eds., *Tra panellenismo e tradizioni locali: generi poetici e storiografia*. Hellenica, 34. Alessandria: Edizioni dell'Orso. Pp. 3–26.
Clader, Linda L. 1976. *Helen: The Evolution from Divine to Heroic in Greek Epic Tradition*. Mnemosyne Suppl., 42. Leiden: Brill.
Cohen, David. 1991. *Law, Sexuality and Society: The Enforcement of Morals in Classical Athens*. Cambridge: Cambridge University Press.
Cole, Susan G. 1984. "Greek Sanctions Against Sexual Assault." *CP* 79.2: 97–113.
Combellack, Frederick M. 1959. "Milman Parry and Homeric Artistry." *Comparative Literature* 11: 193–208.
Conti Jiménez, Luz. 1999. "La expresión de la causa en Homero con referentes humanos." *Emerita* 67.2: 295–313.
Coray, Marina. 2009. In Bierl and Latacz, eds. 2000–. Vol. 6 (Book 19). Fasc. 2 (Commentary). Berlin: de Gruyter.
Cosset, Évelyne. 1983. "Choix formulaire ou choix sémantique? La désignation d'Ulysse et de la lance (ἔγχος) dans l'*Iliade*." *REA* 85: 191–98.
Cosset, Évelyne. 1984. "L'*Iliade*, style formulaire ou non-formulaire?" *AC* 53: 5–14.
Crielaard, Jan Paul. 2002. "Past or Present? Epic Poetry, Aristocratic Self-Representation and the Concept of Time in the Eighth and Seventh Centuries BC." In Montanari and Ascheri 2002: 239–95.
Currie, Bruno. 2015. "*Cypria*." In Fantuzzi and Tsagalis 2015: 281–306.
Danek, Georg. 1998. *Epos und Zitat: Studien zu den Quellen der Odyssee*. Wiener Studien, 22. Vienna: Österreichische Akademie der Wissenschaften.
Davies, Malcolm. 1995. "Agamemnon's Apology and the Unity of the *Iliad*." *CQ* 45: 1–8.
de Sanctis, Dino. 2012. "La Helenes apaitesis attraverso epica, lirica, tragedia." *Prometheus* 38: 35–59.
Debiasi, Andrea. 2004. *L'Epica perduta: Eumelo, il Ciclo, l'occidente*. Rome: "L'Herma" di Bretschneider.
Dee, James H. 2000. *Epitheta Hominum Apud Homerum = The Epithetic Phrases for the Homeric Heroes: A Repertory of Descriptive Expressions for the Human Characters of the* Iliad *and the* Odyssey. Hildesheim: Olms-Weidmann.
Denniston, J.D. 1952. *Greek Prose Style*. Oxford: Oxford University Press.
Denniston, J.D. 1966. *The Greek Particles*. 2nd ed. Oxford: Oxford University Press.
Di Benedetto, Vincenzo. 1998. *Nel laboratorio di Omero*. Turin: Einaudi.
Di Benedetto, Vincenzo. 2010. *Omero: Odissea*. Milan: Rizzoli.
Dodds, E.R. 1951. *The Greeks and the Irrational*. Berkeley: University of California Press.
Ducrot, Oswald and Tzvetan Todorov. 1979[1972]. *Encyclopedic Dictionary of the Sciences of Language*. Trans. by Catherine Porter. Baltimore: Johns Hopkins University Press.
Dué, Casey and Mary Ebbott. 2004. "As Many Homers As You Please: An On-line Multitext of Homer." In C. Blackwell and R. Scaife, edd., *Classics@* 2. The Center for Hellenic Studies of Harvard University. https://chs.harvard.edu/CHS/article/display/1314

Dué, Casey and Mary Ebbott. 2009. "Digital Criticism: Editorial Standards for the Homer Multitext." *Digital Humanities Quarterly (DHQ)* 3.1.
Dué, Casey. 2012. "Hektor's Variation on a Lament by Briseis." In *The Homer Multitext*. http://homermultitext.blogspot.com/2012/03/hektors-variation-on-lament-by-briseis.html
Ebbott, Mary. 1999. "The Wrath of Helen: Self-Blame and Nemesis in the *Iliad*." In Miriam Carlisle and Olga Levaniouk, eds., *Nine Essays on Homer*. Lanham, MD: Rowman & Littlefield. Pp. 3–20.
Edmunds, Lowell. 2005. "Expanding the Context and Audience Response: Reflections on the Methodology of Carlo Brillante's 'Il controverso νόστος di Agamemnone nell'*Odisseia* (IV vv. 512–522)'." *Aevum Antiquum* NS 5: 55–59.
Edmunds, Lowell. 2016a. *Stealing Helen: The Myth of the Abducted Wife in Comparative Perspective*. Princeton: Princeton University Press.
Edmunds, Lowell. 2016b. "Intertextuality without Texts in Archaic Greek Verse and the Plan of Zeus." *Syllecta Classica* 27: 1–27.
Edmunds, Lowell, ed. 2014. *Approaches to Greek Myth*. 2nd ed. Baltimore: Johns Hopkins University Press.
Edwards, G. Patrick. 1971. *The Language of Hesiod in its Traditional Context*. Oxford: Blackwell.
Edwards, Mark W. 1969. "On Some 'Answering' Expressions in Homer." *CP* 64: 81–87.
Edwards, Mark W. 1970. "Homeric Speech Introductions." *HSCP* 74: 1–36.
Edwards, Mark W. 1975. "Type-scenes and Homeric Hospitality." *TAPA* 105: 51–72.
Edwards, Mark W. 1991. *The Iliad: A Commentary*. Vol. 5 (Books 17–20). Cambridge: Cambridge University Press.
Edwards, Mark W. 1997. "Homeric Style and Oral Poetics." In Powell and Morris 1997: 261–83.
Edwards, Michael and Stephen Usher. 1985. *Antiphon & Lysias*. Greek Orators; 1. Warminster: Aris & Phillips.
Elmer, David F. 2005. "Helen epigrammatopoios." *ClAnt* 24: 1–39.
Elmer, David F. 2011. "Oral-Formulaic Theory." In Finkelberg 2011: 604–607.
Elmer, David F. 2015. "The 'Narrow Road' and the Ethics of Language Use in the *Iliad* and the *Odyssey*." *Ramus* 44.1–2: 155–183.
Espermann, Ingeborg. 1980. *Antenor, Theano, Antenoriden: ihre Person und Bedeutung in der Ilias*. Beiträge zur klassischen Philologie, 120. Meisenheim am Glan: Anton Hain.
Fantuzzi, Marco. 2012. *Achilles in Love: Intertextual Studies*. Oxford: Oxford University Press.
Fantuzzi, Marco and Christos Tsagalis, eds. 2015. *The Greek Epic Cycle and its Ancient Reception: A Companion*. Cambridge: Cambridge University Press.
Faust, Manfred. 1970. "Die künstlerische Verwendung von κύων 'Hund' in den homerischen Epen." *Glotta* 48: 8–31.
Finkelberg, Margalit, ed. 2011. *The Homer Encyclopedia*. 3 vols. Chichester: Wiley-Blackwell.
Finkelberg, Margalit. 1989. "Formulaic and Nonformulaic Elements in Homer." *CP* 84: 179–97.
Finkelberg, Margalit. 2004. "Oral Theory and the Limits of Formulaic Diction." *Oral Tradition* 19.2: 236–52.
Finkelberg, Margalit. 2011. "Speeches." In Finkelberg 2011.3: 819–20.
Finkelberg, Margalit. 2012. "Oral Formulaic Theory and the Individual Poet." In Montanari, Rengakos and Tsagalis 2012: 73–82.
Foley, John Miles. 1991. *Immanent Art: From Structure to Meaning in Traditional Oral Epic*. Bloomington: Indiana University Press.
Ford, Andrew. 1992. *Homer: The Poetry of the Past*. Ithaca: Cornell University Press.

Fränkel, Hermann. 1951. *Dichtung und Philosophie des frühen Griechentums: Eine Geschichte der griechischen Literatur von Homer bis Pindar*. Philological Monographs, 13. New York: American Philological Association.

Franco, Cristiana. 2003. *Senza ritegno: Il cane e la donna nell'immaginario della Grecia antica*. Bologna: Il Mulino.

Friedrich, Rainer. 2007. *Formular Economy in Homer: The Poetics of the Breaches*. Hermes Einzelschriften, 100. Stuttgart: Steiner.

Friedrich, Rainer. 2011. "Formelsprache." In Antonios Rengakos and Bernhard Zimmermann, eds., *Homer Handbuch: Leben – Werk – Wirkung*. Stuttgart: Metzler. Pp. 45–64.

García, John F. 2001. "Milman Parry and A.L. Kroeber: Americanist Anthropology and the Oral Homer." *Oral Tradition* 16.1: 58–84.

García Ramón, José. 2016. "Hera and Hero: Reconstructing Lexicon and Greek Name." In David M. Goldstein, Stephanie W. Jamison, and Brent H. Vine, eds., *Proceedings of the 27th Annual UCLA Indo-European Conference: Los Angeles, October 23rd and 24th, 2015*. Bremen: Hempen. Pp. 41–60.

Gates, Henry Phelps. 1971. *The Kinship Terminology of Homeric Greek*. Indiana University Publications in Anthropology and Linguistics, 27. Bloomington: Indiana University Press.

Gill, Christopher. 1990. "The Character-Personality Distinction." In Pelling 1990: 1–31.

Goldhill, Simon. 1994. "The Failure of Exemplarity." In Irene J.F. de Jong and J.P. Sullivan, eds., *Modern Critical Theory and Classical Literature*. Leiden: Brill. Pp. 51–73.

Gómez Seijo, Francisca. 2017. "Responsabilidad y ambigüedad de Helena en la épica homérica / Responsibility and Ambiguity of Helen in Homeric Epic." *Humanitas* 69: 9–45.

González, José M. 2013. *The Epic Rhapsode and His Craft: Homeric Performance in a Diachronic Perspective*. Hellenic Studies Series 47. Washington, DC: Center for Hellenic Studies. https://chs.harvard.edu/CHS/article/display/6127

Graf, Fritz, Bierl, Anton, Olson, S. Douglas, et al. 2015. *Homer's* Iliad. *Prolegomena: The Basel Commentary*. Berlin: de Gruyter.

Graver, Margaret. 1995. "Dog-Helen and Homeric Insult." *CA* 14: 41–61.

Graziosi, Barbara and Johannes Haubold. 2010. *Homer:* Iliad *Book VI*. Cambridge: Cambridge University Press.

Griffin, Jasper. 1980. *Homer on Life and Death*. Oxford: Oxford University Press.

Hackstein, Olav. 2010. "The Greek of Epic." In Bakker 2010: 401–23.

Hainsworth, Bryan. 1964. "Structure and Content in Epic Formulae: The Question of the Unique Expression. *CQ* NS 58: 155–64.

Hainsworth, Bryan. 1968. *The Flexibility of the Homeric Formula*. Oxford: Clarendon Press.

Hainsworth, Bryan. 1978. "Good and Bad Formulae." In Bernard C. Fenik, ed., *Homer: Tradition and Invention*. Leiden: Brill. Pp. 41–50.

Hainsworth, Bryan. 1993. *The* Iliad: *A Commentary*. Vol. 3 (Books 9–12). Cambridge: Cambridge University Press.

Heubeck, Alfred, Stephanie West and J.B. Hainsworth. 1988. *A Commentary on Homer's* Odyssey. Vol. 1 (Books 1–8). Oxford: Oxford University Press.

Heubeck, Alfred and Arie Hoekstra. 1989. *A Commentary on Homer's* Odyssey, Vol. 2 (Books IX-XVI). Oxford: Clarendon Press.

Higbie, Carolyn. 1995. *Heroes' Names, Homeric Identities*. Albert Bates Lord Studies in Oral Tradition, 10. New York: Garland Publishing.

Hoekstra, Arie. 1965. *Homeric Modifications of Formulaic Prototypes: Studies in The Development of Greek Epic Diction*. Verhandelingen der Koninklijke Nederlandse Akademie van

Wetenschappen: Section Letterkunde, New Series, Vol. 71, No. 1. Amsterdam: North-Holland.
Hoekstra, Arie. 1991. "Homer, Oral Poetry Theory, and Comparative Literature: Major Trends and Controversies in Twentieth-Century Criticism." In Joachim Latacz, ed., *Zweihundert Jahre Homer-Forschung: Rückblick und Ausblick*. Stuttgart: Teubner. Pp. 456–81.
Hoffmann, Geneviève. 1990. *Le châtiment des amants*. Paris: De Boccard.
Hooker James T. 1979. "Εἴ ποτ' ἔην γε." *AJP* 100: 393–395.
Huld, Martin E. 1988. "Homeric ΔAHP." *AJP* 109: 424–30.
Hunter, Richard, ed. 2005. *The Hesiodic Catalogue of Women: Constructions and Reconstructions*. Cambridge: Cambridge University Press.
Irwin, Elizabeth. 2005. "Gods among Men? The Social and Political Dynamics of the *Catalogue*." In Hunter 2005: 35–84.
Jahn, Thomas. 1987. *Zum Wortfeld "Seele-Geist" in der Sprache Homers*. Zetemata, 83. Munich: Beck.
Janko, Richard. 1981. "Equivalent Formulae in the Greek Epos." *Mnemosyne* 4: 251–64.
Janko, Richard. 1992. *The Iliad: A Commentary*. Vol. 4 (Books 13–16). Cambridge: Cambridge University Press.
Jensen, Minne Skafte et al. 1999. "SO Debate: Dividing Homer. When and How Were the *Iliad* and the *Odyssey* Divided into Songs?" *Symbolae Osloenses* 74: 1–91.
Jörgensen, Ove. 1904. "Das Auftreten der Götter in den Büchern ι-μ der Odyssee." *Hermes* 39: 357–82.
Jong, Irene J.F. de. 1987. *Narrators and Focalizers: The Presentation of the Story in the Iliad*. Amsterdam: B.R. Grüner.
Jong, Irene J.F. de. 1993. "Studies in Homeric Denomination." *Mnemosyne* 46: 289–306.
Jong, Irene J.F. de. 1997. "Narrator Language versus Character Language: Some Further Explorations." In Françoise Létoublon, ed., *Hommage à Milman Parry. Le style formulaire de l'épopée homérique et la théorie de l'oralité poétique*. Amsterdam: Gieben. Pp. 293–302.
Jong, Irene J.F. de. 1998. "Homeric Epithet and Narrative Situation." In Machi Païsi-Apostolopoulou, ed., *Proceedings of the Eighth International Symposium on the Odyssey (1–5 September 1996)*. Ithaca: Kentro Odysseiakōn Spoudōn. Pp. 121–35.
Jong, Irene J.F. de. 2001a. *A Narratological Commentary on the Odyssey*. Cambridge: Cambridge University Press.
Jong, Irene J.F. de. 2001b. "The Origins of Figural Narrative in Antiquity." In Willie Van Peer and Seymour Chapman, eds., *New Perspectives on Narrative Perspective*. Albany: SUNY Press. Pp. 67–81.
Jong, Irene J.F. de. 2004. *Narrators and Focalizers: The Presentation of the Story in the Iliad*. 2nd ed. Bristol: Bristol Classical Press.
Jong, Irene J.F. de. 2012. *Homer: Iliad Book XXII*. Cambridge: Cambridge University Press.
Jouan, François. 1966. *Euripide et les légendes des Chants cypriens: Des origines de la guerre de Troie à l'Iliade*. Paris: Belles Lettres.
Karanika, Andromache. 2014. *Voices at Work: Women, Performance, and Labor in Ancient Greece*. Baltimore: Johns Hopkins University Press.
Katz, Joshua. 2010. "Inherited Poetics." In Egbert J. Bakker, ed., *A Companion to the Ancient Greek Language*. Malden, MA: Wiley-Blackwell. Pp. 357–69.
Katz, Joshua. 2013a. "Saussure's *anaphonie*: Sounds Asunder." In Shane Butler and Alex Purves, eds., *Synaesthesia and the Ancient Senses*. Durham: Acumen. Pp. 167–84.

Katz, Joshua. 2013b. "The Hymnic Long Alpha: Μούσας ἀείδω and Related Incipits in Archaic Greek Poetry." In Stephanie W. Jamison, H. Craig Melchert & Brent Vine, eds., *Proceedings of the 24th Annual UCLA Indo-European Conference, Los Angeles, October 26th and 27th, 2012*. Bremen: Hempen. Pp. 87–101.

Kelly, Adrian. 2007. *A Referential Commentary and Lexicon to Iliad VIII*. Oxford: Oxford University Press.

Kiessling, Adolf and Richard Heinze. 1957. *Quintus Horatius Flaccus: Briefe*. 5th ed. Berlin-Charlottenberg: Weidman.

Köchly, Hermann. 1881. "De Iliadis carminibus dissertatio IV." In *Opuscula philologica*. Vol. 1. Ed. by Gottfried Kinkel. Leipzig: Teubner. Pp. 69–88.

Köstler, Rudolf. 1950. "Die homerische Staats- und Rechtsordnung." In id., *Homerisches Recht*. Vienna: Österreichische Bundesverlag. Pp. 7–25.

Kirk, G.S. 1985. *The* Iliad*: A Commentary*. Vol. 1 (Books 1–4). Cambridge: Cambridge University Press.

Kirk, G.S. 1990. *The* Iliad*: A Commentary*. Vol. 2 (Books 5–8). Cambridge: Cambridge University Press.

Koning, Hugo H. 2017. "Helen, Herakles, and the End of the Heroes." In Christos Tsagalis, ed., *Poetry in Fragments: Studies on the Hesiodic Corpus and its Afterlife*. Berlin: De Gruyter. Pp. 99–114.

Krieter-Spiro, Martha. 2009. In Bierl and Latacz, eds. 2000–. Vol. 3 (Book 3). Fasc. 2 (Commentary). Berlin: de Gruyter.

Kroeber, Alfred L. 1917. "The Superorganic." *American Anthropologist* 19: 163–213.

Kroeber, Alfred L. 1952. *The Nature of Culture*. Chicago: University of Chicago Press.

Kullmann, Wolfgang. 1960. *Die Quellen der* Ilias *(Troischer Sagenkreis)*. Wiesbaden: Steiner.

Kullmann, Wolfgang. 1992. *Homerische Motive: Beiträge zur Entstehung, Eigenart und Wirkung von Ilias und Odyssee*. Stuttgart: Steiner.

Kullmann, Wolfgang. 1992[1955]. "Ein vorhomerisches motiv in Iliasproömium." In id. 1992: 11–35. Orig. pub. in Philologus 99 (1955) 167–92.

Landfester, Manfred. 1966. *Das griechische Nomen 'philos' und seine Ableitungen*. Spudasmata 11. Hildesheim: Olms.

Latacz, Joachim. 2000. "Formelhaftigkeit und Mündlichkeit." In Graf, et al. 2000: 39–59.

Latacz, Joachim, René Nünlist and Magdalena Stoevesandt. 2000. In Bierl and Latacz, eds. 2000–. Vol. 1 (Book 1). Fasc. 2 (Commentary). Munich: Saur.

La Roche, J. 1897. "Die Stellung des attributiven und appositiven Adjectivs bei Homer." *WS* 19: 161–88.

Leaf, Walter. 1900–1902. *The Iliad*. 2 vols. 2nd ed. London: Macmillan.

Létoublon, Françoise and Helma Dik, eds. 1997. *Le style formulaire de l'épopée homérique et la théorie de l'oralité poétique : hommage à Milman Parry*. Amsterdam: Gieben.

Leumann, Manu. 1993[1950]. *Homerische Wörter*. Darmstadt: Wissenschaftliche Buchgesellschaft.

Lohmann, Dieter. 1970. *Die Komposition Der Reden In Der Ilias*. Berlin: de Gruyter.

López Gregoris, Rosario. 1986. "El matrimonio de Helena: solución lexemática". *Epos* 12: 15–30.

Lord, Albert B. 1967. "Homer as Oral Poet." *HSCP* 72: 1–46.

Lowe, Nicholas J. 2000. *The Classical Plot and the Invention of Western Narrative*. Cambridge: Cambridge University Press.

Ludwich, Arthur. 1898. *Die Homervulgata Als Voralexandrinisch Erwiesen*. Leipzig: Teubner.

Macleod, C.A. 1982. *Iliad: Book XXIV*. Cambridge: Cambridge University Press.
Marincola, John, Lloyd Llewellyn-Jones and Calum Maciver, eds., *Greek Notions of the Past in the Archaic and Classical Eras: History without Historians*. Edinburgh: Edinburgh University Press.
Martin, Richard P. 1989. *The Language of Heroes: Speech and Performance in the Iliad*. Ithaca, NY: Cornell University Press.
Martin, Richard P. 1993. "Telemachus and the Last Hero Song." *Colby Quarterly* 29.3: 222–40.
Martin, Richard P. 2003. "Keens from the Absent Chorus: Troy to Ulster." *Western Folkore* 62: 120–42.
Mayer, Roland G. 1994. *Horace: Epistles: Book I*. Cambridge: Cambridge University Press.
Miller, M. 1953. "Greek Kinship Terminology." *JHS* 73: 46–52.
Monsacré, Hélène. 1984. *Les larmes d'Achille: Le héros, la femme et la souffrance dans la poésie d'Homère*. Paris: A. Michel.
Monsacré, Hélène. 2018. *The Tears of Achilles*. Trans. by Nicholas J. Snead. Intro. by Richard P. Martin. Hellenic Studies Series, 75. Washington, DC: Center for Hellenic Studies. http://nrs.harvard.edu/urn-3:hul.ebook:CHS_MonsacreH.The_Tears_of_Achilles.2018.
Montanari. Franco and Paola Ascheri, eds. 2002. *Omero tremila anni dopo*. Rome: Edizioni di Storia e Letteratura.
Montanari, Franco, Antonios Rengakos, Christos Tsagalis, eds. 2012. *Homeric Contexts: Neoanalysis and the Interpretation of Oral Poetry*. Berlin: de Gruyter.
Morris, Ian. 1986. "The Use and Abuse of Homer." *CA* 5: 81–138.Morris, Ian. 1997. "Homer and the Iron Age." In *id.* and Barry Powell, eds., *A New Companion to Homer*. Leiden: Brill. Pp. 535–59.
Muellner, Leonard C. 2016. "Helen's Fatal Attraction and Its Inversion." http://classical-inquiries.chs.harvard.edu/helens-fatal-attraction-and-its-inversion/
Mureddu, Patrizia. 1983. *Formula e tradizione nella poesia di Esiodo*. Rome: Ateneo.
Naafs-Wilstra, Marianne C. 1987. "Indo-European 'Dichtersprache' in Sappho and Alcaeus." *The Journal of Indo-European Studies* 15: 273–83.
Nagler, Michael. 1974. *Spontaneity and Tradition: A Study in the Oral Art of Homer*. Berkeley: University of California Press.
Nagy, Gregory. 1974. *Comparative Studies in Greek and Indic Meter*. Cambridge, MA: Harvard University Press.
Nagy, Gregory. 1976. "Formula and Meter." In Benjamin A. Stolz and Richard S. Shannon, eds., *Oral Literature and the Formula*. Ann Arbor: University of Michigan. Pp. 239–60.
Nagy, Gregory. 1990a. *Greek Mythology and Poetics*. Ithaca: Cornell University Press. Available at http://chs.harvard.edu/CHS/article/display/1283.
Nagy, Gregory. 1992. "Homeric Questions." *TAPA* 122: 17–60. Rev. in 1996a: 29–63.
Nagy, Gregory. 1996a. *Homeric Questions*. Austin, TX: University of Texas Press.
Nagy, Gregory. 1996b. *Poetry as Performance: Homer and Beyond*. Cambridge: Cambridge University Press.
Nagy, Gregory. 1999[1979]. *The Best of the Achaeans: Concepts of the Hero in Archaic Greek Poetry*. Rev. ed. Baltimore: The Johns Hopkins University Press.
Nagy, Gregory. 2001. "Homeric Poetry and Problems of Multiformity: The 'Panathenaic Bottleneck'." *CP* 96.2: 109–119.
Nagy, Gregory. 2002. "The Language of Heroes as Mantic Poetry." In Michael Reichel and Antonios Rengakos, ed., *Epea Pteroenta: Beiträge zur Homerforschung*. Festschrift für Wolfgang Kullmann zum 75. Geburtstag. Stuttgart: Franz Steiner. Pp. 141–50.

Nagy, Gregory 2004. *Homer's Text and Language*. Chicago: University of Illinois Press.
Nagy, Gregory 2007. "Homer and Greek Myth." In Roger D. Woodard, ed., *The Cambridge Companion to Greek Mythology*. Cambridge: Cambridge University Press. Pp. 52–82.
Nagy, Gregory 2014. Rev. of Jensen 2011. *Gnomon* 86 (2014) 97–101.
Nagy, Gregory 2016a. "Helen of Sparta and Her Very Own Eidolon." In *Classical Inquiries: Studies on the Ancient World from CHS*. Available at http://classical-inquiries.chs.harvard.edu/helen-of-sparta-and-her-very-own-eidolon/
Nagy, Gregory 2016b. "Revisiting the Question of Etymology and Essence." http://classical-inquiries.chs.harvard.edu/revisiting-the-question-of-etymology-and-essence/
Nannini, Simonetta. 1995. *Nuclei tematici dell'*Iliade: "Il duello in sogno". Firenze: L.S. Olschki.
Neuberger-Donath, Ruth. 1977. "Sappho 31.2s...ὅττις ἐνάντιός τοι / ἰσδάνει." *AC* 20: 199–200.
Nünlist, René and Irene J.F. de Jong. 2000. "Homerische Poetik in Stichwörtern." In Graf *et al.* 2000: 159–71.
Olson, S. Douglas. 1994. "Equivalent Speech-Introduction Formulae in the *Iliad*." *Mnemosyne* 47.2: 145–51.
Ormand, Kirk. 2014. *The Hesiodic* Catalogue of Women *and Archaic Greece*. Cambridge: Cambridge University Press.
Osborne, Robin. 2005. "Ordering Women in Hesiod's Catalogue." In Hunter 2005: 5–24.
Page, Denys L. 1959. *History and the Homeric* Iliad. Berkeley: University of California Press.
Palmer, Leonard R. 1980. *The Greek Language*. London: Faber and Faber. Repr. Norman, OK: University of Oklahoma Press, 1996.
Pape, Wilhelm. 1888. *Griechisch-deutsches Handwörterbuch*. 2 vols. 3rd ed. Braunschweig: F. Vieweg.
Parlato, Giorgia. 2010. "Note di lettura al 'Cypria': frr. 4.3, 9.1, 32.2 Bernabé." *Lexis* 28: 291–96.
Parry, Adam. 1956. "The Language of Achilles." *TAPA* 87: 1–7.
Parry, Adam. 1966. "Have We Homer's *Iliad*?" *YCS* 20: 177–216.
Parry, Adam. 1971. "Introduction." In *id.*, ed., *The Making of Homeric Verse*. Oxford: Oxford University Press. Pp. ix–lxii.
Parry, Anne Amory. 1966. "The Gates of Horn and Ivory." *YCS* 20: 3–57.
Parry, Anne Amory. 1971. "Homer as Artist." *CQ* 21: 1–15.
Parry, Anne Amory. 1973. *Blameless Aegisthus: A Study of* ἀμύμων *and Other Homeric Epithets*. Leiden: Brill.
Parry, Milman. 1971[1928]. *The Traditional Epithet in Homer*. In Parry 1971: 1–190.
Parry, Milman. 1971. *The Making of Homeric Verse*. Ed. Adam Parry. Oxford: Oxford University Press.
Pelling, Christopher, ed. 1990. *Characterization and Individuality in Greek Literature*. Oxford: Oxford University Press. Pp. 137–61.
Perkell, Christine. 2008. "Reading the Laments of *Iliad* 24." In Ann Suter, ed., *Lament: Studies in the Ancient Mediterranean and Beyond*. New York: Oxford University Press. Pp. 93–117.
Perotti, Pier Angelo. 1990. "A propos de l'adjectif 'dios'." *RPh* 64: 163–71.
Pucci, Pietro. 1987. *Odysseus Polutropos: Intertextual Readings in the* Odyssey *and the* Iliad. Ithaca: Cornell University Press.
Rabel, Robert J. 1997. *Plot and Point of View in the Iliad*. Ann Arbor: University of Michigan Press.
Ramersdorfer, Hans. 1981. *Singuläre Iterata der Ilias (A-K)*. Königstein/Ts.: Verlag Anton Hain.

Ready, Jonathan L. 2018. *The Homeric Simile In Comparative Perspectives: Oral Traditions From Saudi Arabia to Indonesia*. Oxford: Oxford University Press.
Reckford, Kenneth. 1964. "Helen in the *Iliad*." *GRBS* 5.1: 5–20.
Reece, Steve. 2009. *Homer's Winged Words: The Evolution of Early Greek Epic Diction in the Light of Oral Theory*. Leiden: Brill.
Reichel, Michael. 1994. *Fernbeziehungen in der Ilias*. Tübingen: Narr,
Reichel, Michael. 1999. "Die homerische Helenagestalt aus motivgeschichtlicher und motivvergleichender Sicht." In John N. Kazazis and Antonios Rengakos, eds., *Euphrosyne: Studies in Ancient Epic and its Legacy in Honor of Dimitris N. Maronitis*. Stuttgart: Steiner. Pp. 291–307.
Reichel, Michael. 2002. "Zur sprachlichen und inhaltlichen Deutung eines umstrittenes Iliasverses (*Il.* II, 356 = 590)." In *id.* and Antonios Rengakos, eds., *Epea Pteroenta: Beiträge zur Homerforschung*. Festschrift für Wolfgang Kullmann zum 75. Geburtstag. Stuttgart: Franz Steiner. Pp. 163–72.
Richardson, Nicholas. 1993. *The* Iliad: *A Commentary*. Vol. 6 (Books 21–24). Cambridge: Cambridge University Press.
Rousseau, Philippe. 1990. "Le deuxième Atride: Le type épique de Ménélas dans l'*Iliade*." In Marie-Madeleine Mactoux and Evelyne Geny, eds., *Mélanges Pierre Lévêque*. Vol. 5. Paris: Belles Lettres. Pp. 325–54.
Russell, D.A. 1964. *'Longinus': On the Sublime*. Oxford: Oxford University Press.
Russo, Joseph. 1963. "A Closer Look at Homeric Formulas." *TAPA* 94: 235–47.
Russo, Joseph. 1966. "The Structural Formula in Homeric Verse." *YCS* 20: 219–40.
Russo, Joseph. 1997. "The Formula." In Powell and Morris 1997: 238–60.
Russo, Joseph. 2011. "Formula." In Finkelberg 2011: 296–98.
Russo, Joseph, Manuel Fernández-Galiano, and Alfred Heubeck, eds. 1992. *A Commentary on Homer's* Odyssey, Vol. III: Books XVII–XXIV. Oxford: Clarendon Press.
Sacks, Richard. 1987. *The Traditional Phrase in Homer: Two Studies in Form, Meaning, and Interpretation*. Leiden: Brill.
Sale, Mary. 2001. "The Oral-Formulaic Theory Today." In Janet Watson, ed., *Speaking Volumes*. Mnemosyne Suppl., 218. Leiden: Brill. Pp. 53–80.
Sale, W. Merritt. 1989. "The Trojans, Statistics, and Milman Parry." *GRBS* 30: 341–410.
Sammons, Benjamin. 2017. *Device and Composition in the Greek Epic Cycle*. Oxford: Oxford University Press.
Saussure, Ferdinand de. 1972. *Cours de Linguistique Général*. Edited by Charles Bally and Albert Sechehaye with the collaboration of Albert Riedlinger. Paris: Payot.
Saussure, Ferdinand de. 1986. *Course in General Linguistics*. Trans. of Saussure 1972 by Roy Harris. La Salle, Ill.: Open Court.
Sbardella, Livio. 1994. "La 'variatio' formulare nella dizione epica." *QUCC* 47: 21–45.
Scafoglio, Giampiero. 2015. "I due volti di Elena: Sopravvivenze della tradizione orale nell'*Odissea*." *Gaia* 18: 133–44.
Schadewaldt, Wolfgang. 1966[1943]. *Iliasstudien*. Repr. of 2nd ed., Leipzig, 1943. Darmstadt: Wissenschaftliche Buchgesellschaft.
Scheid, John and Jesper Svenbro. 1996. *The Craft of Zeus: Myths of Weaving and Fabric*. Cambridge, MA: Harvard University Press.
Scheid, John and Jesper Svenbro. 1994. *Le métier de Zeus*. Paris: Éditions de la Découverte.
Schmiel, Robert. 1984. "Metrically-interchangeable formulae and phrase-clusters in Homer." *LCM* 9.3 (March): 34–38.

Schuster, Albrecht. 1866. *Untersuchungen über die homerischen stabilen Beiwörter*. Stade: A. Pockwitz.
Schwenn, Friedrich. 1927. *Gebet und Opfer: Studien zum griechischen Kultus*. Heidelberg: Winter.
Schwyzer = Schwyzer, Eduard. 1939–1971. *Griechische Grammatik auf der Grundlage von Karl Brugmanns Griechischer Grammatik*. Vol. 1 (Allgemeiner Teil; Lautlehre; Wortbildung; Flexion) by Schwyzer (1939). Vol. 2 (Syntax and Syntaktische Stylistik) by Albert Debrunner (1950). Vol. 3 (Register) by Demetrius J. Georgacas (1953). Vol. 4 (Stellenregister) by Fritz Radt and Stefan Radt (1971). Munich: Beck.
Scodel, Ruth. 2002. *Listening to Homer: Tradition, Narrative, and Audience*. Ann Arbor: University of Michigan Press.
Scodel, Ruth. 2008. *Epic Facework: Self-Presentation and Social Interaction in Homer*. Swansea: Classical Press of Wales.
Shannon, Richard S., III. 1975. *The Arms of Achilles and Homeric Compositional Technique*. Mnemosyne Suppl., 36. Leiden: Brill. Pp. 31–94.
Smith, Ian. 2002. "European Divorce Laws, Divorce Rates, and Their Consequences." In Antony W. Dnes and Robert Rowthorn, eds., *The Law and Economics of Marriage and Divorce*. Cambridge: Cambridge University Press. Pp. 212–29.
Stanford, W. B. 1958–1959. *The* Odyssey *of Homer*. 2nd ed. 2 vols. London: Macmillan.
Suzuki, Mihoko. 1989. *Metamorphoses of Helen: Authority, Difference, and the Epic*. Ithaca, NY: Cornell University Press.
Taplin, Oliver. 1992. *Homeric Soundings: The Shaping of the* Iliad. Oxford: Clarendon Press.
Tosetti, Giovanni. 2006. "La dernière generation héroïque: un parcours historico-réligieux et sémio-narratif, d'Hésiode au ps.-Apollodore." *Kernos* 19: 113–30.
Tsagalis, Christos C. 2004. *Epic Grief*. Untersuchungen zur antiken Literatur und Geschichte, 70. Berlin: de Gruyter.
Tsagalis, Christos C. 2008. *The Oral Palimpsest: Exploring Intertextuality in the Homeric Epics*. Washington, DC: Center for Hellenic Studies.
Tsagalis, Christos C. 2009. "Naming Helen: Localization, Meter and Semantics of a Homeric Character." In Eleni Karamalengou and Eugenia Makrygianni, eds., Ἀντιφίλησις: *Studies on Classical, Byzantine, and Modern Greek Literature and Culture in Honour of John-Theophanes Papademetriou*. Stuttgart: Franz Steiner. Pp. 39–47.
Usener, Kurt. 1990. *Beobachtungen zum Verhältnis der* Odyseе *zur Ilas*. Tübingen: Narr.
Van Leeuwen, Jan. 1912–1913. *Ilias*. 2 vols. Leiden: A.W. Suthoff.
van Thiel, Helmut. 2010. *Homeri* Ilias. 2nd ed. Hildesheim: Olms.
Vanséveren, Sylvie. 1998. "Skhetlios dans l'épopée homérique: Étude sémantique et morphologique." In Lambert Isebaert and René Lebrun, eds., *Quaestiones Homericae: Acta Colloquii Namurcensis*. Louvain-Namur: Peeters. Pp. 253–73.
Versnel, H.S. 2011. *Coping with the Gods: Wayward Readings in Greek Theology*. Leiden: Brill.
Visser, Edzard. 1987. *Homerische Versifikationstechnik. Versuch einer Rekonstruktion*. Frankfurt am Main: Lang.
Visser, Edzard. 1989. "Formulae or Single Words? Towards a New Theory on Homeric Verse-Making." *Würzburger Jahrbücher* 14: 21–37.
Vivante, Paolo. 1982. *The Epithets in Homer. A Study in Poetic Values*. New Haven: Yale University Press.
Vox, Onofrio. 1975. "Epigrammi in Omero." *Belfagor* 30: 67–70.
Wachter, Rudolf. 2000. "Grammatik der homerischen Sprache." In Graf *et al*. 2000: 61–108.

Wathelet, Paul. 1995. "Athéna chez Homère ou le triomphe de la déesse." *Kernos* 8: 167–85.
Wendel, Thilde. 1929. *Die Gesprächsanrede im griechischen Epos und Drama der Blütezeit*. Tübinger Beiträge zur Altertumswissenschaft, 6. Stuttgart: W. Kohlhammer.
West, M.L. 1966. *Hesiod: Theogony*. Oxford: Clarendon Press.
West, M.L. 1985. *The Hesiodic Catalogue of Women*. Oxford: Clarendon Press.
West, M.L. 2001. *Studies in the Text and Transmission of the* Iliad. Munich: Saur.
West, M.L. 2007. *Indo-European Poetry and Myth*. Oxford: Oxford University Press.
West, M.L. 2011a. *The Making of the* Iliad. Oxford: Oxford University Press.
West, M.L. 2011b[1999]. "The Invention of Homer." In West 2011b: 408–36. Orig. pub. in *CQ* 49 (1999) 364–82.
West, M.L. 2013. *The Epic Cycle: A Commentary on the Lost Troy Epics*. Oxford: Oxford University Press.
West, M.L. 2014. *The Making of the* Odyssey. Oxford: Oxford University Press.
West, Stephanie. 1988. In Alfred Heubeck, Stephanie West and J.B. Hainsworth, *A Commentary on Homer's* Odyssey. Vol. I: Books I–VIII. Oxford: Clarendon Press.
Whallon, William. 1961. "The Homeric Epithets." *Yale Classical Studies* 17: 97–142.
Whitman, Cedric H. 1958. *Homer and the Heroic Tradition*. Cambridge, MA: Harvard University Press.
Wickert-Micknat, Gisela. 1982. *Die Frau*. Archaeologia Homerica, R. Göttingen: Vandenhoeck & Ruprecht.
Wilamowitz-Moellendorff, Ulrich von. 1931–1932. *Die Glaube der Hellenen*. 2 vols. Berlin: Weidmann.
Worman, Nancy. 2001. "The Voice Which is Not One: Helen's Verbal Guises in Homeric Epic." In André Lardinois and Laura McLure, eds., *Making Silence Speak: Women's Voices in Greek Literature and Society*. Princeton: Princeton University Press. Pp. 19–37.
Worman, Nancy. 2002. *The Cast of Character: Style in Greek Literature*. Austin, TX: University of Texas Press.
Worth, Robert F. 2010. "Crime (Sex) and Punishment (Stoning)." *The New York Times* Aug 22: WK 1,4.
Zink, Norbert. 1962. *Griechische Ausdrucksweisen für warm und kalt im seelischen Bereich*. Diss. Johannes Gutenberg University. Heidelberg.

Index nominum et rerum

Modern authors cited in the text of this monograph are listed in this index.

Achilles 38, 39, 44, 45, 48, 53, 60, 70, 72, 78, 81, 84–86, 88, 89, 90, 91, 92, 105, 106, 119, 135, 143, 144, 145; as speaker 28
Aegisthus 50–51, 108, 129
Agamemnon 18, 20, 24, 27, 28, 29, 35, 36, 41, 42, 43, 44, 45, 51, 53, 54, 67, 73, 89, 90, 100, 115, 135, 136, 147
Andromache 13, 15, 18, 33, 38, 60, 93, 97, 98, 102, 148
Antenor 15, 17, 25, 44, 54, 57, 100, 106, 146
Aphrodite 2, 9, 21–22, 29, 31–33, 36, 39, 45, 50, 55, 57, 62, 70, 86, 100, 103, 105, 107, 116–17, 120, 121, 124, 129, 135, 141, 142, 147
Apple of Discord 86
Arētē 48, 93, 98, 101
Athena 2, 11, 14, 42, 45, 71, 82, 83–84, 88, 90, 93, 94, 95–96, 97, 101–102, 106, 119–21, 125, 126–27, 128, 132, 133, 141, 142, 143, 145
Bilhah 104
bride contest 109
Brillante, Carlo 51
Brisēís 48, 78, 82, 83, 84, 103, 105, 106, 111, 135
Brunot, Ferdinand 1
Charites 103, 105
Chloris 127, 129, 130, 133
Chryses 67
Chrysēís 74, 104, 105
Clytemestra 140; cf. Clytemnestra
Clytemnestra 36, 50, 51, 54, 55, 73, 126; cf. Clytemestra
Conti Jiménez, Luz 89
de Jong, Irene 80, 95, 120
Deïphobus 20, 21, 21n7, 30, 38, 122n2
Di Benedetto, Vincenzo 78, 86
Diomedes 41, 54, 60

divorce law, Athenian 37; in the United States 37–38
Edwards, Mark W. 120
Eris 32, 86
Eumaeus 55, 73, 76
Eurycleia 16, 36, 48, 65
Eurymachus 103, 108
Foley, John Miles 11–12
Gadatas 104
García, John F. 12
Hackstein, Olav 142
Hainsworth, J.B. V, 75–76, 134
Hector 23–24, 33–35, 38–39, 43, 44, 46–47, 50, 52, 53, 56, 57–58, 59–61, 62, 68, 71, 83, 85, 91, 95, 98, 100, 102, 131, 148, 149
Hecuba 18, 38, 58, 71, 125, 126, 128
Helen, "archaic vulgate," in 86n18, 138, 139, 144; as cause of the war 27; as prize by capture 15, 19, 20–21, 23, 91; blame of by in-laws 26; focalization 22n1, 52n1, 53, 57, 57n7, 91, 91n30, 126; name, with and without digamma 61n23; pairs of epithets for 7, 69, 76, 77, 94, 102, 126; self-reproach of V, 1, 39, 58, 69, 76, 80, 149; speeches 1, 29, 35, 61n20, 67, 68, 72, 122; two perspectives on in *Il.* 100; Trojan view of 91; wife, fundamental identity as 25
Helenus 21, 83, 84
Hephaestus 36, 58
Hera 11, 25, 36, 42, 45, 82, 83, 90, 93, 97, 101, 107, 111, 112, 113
Hermione 18, 62, 148, 149
Heubeck, Alfred 96
Hirschberger, Martina 140
Hoekstra, Arie 131–32, 143
Homer: embassy before fighting started 15; formular economy, violation of, 9n36, 74–75; in-laws, words for 17–

18, 24; kinship, words for 18–19; narrator 2; semantic field of κρυοέσση 30–31; sister-in-law, words for 16; tradition VI, 9, 11–12; "traditional referentiality" 11–12; typical scene 14, 48, 80, 125n1; verbs for leading and following 21; wife, words for 24–25; xenia 19

Idomeneus 21, 41

Iris 16, 20, 25, 53, 86, 96, 97, 100

Jacob 104

Jörgensen's Law 3

Judgment of Paris 86, 135

Katz, Joshua 134

Kirk, G.S. 9, 32, 75

Köchly, Hermann 67

Kroeber, A.L. 12

Kullmann, Wolfgang 139

Leah 104

Leto 82, 103, 106, 131, 132

Martin, Richard 58, 70, 109

Megapenthes 56, 61, 62, 70, 79, 149

Melantho 104, 107, 108

Memnon 143

Mētis 107

Monsacré, Hélène 148

Mureddu, Patrizia 87

Mycenae 107

Nagy, Gregory V–VI, 11–12, 109

Nemesis 103, 140

Nestor 41, 46, 47, 48, 49, 50, 51, 56, 110, 118, 120, 127, 143, 146

Odysseus 15, 26, 36, 41, 42, 45, 48, 49, 54–55, 60, 65, 67, 68, 69, 72, 74, 76, 78, 79, 92, 93, 94, 95, 96, 97, 98, 101, 103, 106, 107, 108, 109, 110, 116, 118, 120, 121, 123, 125, 127, 128, 129–30, 132, 147, 149

Orestes 50, 51

Paris/Alexander 6, 15, 16, 18, 19–20, 21, 22–25, 29–30, 32, 33, 34, 35, 37, 38, 39, 43, 44, 45, 46, 47, 50, 52, 53, 54, 57, 58, 59, 60, 62–63, 69, 70, 81, 82–83, 86, 90, 95, 100, 112, 116, 117, 118, 121, 123, 124, 128, 135, 146, 147, 148, 149

Parry, Milman V, 1, 3–5, 7, 10, 11, 12, 93

Patroclus 28, 38, 48, 85, 110, 136, 143, 147

Peleus 26, 58, 85–86, 127

Penelope 2, 13, 16, 27, 38, 48, 49, 50, 66, 70, 71, 72, 77, 88, 96, 102, 107, 116, 119, 123, 124, 126, 127, 138, 145, 148, 149

Pero 127, 129, 130–32, 133

Philoctetes 20

Phoenix 26, 35, 48, 103, 104, 105, 111, 112

Phylonoē 55, 140

Pisistratus 47, 49, 71, 120

Priam, 15, 16, 17, 19, 21, 22, 25, 27, 35, 38, 39, 42, 48, 53, 57, 58, 61, 66–68, 69, 70, 76, 78, 85, 91, 92, 96, 100, 114–15, 144

Proteus 51, 52, 63, 122, 138, 140

Rachel 104

Reichel Michael 55

Reuben 104

Salmoneus 127, 128–29

Scheid, John and Jesper Svenbro 77

Telegonus 109

Telemachus 27, 36, 46, 47–48, 49, 51, 52, 56, 61, 63, 68, 70–71, 79–80, 90, 92, 103, 104, 108–109, 110, 112, 118, 120, 128, 138, 148, 149

Telephus 85

Theano 83, 103, 106, 112, 113, 131, 136

Themis 85, 103, 106

Thersites 28, 147

Thetis 13, 58, 73, 76, 82, 83, 85–86, 87–88, 140

Timandra 55, 140

Tyndareus 55, 115, 126, 128, 140

Tyro 11, 14, 94, 125, 127–29, 133

Zeus Xenios 147

Index locorum

Aesch.
Ag.
399–402   19n22
1469–71   55
Pers.
970   128

Alcaeus
fr. 42 V   92
fr. 206.1 V   142
fr. 283.4 V   40

Anacreon
15 Page   103n2

Anth. Pal.
6.144 (Anacreon)   103n2

Apollodorus
Epit.
3.28   15
5.9   21
5.22   21n27, 30n21
6.29   109n14

Apollonius Dysc.
De constructione
Uhlig, *Gramm. Graec.* vol. 2.2:   101

Apollonius Rhod.
1.570   132
4.1343   28
fr. 7 Powell   132

Apollonius Soph.
p. 149 Bekker   73

Aristophanes
Pax 798   103n2

Bacchylides
8.18 S–M   26
15(14) S–M   15n3, 44n10
15(14).7 S–M   106n8

Conon
FGrH 26 F 1 (XXXIV)   21

Demetrius
Eloc. 194   94

Demosthenes
23.53   37
59.87   37

Epic Cycle
Cypria
Arg. 4–9 B   145n31
Arg. 19–20 B   21n30
Arg. 55–57 B   15n3, 44n10, 106n8
fr. 1 B   90
fr. 9.1 B   1, 130, 131
fr. 9.2 B   103, 103n1
Il. Parv.
Arg. 1.6–7 B   21n26
Arg. 1.10 B   20
frs. 6–7 B   120
Ilioupersis
Arg. 14–15 B   21n27, 30n21
Telegonia
Arg. 17–20 B   109n19
fr. 5 B   109n19

Epimenides
fr. 19.1 D–K   103

Euripides
frag. 81.8 Austin (1968)   133n23
Hipp.
68   132
IA
201–202   130n13
Tro.
647–50   102n27
864–66   37

Eustathius

I.617.23 (*Il.*)	16
II.326.13 (*Il.*)	27n8
I.154.31 (*Od.*)	74n7
II.94.24 (*Od.*)	110

Frag. adesp. PMG

96	7, 94n9

Gorgias
Helen

4	88
6	22n35
20	22n35

Hesiod
Astronomica

291 M–W	73

Catalogue

fr. 10(a).21 M–W	105, 111n23
fr. 10(a).24 M–W	24n40
fr. 10(a).32 M–W	110n21
fr. 10(a).34 M–W	24n40
fr. 10a.46 M–W	24n41
fr. 10(a).59 M–W	24n40
fr. 17a.3 M–W	105, 111n23
fr. 17a.7 M–W	110n21
fr. 20.25 M–W	129
fr. 23a.7–10 M–W	140n19
fr. 26.36 M–W	24n41
fr. 30.25 M–W	129, 135n4
fr. 30.29 M–W	24n41
fr. 30.31 M–W	110n21
fr. 37.8–9 M–W	131n18
fr. 43a.19 M–W	105, 111n22
fr. 85.6 M–W	105, 111n23
fr. 105.3 M–W	24n41
fr. 129.13 M–W	105n5, 111n23
fr. 141.10 M–W	103n1
fr. 180.13 M–W	105n5, 111n23
fr. 185.8 M–V	87n23
fr. 190.3 M–W	65n4
fr. 193.11 M–W	24n41
fr. 199.2 M–W	8n27
fr. 200.2 M–W	7n22, 8n26, 94n9
fr. 200.11 M–W	89n24
fr. 204.43 M–W	7n22, 8n26, 94n9
fr. 204.55 M–W	94n9
fr. 204.49–54 M–W	29n14
fr. 204.55 M–W	94n9, 97n20
fr. 204.62 M–W	97n20
fr. 205.2 M–W	110n21
fr. 217.6 M–W	137n12
fr. 251a.5 M–W	24n41
fr. 280.20 M–W	87n23
fr. 305.1 M–W	110
fr. 343.5 M–W	107, 111

Fr. dub.

fr. 343.4 M–W	87n23

Meg.

fr. 252.4 M–W	24n40

Op.

75	103
161–65	86
163	90
165	89, 89n24, 90, 91, 137
256	11, 142
608–701	31
702–703	31
739	110

Scut.

83	73

Theogony

11–12	11
15	106
26–28	121
27	121n29
76	11, 142
238	106
241	87n23
250	24, 24n39
266	24n41
270	106
298	107
298	111n22
354	24
404	110
410	24n41
508	24n41
901	24n41, 106
907	105, 111
908	110n21
915	103n1

921	25	2.356	55
960	105	2.394	41n4
976	105n5	2.484–85	126n5
		2.484–87	69
Hereas		2.488	69, 121
FGrH 486 F 2	89n24	2.491	117n12
		2.548	126n5
Herodotus		2.590	55, 56
1.3.1	24n44	2.594	126n5
2.118	15	2.598	117n12
2.120.5	135n6	2.689	82n2, 84, 87n23
		2.714	65, 65n4
Homer		3.39	83
Iliad		3.40	35n42
1.36	82	3.45–51	83
1.115	73	3.48	100
1.143	105	3.69–70	95
1.158–60	29	3.46–53	23
1.159	36, 136, 147	3.48	6, 22, 22n33, 134
1.159–60	136n8, 147n7	3.48–51	24
1.184	105	3.49	24
1.202	117n12, 126n5	3.53	6, 25
1.222	117n12	3.67–70	43, 136n8, 147n7
1.225	36	3.70	53, 100
1.307	143	3.72	19n20, 53, 100
1.310	105	3.82	41n4
1.323	105	3.88–91	43, 95
1.346	105	3.91	53, 100
1.369	105	3.93	19n20, 53, 100
1.414	31	3.121	10, 66, 93, 96, 97, 115
1.505–10	85		
1.508–10	85n16, 86	3.121–24	16
2.109	41n4	3.121–244	74
2.111	35	3.122	16, 18
2.115	51	3.125	96
2.120	147	3.126	91
2.157	117n12, 126n5	3.126–28	91
2.160–62	42	3.130	16, 16n7, 100
2.161	66, 97, 90	3.136–37	20
2.173–78	42	3.137	53
2.177	66, 90, 97	3.139–40	149
2.212–77	147	3.139–45	114
2.284	41	3.140	115
2.287	41	3.154	66
2.332	41n4	3.156–58	62, 66, 67, 81
2.346–49	41	3.157	19n20, 53, 100
2.354–56	56	3.158	134

3.159–60	53, 81	3.351–54	135, 147
3.161	57, 114, 135n3	3.374	126n5
3.162	17, 66, 100, 114, 114n3	3.383	57
		3.383–94	29, 116
3.164	91	3.395–412	116
3.166	66	3.399	29, 29n18
3.171	48, 66, 74, 75, 76, 99, 101	3.400–401	55
		3.400–402	29
3.172	15, 17	3.403–405	29
3.173–74	35, 58	3.404	26, 29, 100
3.174	22	3.406–409	116
3.175	18, 149	3.410–12	30
3.177	67	3.411–12	30, 32, 147
3.177–80	67	3.412	86
3.178	68n13	3.412–17	31
3.178–79	67	3.413	32, 116
3.178–80	67	3.414	2, 26, 31, 39, 100
3.179	67	3.418	32, 33, 99, 116, 117, 126
3.180	18, 18n13, 26, 35, 36, 100, 118	3.418–20	32
3.192	17, 100, 115	3.419	86
3.199	74, 75, 99, 114, 115, 118, 123, 126	3.420	32, 116, 117
		3.423	33, 65, 69, 70, 99, 116, 117
3.200	68n13		
3.200–202	67	3.424	32
3.204	15	3.424	116
3.204–24	15, 100	3.424–27	116
3.204–207	106n8	3.425	117
3.228	7, 66, 69, 71, 73, 74, 75, 76, 79, 86, 94, 99, 105n4	3.426	32, 33, 99, 116, 117, 126
		3.427	116
3.229	68n13	3.428	86, 35n42
3.234–35	69	3.428–36	34, 59
3.238	18	3.429	19
3.242	19, 28, 32, 69, 92, 148	3.437	118
		3.438	15, 33
3.254	100	3.443–44	22
3.254–55	53	3.447	21n30, 33
3.255	23, 100	3.448	20
3.281–85	43	3.456–60	20, 44
3.282	54, 100	3.458	52
3.285	54	3.767–71	147
3.313–82	29, 116	4.8	11
3.329	81, 82, 99	4.9	45, 97
3.321	101	4.18–19	45
3.395–412	29	4.19	21n27
3.396	100	4.59–61	101

Index locorum — 177

4.60	25n46	6.291	22
4.128	126n5	6.292	22, 22n33, 128
4.145	92	6.293–303	83
4.156	49	6.298–99	106
4.174	42	6.300	106
4.184	94	6.302	131
4.234	41n4	6.302–303	106, 107n10
4.235–64	119n20	6.303	82n2, 83
4.242	41n4	6.304	126n5
4.291	49	6.305	84
4.316	49	6.312	126n5
4.392–97	60	6.316	33
4.444	32	6.318–20	57
4.512	82n2.88	6.321–22	57
4.512–13	85n13	6.321–24	46
4.515	126n5	6.323–24	10
5.55–53	136	6.325–31	58
5.115	117n12, 126n5	6.328	60
5.131	126n5	6.328–29	22, 47
5.312	126n5	6.332–41	58
5.348	126n5	6.337	20n24, 60
5.348–49	29n18	6.343	7, 34, 58, 59, 94
5.373	17n8	6.344	6, 15, 17, 26, 33, 34, 60
5.396	117n12, 126n5, 143	6.344–58	148
5.498	41n4	6.345	18
5.550–53	147	6.345–48	35
5.635	117n12	6.348	26, 34
5.712	41n4	6.349–50	34
5.714	117n12, 126n5	6.350–53	60
5.733	117n12, 126n4	6.351	20n24
5.815	117n12	6.354	58
5.820	126n5	6.355	15, 17
5.824	41n4	6.355–56	91
5.908	11, 45, 97	6.355–57	33
6.86–92	83	6.355–57	91
6.92	82n2, 83	6.356	33, 60
6.107	41n4	6.357	35
6.151	126n5	6.357–58	62, 149
6.214	60	6.360	17, 17n10, 60
6.229	11	6.370–71	98
6.269–73	83	6.371	93, 102
6.273	82n2, 83	6.377	93, 98, 102
6.281–85	35n42	6.378	16n5
6.288	126	6.383	16n5
6.288–92	71, 125	6.394	102
6.289	126	6.395	102

178 — Index locorum

6.408	38	9.665	106
6.420	117n12, 126n5	10.5	82n2 87n23
6.441	15	10.27–28	136n7, 147n6
6.490–93	102n27	10.278	117n12, 126n5
7.24	126n5	10.288–90	60
7.156–60	57	10.296	126n5
7.345–78	54	10.329	82n3
7.347–53	146n3	10.391	35
7.350	10, 44, 57, 52	10.553	117n12
7.354–64	146n3	11.73–83	85n16
7.355	81, 82	11.125	53
7.362	54	11.138–42	15n3
7.362–64 20, 146		11.140	106n8
7.368–78	146n3	11.216	41n4
7.392–93	20, 54	11.224	106
7.400–401	54	11.362	33n32
7.411	82n3	11.369	81, 82, 8n28
8.39	17n8	11.385	83n7
8.82	81	11.505	81, 82
8.228	41n4	11.638	62n24, 135n3
8.236–37	35	12.2	41n4
8.304–305	62n24	12.14	41n4
8.305	135n3	12.37	41n4
8.352	117n12, 126n5	12.178	41n4
8.384	117n12, 126n4	12.293	41n4
8.423	33n32	12.415	41n4
8.427	117n12, 126n5	13.154	82n3
9.16	41n4	13.227	41
9.18	35	13.347–50	85n16
9.139–40	44	13.622–27	135, 147
9.140	135	13.623–27	19
9.257	26	13.626–27	22, 83
9.281–82	45	13.627	22n33
9.282	135	13.766	81, 82
9.339	2, 81, 89, 89n24, 145	13.769	83
		13.825	117n12
9.339–43	84	14.156	18n13
9.437	17n8	14.190	17n8
9.444	17n8	14.193	126n5
9.448–49	104	14.198	107
9.449	103, 111	14.213	107
9.502–12	35	14.214	107
9.536	126n5	14.224	126n5
9.590	25	14.325	131
9.658–62	48	14.346	25n46
9.663–68	48	14.470	49
9.664–65	105	15.52	49

Index locorum — **179**

15.57–58	88	19.325	2, 5, 11, 26, 28, 39, 89, 90, 148
15.64	49		
15.87	49, 106, 111	19.329–31	91
15.121	49	19.331	11, 92
15.202	41n4	19.413	82
15.560	41n4	20.193	119
15.592–603	85n16	20.449	33n32
15.598	86	21.416	126n5
16.20	143	21.420	126n5
16.73	41n4	21.429	117n12
16.88	82n3	21.479	25n46
16.744	143	21.481	33n32
16.860	82n2, 88	21.509	17n8
16.860–61	85n14	22.34	33n32
17.92	136, 147	22.38	17n8
17.116	46	22.65	24n43
17.118–19	46	22.84	17n8
17.120	46	22.111–25	53
17.147	49	22.183	17n8
17.431	60	22.221	117n12
18.45	24n39	22.428	38
18.63	17n8	22.473	16n5, 18n15
18.86–87	35n42	22.481	35n42
18.184	25n46	22.485	38
18.364–67	101	23.81a	89n24
18.365	25n46	23.140	119
18.385	73, 86	23.185	126n5
18.396	36	23.218	94
18.424	73, 86	23.271	41n4
18.429–61	58	23.471	41
18.432–35a	58	23.535	41n4
18.435b–41	58	23.619	110
18.442–56	58	23.658	41n4
18.457–61	58	23.706	41n4
18.489	38n58	23.753	41n4
19.59–60	35n42	23.801	41n4
19.86–96	35	24.29–30	145n3
19.91	126n5	24.60	25n46
19.175	41n4	24.91	86
19.246	105	24.95	86
19.250	62n24	24.104	86
19.255	41n4	24.166	24n43
19.282	135n4	24.200	58
19.286	135	24.300	15
19.315	38	24.373	17n8
19.320	28	24.466	87
19.323–35	28	24.466–67	85n15

Index locorum

24.602	82	3.337	120, 126n5
24.607	106, 111	3.371–79	120
24.643–48	48	3.378	120, 126n5
24.643–76	78	3.394	126n4
24.675–76	48	3.397–401	48
24.676	105, 111	3.399–412	50
24.699	135n4	3.402–3	48
24.723	61n19, 93, 102	3.451	24n43
24.723–74	102	4.12–14	62, 149
24.724	102	4.21	143
24.725	102	4.98–107	49
24.727	38	4.103	143
24.747	61n19, 102	4.104–12	120
24.748	18n15	4.116–46	80
24.761	6, 56, 60, 131	4.122	73
24.761–76	68	4.130	63, 74
24.762	18, 18n13, 18n15	4.145	6, 36, 78, 91, 118
24.762–75	18	4.145–46	26, 35
24.763	18, 121	4.148	15, 138
24.763–64	21	4.151–53	49
24.763–67	18n14	4.174	118
24.764	35	4.183–86	47, 48
24.765–66	18	4.184	7, 10, 49, 76n13
24.766	21, 61	4.184–187	118
24.769	16n5, 18n13	4.188	143
24.769–70	18	4.190–202	120
24.770	17	4.219	7, 119, 120, 122
24.773	6, 28	4.220–26	120
24.775	28, 31, 32, 91, 147	4.227	6, 14, 78, 119, 120, 122
Odyssey		4.234	120
1.10	126n5	4.238–40	68, 121
1.29	108n12, 129	4.242–59	121
1.332	65	4.259–64	121
2.116–19	127	4.261–62	22, 50, 55
2.296	126n4	4.263	149
2.363	17n8	4.266	15, 122, 138
2.382	119n22	4.277–79	122
2.393	119n22	4.296	47n12, 48
3.154–55	57	4.296–97	47
3.156–58	57	4.296–305	78
3.184	17n8	4.302–305	47
3.247–52	51	4.304–305	70, 77, 105
3.256–57	51	4.305	73, 76, 79, 86, 94
3.305	51	4.512–22	51
3.309–10	50	4.544–47	51
3.311	51	4.561–69	138

4.564	63n26	11.427	36
4.569	63, 122	11.436–37	54
4.611	17n8	11.438	90
4.743	16, 16n7	11.438–39	54
4.752	126n4	11.522	143
4.762	126n5	12.375	86n19
4.795	119n22	12.389	82n2, 87n23
5.198	116	13.190	126n4
5.308–10	35n42	13.252	126n4
5.382	126n4	13.291	121
6.101	93	13.291–99	121
6.105	126n5	13.297	121
6.107–8	73	13.318	126n4
6.112	119n22	13.359	126n5
6.148	60	13.371	126n4
6.186	93	14.67–69	55
6.239	93	14.68	8n30
6.251	93	14.518–22	48
6.323	126n5	15.14	27n4
6.324	126n5	15.56–66	79
6.344	27	15.57–58	104
7.12	93	15.58	70, 77, 112
7.230	98	15.67–91	79
7.233	98	15.92–98	79
7.334	98	15.93	25, 138
7.335	98	15.99–108	79
7.335–38	98	15.100	61
7.335–42	48	15.103	61
7.339	98	15.107	70
7.346–47	48	15.109	71
8.308	126n5	15.109–30	79
8.312	35n42	15.122	61
8.319	36	15.122–23	61
8.452	82n2, 87n23	15.123	V, 4, 7, 111, 128
8.516–18	21n27	15.123–30	108
9.64	27n6	15.125	17n8
9.154	126n5	15.126	6, 61, 110
11.217	126n5	15.131–59	79
11.235	11, 94, 125	15.144	143
11.235–36	127	15.160–68	80
11.236	129	15.169–70	80
11.281	127	15.170–71	68, 80
11.287	1, 127, 131	15.171	71, 73
11.287–88	130	15.171	86
11.298–99	126	15.304–305	77
11.328	121	15.305	77, 80
11.424	36	15.363	73, 86n19

15.366	110n21	24.199	126
15.509	17n8	24.502	126n5
16.25	17n8	24.521	126n5
16.409	119n22	24.529	126n4
16.414	65	24.547	126n4
16.418	27		
16.421–22	27	**Homeric Scholia**	
17.118	90, 148	AbT *Il.* 3.458	42
18.187	119n22	BEQ *Od.* 4.305	73n3
18.198	93	bT	*Il.* 3.329 82
18.208	65	bT *Il.* 11.715	96n18
18.302	65	bT *Il.* 17.49	121n27
19.317–19	48	bT *Il.* 348c	27
18.321	103	bT *Il.* 6.377	97
18.321–25	107	D *Il.* 1.5	90
19.60	93	D *Il.* 3.228	73n4
19.203	121n29	T *Il.* 13.516	21
19.315	68	T *Il.* 1.346	106n6
19.372	36	T *Il.* 11.715	96n18
19.474	17n8	T *Il.* 3.121	97
20.60	66	T *Il.* 3.178	67
20.61	126n5	T *Il.* 4.19	82
20.61–65	35n42	T *Il.* 5.549	29n18
20.147–48	65n4	H *Od.* 11.236	129
21.38–41	110	QT *Od.* 11.236	129
21.42	65	ZM *Od.* 11.235	129
21.63	65		
22.205	126n5	*Hymn Hom.*	
22.226–29	93	*Ap.*	
22.227	2, 7, 76n13, 125, 128	25	131
		198–99	73
22.464	36	*Cer.*	
23.5	17n8	31	110n21
23.89	116	*Ven.*	
23.150	26	225	110n21
23.165	116	274	110n21
23.177–80	48	27 (To Artemis)	
23.218	2, 7, 76n1, 123, 127, 141	21	87n23
23.218–21	38, 49	**Horace**	
23.218–24	72	*Epist.* 1.2	146
23.218–221	123, 148	*Sat.* 1.3.107–108	29n16
23.242	119n22		
23.302	65	**Ibycus**	
23.344	119n22	fr. 297 PMG	21
23.354	110	fr. 282a.1–9 PMG = S151.1–9 PMGF	86n18, 92n36
24.196–97	149		

| fr. 288.1–2 PMG | 103n2 |
| fr. S174 SLG = PMGF | 132 |

Inscriptions
IG 13 983 = CEG 312 = 119 Friedlander
	103n2
SEG 26: 457–58	8n28
SEG 36: 356	8n28

Isocrates
Enc. Hel.
| 61 | 88 |
| 62 | 63 |

Lysias
| 1.26–31 | 37 |

Menander
| fr. 151.465 | Austin (1973) |

Moschus
Europa
| 29 | 133 |

Old Testament
Genesis
| 35.22 | 104n3 |
| 49.4 | 104n3 |

Ovid
Tristia II 371–72   29n16

Priapea
| 68.9–10 | 29n16 |

Papyri
P480a (6.288a–b)	71
P. Oxy. 2481	129
P. Oxy. 2485	129

Pindar
| *Isth.* 8.29–61 | 85 |

Pyth. 9.106	103
schol. *Isth.* 2.17	41n7
schol. *Nem.* 10	140

Plutarch
| *Sol.* 23.1 | 37 |

Rhianus
| fr. 56 Powell | 132 |

Sappho
| fr. 128 V | 103n2 |

Semonides
| fr. 6 W² | 31 |
| fr. 7.115–18 W² | 86 |

Simonides
| fr. 561 PMG | 21 |

Sophocles
Ἑλένης Ἀπαίτησις frs. 176–180a Radt
| | 15n3, 44n10 |
| *OC* 771 | 17 |

Stesichorus
| fr. 46 PMG | 55 |
| fr. 209 PMG | 16 |

Strabo
| 8.6.5 | 41 |
| 8.6.19 | 51 |

Theognis
| 1305 | 110n21 |

Theocritus
| *Idyll* 18 | 77 |

Xenophon
| *Cyr.* 5.2.28 | 104 |
| *Hier.* 3.3 | 37 |

www.ingramcontent.com/pod-product-compliance
Lightning Source LLC
Chambersburg PA
CBHW021914180426
43198CB00035B/566